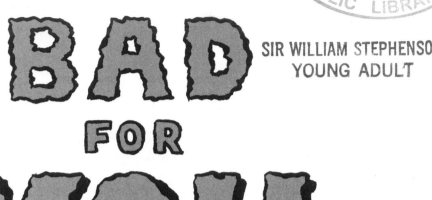

SIR WILLIAM STEPHENSON
YOUNG ADULT

EXPOSING THE WAR ON FUN!

KEVIN C. PYLE
SCOTT CUNNINGHAM

ILLUSTRATED BY KEVIN C. PYLE

HENRY HOLT AND COMPANY · NEW YORK

TO CALVIN, WHO HAS ALWAYS KNOWN THE DIFFERENCE BETWEEN
FANTASY AND REALITY AND HAS TAUGHT ME SO MUCH ABOUT BOTH
—K. P.

TO MY WIFE, ELENA, AND MY DAUGHTER, JO, FOR THEIR CONSTANT LOVE,
SUPPORT, AND INSPIRATION (PLUS, THEY'RE REALLY CUTE!)
—S. C.

Many thanks to Melanie Comer, Dr. Elena Cunningham, Ana Deboo, Kate Farrell, Todd Hamilton, Peter Kuper, Phillip S. Pittz, Calvin Pyle, and all the journalists, activists, scholars, and scientists who did the primary research that made this book possible.

Henry Holt and Company, LLC
Publishers since 1866
175 Fifth Avenue
New York, New York 10010
macteenbooks.com

Henry Holt® is a registered trademark of Henry Holt and Company, LLC.
Text copyright © 2014 by Kevin Pyle and Scott Cunningham
Illustrations copyright © 2014 by Kevin Pyle
All rights reserved.

Library of Congress Control Number: 2012953810
ISBN 978-0-8050-9289-9

Henry Holt books may be purchased for business or promotional use. For information on bulk purchases, please contact Macmillan Corporate and Premium Sales Department at (800) 221-7945 x5442 or by e-mail at specialmarkets@macmillan.com.

First Edition—2014
Printed in the United States of America

1 3 5 7 9 10 8 6 4 2

INTRODUCTION

KIDS USUALLY SKIP INTRODUCTIONS, AND SINCE THAT'S
WHO THE "YOU" IS IN THE TITLE, LET'S KEEP THIS QUICK.

THIS IS THE HISTORY OF STUFF THAT'S SUPPOSED TO BE

TO FIND OUT WHY MOST OF IT ISN'T, KEEP READING.

GLOSSARY

Some scientific terms used in *Bad for You* get defined in detail within the book. Other terms, scientific and not, sometimes get glossed over. For those terms, there's the . . . glossary. If you want to know the meaning before you start a-reading, continue on. Glossaries are usually at the end of a book, so glossary traditionalists can wait until then before reading this (but hey, they've probably skipped this anyway).

ABSTINENCE: Not doing a thing . . . EVER (and if you are doing it, stop right now!).

ALLEGORY: A story or image that has a hidden meaning or underlying symbolism (could be a myth or fairy tale or fable or poem, or pretty much anything made up). Bet you have to use this word in an essay someday.

COGNITION: Hold on a second. I'm thinking about it. Hmm, thinking . . . thinking . . . Wait, cognition is thinking! Thinking, remembering, decision making, problem solving, language decoding—ALL mental, aka "cognitive," processes.

COMMITTEES: As far as this book goes, committees are a bunch of elected government representatives who are appointed to investigate whatever. Sometimes these investigations lead to new legislation or regulations. There are Senate and Congressional committees, as well as subcommittees (note: subcommittees do not meet on subs, though they could investigate them). Committees usually have hearings to hear (get it?) the testimony of witnesses.

CRITICAL THINKING: What's with all the questions? That's because you're thinking critically—i.e., questioning assumptions. That's what you're supposed to be doing while you read this book (but don't be too critical, because the authors are very sensitive).

DISBARRED: This is what happens to a lawyer when other lawyers and judges think he or she is too dishonest, incompetent, or crazy to practice law. In other words, when a lawyer is not allowed, by law, to be a lawyer anymore.

INDUSTRIAL REVOLUTION: We're not talking cyber-robots overthrowing humanity here. That's a few years off. The actual Industrial Revolution started in England around 1760 but still involved the rise of machines. New inventions created more efficient factories, which, in turn, brought more people to cities. Living standards for workers improved, allowing them to buy all the things they were busy making. Though a slow revolution, taking nearly a hundred years, it altered society almost as much as if it had been overthrown by cyber-robots.

JUVENILE DELINQUENT: An underage "criminal"; though, since you're a kid, anything from being busted for skateboarding to breaking a curfew (or, in extreme cases, murder) could be called "juvenile delinquency."

LITIGATION: It's all about courts, judges, lawyers, suing, going to jail and not going to jail. You know, doing legal stuff.

MEDIA: Turn on the TV, visit a website, listen to the radio, watch a movie, read a newspaper (HA—read a newspaper!) . . . do any of that, and you're using a form of mass media communication. Pass a note to a friend in class . . . that's not media.

MORAL: Defining moral is easy: If you're good, if you're on the side of what's right, then you're acting "moral." And if you're "immoral," that's baaaaad. What's a lot harder, though, is defining "good" and "bad."

PROFILING: Not a side-view "selfie," but when law enforcement authorities decide someone is suspicious based on race or looks, as opposed to actual behavior. Often used with "racial" as in "racial profiling."

PSEUDOSCIENCE: Literally, fake science; different theories or systems that pretend to be like science but do not use the scientific method of investigation* (like astrology).

PSYCHOLOGY: When a bunch of psychologists get together, one of them is bound to say "cognition" before the night's over. That's because psychology is the study of how the mind works and its effect on behavior.

RESEARCHER: Someone who does a careful, systematic, objective investigation of something (if they're a good researcher, at least). Researchers publish their results as papers, surveys, studies, books, and dissertations (which the authors would like to thank them all for).

SOCIOLOGY: How many sociologists does it take to screw in a lightbulb? At least two . . . since sociology is the study of people in groups—i.e., society.

STATISTICS: Numbers, numbers, numbers—collecting them, organizing them, interpreting them, turning them into bar graphs and pie charts (mmm . . . pie). That's all the stuff (or "data") of statistical studies. But the numbers aren't just numbers. They represent the amounts of real things; for example,

a study of kids doing this, or watching that, or playing there. Whenever you see a headline proclaiming an increase in kids doing _____ (fill in the blank), it's because of how certain statistics have been collected and interpreted.

SUPREME COURT: When someone says, "That's the law of the land," these nine hotshot judges can say, "Hold it—not so fast!" Everyone knows about the president and Congress, but the Supreme Court is the often-forgotten third branch of our government. Cases that the Supreme Court decides have usually gone through a bunch of appeals from lower courts before reaching them. But what they say goes (unless they overturn their own decision years later, which happens).

SURGEON GENERAL: Imagine an army of surgeons, scalpels ready, waiting for the command from their all-powerful general to attack a slew of zombie invaders! Pretty cool, huh? Unfortunately, nothing like the real job of the surgeon general, who serves as the leading spokesperson on the public health of the USA.

SURVEILLANCE: You know that creepy feeling you get when you think someone's secretly watching you? Well, they are.†

UNINTENDED CONSEQUENCES: This refers to how something can unexpectedly result from an action (sometimes the opposite of what you're going for). Example: The action of requiring kids to wear helmets has the intended consequence of keeping them safe and therefore healthy. Unintended consequence: Kids don't like wearing helmets, so they're less and less likely to ride bikes, leading to kids who are overweight and unhealthy.

*For further explanation of the scientific method, see page 22.

†See—and we do mean see—page 173.

CONTENTS

BAD FOR YOU: COMICS

BAD FOR YOU: GAMES

BAD FOR YOU: TECHNOLOGY

BAD FOR YOU: PLAY

BAD FOR YOU: THOUGHT

GOOD FOR YOU

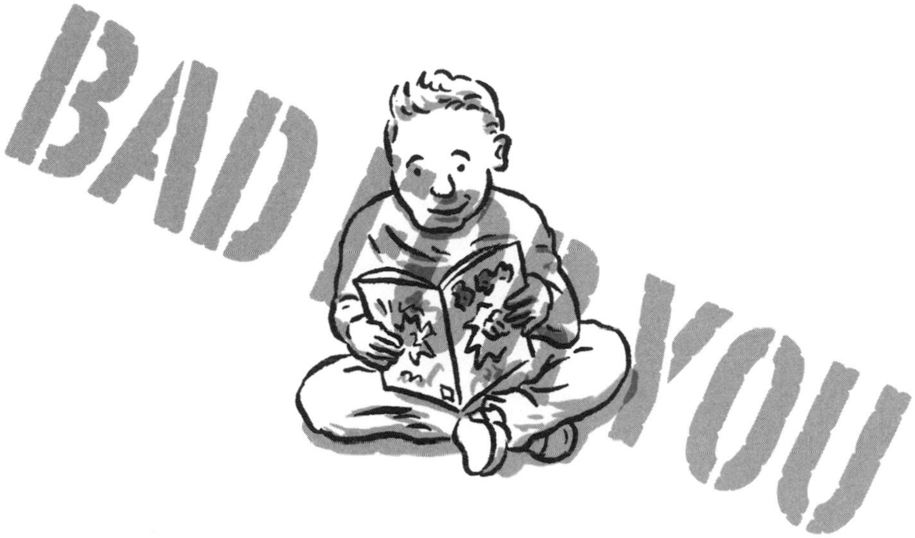
BAD
YOU

COMICS

IT WAS A COOL OCTOBER DAY IN 1948 WHEN HUNDREDS OF CHILDREN IN SPENCER, WEST VIRGINIA, MADE A PILE OF COMICS ON THE GROUNDS BEHIND THEIR SCHOOL. UNDER THE WATCHFUL EYES OF THE PRINCIPAL, TEACHERS, AND REPORTERS, A STUDENT LIT THE COVER OF A *SUPERMAN* COMIC AND THREW IT ON THE MOUNTAIN OF PAPER. IT WAS THE FIRST OF AMERICA'S COMIC BOOK BONFIRES, BUT THE FIRE LIT THERE WOULD SPREAD. SOON, ALL ACROSS AMERICA, COMIC BOOKS WOULD BE CONSUMED IN FLAMES.

FLAMES OF FEAR

IN 1933, MAXWELL GAINES OF THE EASTERN COLOR PRINTING COMPANY WAS LOOKING FOR A WAY TO KEEP THE PRINTING PRESSES RUNNING BETWEEN JOBS AND TO KEEP HIS WORKERS BUSY.

EASTERN REPRINTED POPULAR COMIC STRIP SECTIONS FROM THE SUNDAY NEWSPAPERS. GAINES HAD THE IDEA TO TAKE THOSE STRIPS AND PUT THEM IN A BOOKLET FORM. THUS THE FIRST COMIC BOOK, *FUNNIES ON PARADE*, WAS BORN.

FUNNIES ON PARADE WAS GIVEN AWAY FOR FREE AS A WAY TO GET PEOPLE TO SEE THE ADS FOR SOAP ON ITS PAGES. IT WAS SO POPULAR THAT EASTERN STARTED PRODUCING SIMILAR COMICS FOR OTHER PRODUCTS.

IN 1934, EASTERN COLOR STARTED PRINTING FAMOUS FUNNIES, THE FIRST COMIC BOOK SOLD ON NEWSSTANDS. COSTING ONLY TEN CENTS, IT WAS AN INSTANT HIT AND LAUNCHED A NEW INDUSTRY.

BROTHER, CAN YOU SPARE A DIME . . . FOR A COMIC?

MAX GAINES SOON LEFT EASTERN COLOR PRINTING TO WORK FOR ANOTHER PRINTER.

IN MAY 1936, "WAR ON CRIME," THE FIRST TRUE-CRIME COMIC STORY, APPEARED IN FAMOUS FUNNIES, BASED ON AN IDEA BY FBI DIRECTOR J. EDGAR HOOVER, USING STORIES OF ACTUAL AGENTS.

BOSS! DAT LOOKS JUST LIKE YOU!

SHADAP, YOUSE!

MEANWHILE, ACROSS TOWN, THE TEAM OF JERRY SIEGEL AND JOE SHUSTER CREATED SUPERMAN. WITHIN TWO YEARS, MILLIONS OF SUPERHERO COMICS WERE SELLING EVERY MONTH.*

*SPEAKING OF MILLIONS, THE FIRST ISSUE FEATURING SUPERMAN RECENTLY SOLD FOR A RECORD $2.2 MILLION. IN 1939, IT COST ONLY A DIME!

BY THE MID-40s, HOWEVER, SALES OF SUPERHERO COMICS SLIPPED AS NEW GENRES GAINED IN POPULARITY. A DRIVING FORCE BEHIND THIS CHANGE WAS EC COMICS.

IN 1944, MAX GAINES HAD STARTED EDUCATIONAL COMICS (EC), WITH THE IDEA TO MAKE COMICS ABOUT SCIENCE, HISTORY, AND THE BIBLE TO SELL TO SCHOOLS AND CHURCHES.

THREE YEARS LATER, MAX GAINES DIED TRAGICALLY IN A BOATING ACCIDENT. HIS SON, 25-YEAR-OLD WILLIAM GAINES, TOOK OVER THE COMPANY.

THE YOUNGER GAINES CHANGED THE NAME FROM EDUCATIONAL COMICS TO ENTERTAINING COMICS AND EC, AS IT WAS STILL CALLED, SOON BECAME KNOWN FOR ITS SURPRISING STORIES ILLUSTRATED BY ARTISTS DESTINED TO BECOME SOME OF THE MOST ACCLAIMED OF THEIR GENERATION.

THESE STORIES WERE IN GENRES PREVIOUSLY RARE IN COMICS. WITH ITS HORROR, SUSPENSE, SCIENCE FICTION, MILITARY, AND CRIME COMICS, EC SPARKED A MARKET THAT WOULD SOON EXPLODE.

IN THE YEARS AFTER WORLD WAR II, KIDS IN AMERICA WERE CRAZY FOR COMICS. IN 1948, 80 TO 100 MILLION COMIC BOOKS WERE SOLD PER MONTH.

THERE WERE COMICS ON EVERYTHING—FUNNY ANIMALS, ROMANCE, WAR, AND, MOST NOTORIOUSLY, CRIME.

ENTER DR. FREDRIC WERTHAM, A GERMAN-BORN PSYCHIATRIST AND DIRECTOR OF THE PSYCHIATRIC CLINIC AT QUEENS HOSPITAL CENTER.

IN 1948, DR. WERTHAM ORGANIZED A SYMPOSIUM, "PSYCHOPATHOLOGY OF COMIC BOOKS," TO PRESENT HIS THEORY THAT COMIC BOOKS WERE RESPONSIBLE FOR THE POSTWAR RISE IN JUVENILE DELINQUENCY.

THEN THE MOB WENT ON A RAMPAGE!

BURNING AND SMASHING!

IN ADDITION TO INSPIRING CRIME, WERTHAM BELIEVED, COMICS TURNED KIDS AGAINST THEIR PARENTS . . .

RUINED THEIR READING HABITS...

"MAYBE IT'S MY IMAGINATION...

"...DOING HARM [TO] THE ACQUISITION OF FLUENT LEFT-TO-RIGHT EYE MOVEMENTS,

"...BUT THIS COMIC MIGHT BE...

"WHICH IS SO INDISPENSABLE FOR GOOD READING."*

*ALL QUOTES FROM WERTHAM.

AND INSPIRED A FASCIST MODEL OF VIOLENT JUSTICE.

"THE BIG S ON HIS UNIFORM— WE SHOULD, I SUPPOSE, BE THANKFUL THAT IT IS NOT AN SS."†

†THE SS WAS THE ELITE MILITARY FORCE OF NAZI GERMANY.

SOON ARTICLES BASED ON WERTHAM'S IDEAS APPEARED IN POPULAR MAGAZINES LIKE *TIME* AND *COLLIER'S*, SPREADING THE FEAR OF COMICS LIKE A VIRUS.

THIS SUPPOSED THREAT TO AMERICA'S CHILDREN DEMANDED ACTION AND, IN APRIL OF 1948, DETROIT POLICE OFFICERS SEIZED COMICS FROM NEWSSTANDS.

"IF YOU WANT TO RAISE A GENERATION THAT IS HALF STORM-TROOPERS AND HALF CANNON FODDER ...

"WITH A DASH OF ILLITERACY, THEN COMIC BOOKS ARE GOOD.

"IN FACT, THEY ARE PERFECT."‡

‡ALL QUOTES FROM WERTHAM.

THE NEW YORK STATE PHARMACEUTICAL ASSOCIATION CALLED UPON ITS MEMBERS TO STOP SELLING COMICS THAT DIDN'T UPHOLD THE STANDARDS OF THE NATIONAL ORGANIZATION FOR DECENT LITERATURE.

"BUT THE ANTIDOTE TO THE 'COMIC' MAGAZINE POISON CAN BE FOUND IN ANY LIBRARY OR GOOD BOOK- STORE.

"THE PARENT WHO DOES NOT ACQUIRE THE ANTIDOTE FOR HIS CHILD IS GUILTY OF CRIMINAL NEGLIGENCE."§

§STERLING NORTH, CHILDREN'S AUTHOR AND COMICS CRITIC

IN JANUARY OF '49 THE U.S. ARMY CHARACTER GUIDANCE COUNCIL ADVISED PURCHASING OFFICERS NOT TO ORDER COMICS "BEYOND THE LINE OF DECENCY."

VA VOOM

POW POW

CRACK

IN 1948, LAWS TO BAN OR CENSOR COMIC BOOKS SPREAD LIKE WILDFIRE TO 50 CITIES ACROSS THE NATION. AND THEN THEY JUST KEPT SPREADING . . . ACROSS THE GLOBE . . . TO FRANCE AND CANADA—AND EVEN FRENCH CANADA!

THEN, THE "WILDFIRES" BECAME REAL FIRES, AS CHURCHES AND SCHOOLS IN NEW YORK, WISCONSIN, ILLINOIS, MISSOURI, AND WEST VIRGINIA BEGAN TO TORCH THEIR COMICS.

DEFENDERS OF FREE SPEECH WROTE EDITORIALS IN NEWSPAPERS COMPARING THE COMIC-BURNING CRAZE TO THE BOOK BURNING IN NAZI GERMANY.

AND IN APRIL OF 1949, THE GOVERNOR OF NEW YORK, THOMAS E. DEWEY, BOLDLY VETOED A BILL THAT WOULD HAVE GIVEN THE STATE DEPARTMENT OF EDUCATION THE AUTHORITY TO REGULATE COMICS.

A LOS ANGELES COURT RULED AGAINST A LAW BANNING CRIME COMICS, AND ARTICLES IN *NEWSWEEK* AND THE *NEW YORK TIMES* REPORTED ON SCIENTIFIC STUDIES THAT FOUND "NO STATISTICALLY SIGNIFICANT EFFECT OF THE COMICS UPON THE PERSONALITIES OF THEIR YOUNG DEVOTEES."

BUT DR. WERTHAM WASN'T DONE YET.

IN APRIL 1954, DR. WERTHAM'S ANTI-COMICS BOOK, *SEDUCTION OF THE INNOCENT*, WAS PUBLISHED.

WHILE THE BOOK WAS POPULAR, IT WAS WERTHAM'S MAGAZINE ARTICLES THAT REALLY STIRRED UP MOMS AND DADS.

DAYS AFTER THE PUBLICATION OF *SEDUCTION OF THE INNOCENT*, THE U.S. SENATE SUBCOMMITTEE ON JUVENILE DELINQUENCY HELD HEARINGS FOCUSED ON THE EVILS OF COMIC BOOKS.

IN A STATEMENT ISSUED BY THE CO-SPONSORS OF THE INITIATIVE, SENATORS ESTES KEFAUVER AND ROBERT C. HENDRICKSON LABELED DELINQUENCY THE "FIFTH HORSEMAN OF DOOM" AND A POSSIBLE WEAKNESS IN THE FIGHT AGAINST COMMUNISM.

"IT ENDS UP BY SANTA CLAUS GOING OFF WITH 'JUST DIVORCED' ON THE BACK. THAT IS THE KIND OF COMPLETE AND UTTER ROT WE ARE GIVING TO CHILDREN UNDER THE GUISE OF SOMETHING THAT ORIGINALLY STARTED OUT SUPPOSEDLY TO BE FUNNY."

"EXCESSIVE READING OF MATERIALS OF THIS KIND IN ITSELF IS SYMPTOMATIC OF SOME EMOTIONAL MALADJUSTMENT IN A YOUNGSTER."

"THIS COUNTRY CANNOT AFFORD THE CALCULATED RISK INVOLVED IN FEEDING ITS CHILDREN, THROUGH COMIC BOOKS, A CONCENTRATED DIET OF CRIME, HORROR, AND VIOLENCE."

SENATOR JAMES A. FITZPATRICK

SENATOR RICHARD CLENDENEN

WILLIAM GAINES

SENATOR ESTES KEFAUVER

"WHAT ARE WE AFRAID OF? ARE WE AFRAID OF OUR OWN CHILDREN? WE THINK OUR CHILDREN SO EVIL, SIMPLEMINDED, THAT IT TAKES A STORY OF MURDER TO SET THEM TO MURDER."

"MR. CHAIRMAN, AS LONG AS THE CRIME COMIC BOOKS INDUSTRY EXISTS IN ITS PRESENT FORM THERE ARE NO SECURE HOMES."

DR. FREDRIC WERTHAM

AND THE BURNINGS STARTED AGAIN.

Pendleton, OR 1955:
More than 1,250 comics were handed over by 140 kids.

Los Angeles, CA 1953: Ray Bradbury writes *Fahrenheit 451*—a science-fiction novel in which books are outlawed and a firefighter's job is to burn any house where they are found.

COMICS BURNINGS 1945–55

Fueled by headlines such as "Horror in the Nursery" and "Depravity for Children—Ten Cents a Copy!" churches, schools, and community groups organized book burnings across the nation. In some instances schoolchildren sang anti-comics chants and made signs like "Burn the Bad, Read the Good."

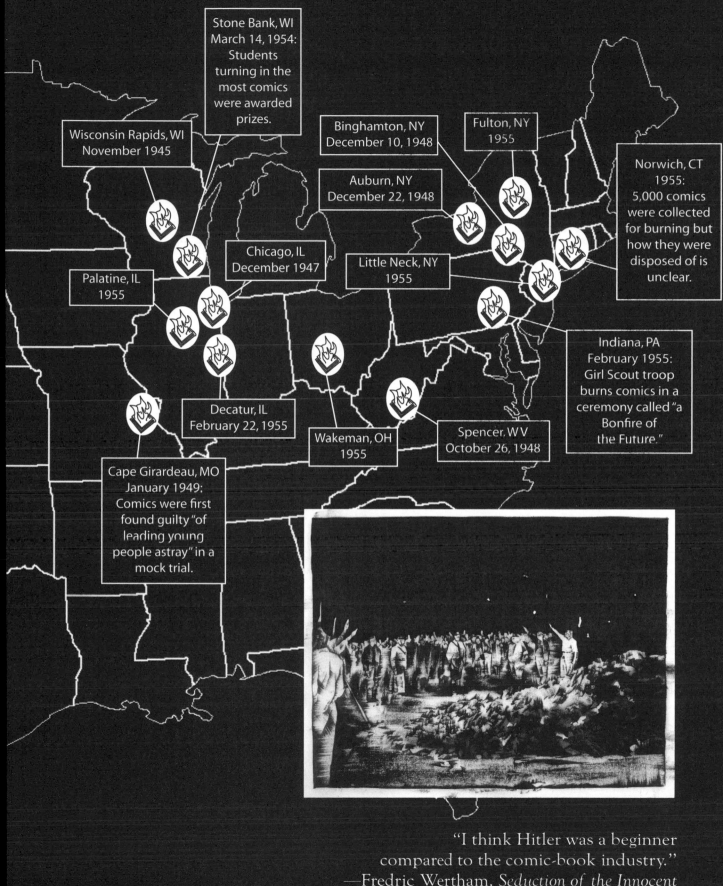

Stone Bank, WI
March 14, 1954:
Students turning in the most comics were awarded prizes.

Wisconsin Rapids, WI
November 1945

Binghamton, NY
December 10, 1948

Fulton, NY
1955

Norwich, CT
1955:
5,000 comics were collected for burning but how they were disposed of is unclear.

Auburn, NY
December 22, 1948

Chicago, IL
December 1947

Little Neck, NY
1955

Palatine, IL
1955

Indiana, PA
February 1955:
Girl Scout troop burns comics in a ceremony called "a Bonfire of the Future."

Decatur, IL
February 22, 1955

Wakeman, OH
1955

Spencer, WV
October 26, 1948

Cape Girardeau, MO
January 1949:
Comics were first found guilty "of leading young people astray" in a mock trial.

"I think Hitler was a beginner compared to the comic-book industry."
—Fredric Wertham, *Seduction of the Innocent*

IN RESPONSE TO THE LEGISLATIVE AND PUBLIC OUTCRY, THE COMIC MAGAZINE ASSOCIATION OF AMERICA ADOPTED THE ORIGINAL COMICS CODE ON OCTOBER 26, 1954. IT WAS ENFORCED BY A "COMICS CZAR," CHARLES F. MURPHY.

THE COMICS CODE HAD STRICT RULES FOR DEPICTION OF CONTENT, INCLUDING . . .

"NO COMIC MAGAZINE SHALL USE THE WORD 'HORROR' OR 'TERROR' IN ITS TITLE.

"SCENES DEALING WITH . . . VAMPIRES AND VAMPIRISM, GHOULS, CANNIBALISM, AND WEREWOLFISM ARE PROHIBITED.

"ADVERTISEMENT OF . . . TOILETRY PRODUCTS OF QUESTIONABLE NATURE ARE TO BE REJECTED.

"ALL LURID, UNSAVORY, GRUESOME ILLUSTRATIONS SHALL BE ELIMINATED!"

BETWEEN 1954 AND 1956, EIGHTEEN COMIC BOOK PUBLISHERS STOPPED PRINTING COMIC BOOKS.

NEARLY ALL THOSE REMAINING SUBMITTED TO THE COMICS CODE AUTHORITY. ONE WHO DID NOT WAS WILLIAM GAINES AT EC, THE PUBLISHER OF CLOSE TO 20 CRIME AND HORROR COMICS.

BUT WHEN RETAILERS AND DISTRIBUTORS REFUSED TO HANDLE EC TITLES, GAINES WAS FORCED TO STOP PRODUCTION OF ALL HIS HORROR AND CRIME COMICS.

"WITH COMIC MAGAZINE CENSORSHIP NOW A FACT, WE AT EC LOOK FORWARD TO AN IMMEDIATE DROP IN THE CRIME AND JUVENILE DELINQUENCY RATE IN THE UNITED STATES."*

BY 1956, WILLIAM GAINES HAD ONLY ONE COMIC LEFT, WHICH HE TRANSFORMED INTO A BLACK-AND-WHITE HUMOR MAGAZINE. IT WAS CALLED MAD MAGAZINE.

WHAT... ME WORRY? HA-HA-HA-HA-HAAAA!

*ACCORDING TO FBI RECORDS, THE NUMBER OF ARRESTS OF KIDS GREW "DRAMATICALLY" THROUGHOUT THE 1950s. IN FACT, IT WASN'T UNTIL THE 1990s THAT JUVENILE HOMICIDE RATES FINALLY PEAKED.

Fredric Wertham's ideas influenced a lot of people and changed the world of comics forever. He was a doctor and a scientist, but was there any science behind what he said?

Did he use...

THE SCIENTIFIC METHOD?

IT'S THE WAY SCIENTISTS STUDY THE WORLD.

And the great thing about the scientific method is that you can use it to study anything:

BIRDS...

BUGS...

PLANETS...

YOU COULD EVEN STUDY KIDS WHO READ COMICS!

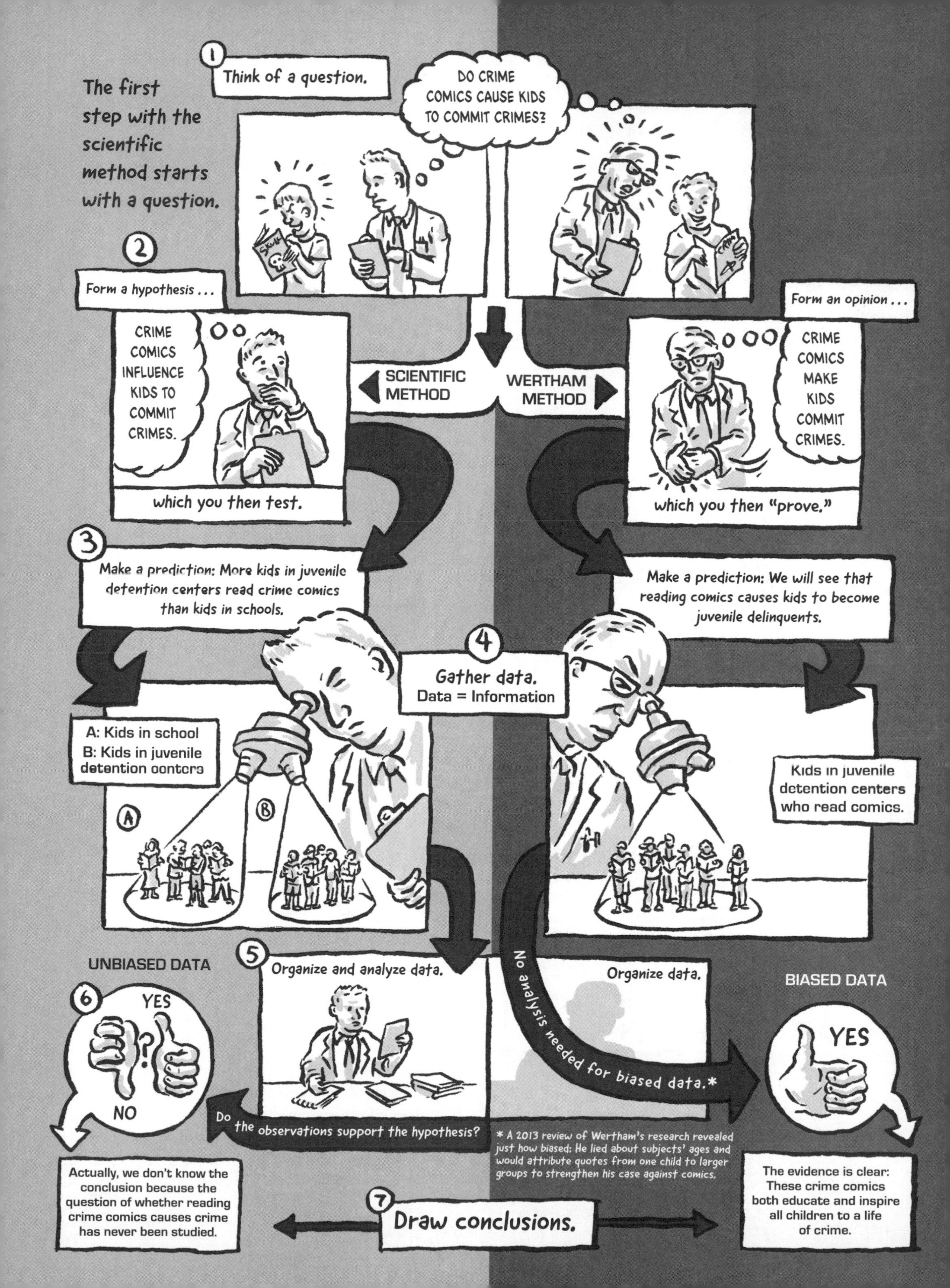

The first step with the scientific method starts with a question.
1
Think of a question.
DO CRIME COMICS CAUSE KIDS TO COMMIT CRIMES?
2
Form a hypothesis . . .
CRIME COMICS INFLUENCE KIDS TO COMMIT CRIMES.
which you then test.
Form an opinion . . .
CRIME COMICS MAKE KIDS COMMIT CRIMES.
which you then "prove."
SCIENTIFIC METHOD
WERTHAM METHOD
3
Make a prediction: More kids in juvenile detention centers read crime comics than kids in schools.
Make a prediction: We will see that reading comics causes kids to become juvenile delinquents.
4
Gather data.
Data = Information
A: Kids in school
B: Kids in juvenile detention centers
A
B
Kids in juvenile detention centers who read comics.
5
Organize and analyze data.
Organize data.
No analysis needed for biased data.*
UNBIASED DATA
BIASED DATA
6
YES
?
NO
YES
Do the observations support the hypothesis?
* A 2013 review of Wertham's research revealed just how biased: He lied about subjects' ages and would attribute quotes from one child to larger groups to strengthen his case against comics.
Actually, we don't know the conclusion because the question of whether reading crime comics causes crime has never been studied.
7
Draw conclusions.
The evidence is clear: These crime comics both educate and inspire all children to a life of crime.

Wertham saw criminal kids reading crime comics and thought comics were causing crime. But you know what?

He was making... **the Common Correlation Mistake.**

The fact that two things are related does not mean one thing causes the other. You would have to do more investigation to see if there could be another reason (or several reasons) for what appears to be happening.

I'M AFRAID TO GO TO SCHOOL!

HOW COME?

I REALIZED THAT WE LIVE IN A CITY WITH A LOT OF CRIME!

YEAH...

AND A LOT OF SCHOOLS.

So?

DON'T YOU SEE— SCHOOLS CAUSE CRIME!

CORRELATION IS NOT CAUSATION

Basically, the point here is that just because two things look like they're related doesn't automatically mean that one is causing the other (the scientific way of saying this is "correlation is not causation"). There might be something else causing it. For instance, the "something" that the kid in the comic isn't considering is that a city has more schools and more crime, but that's because CITIES HAVE MORE PEOPLE!

24

GOOD FOR YOU
READING COMICS!

According to Dr. Wertham, comic book fans suffered from "reading disorders," but should we take his word on reading? After all, Wertham never published any studies—ever. When REAL research is done, look what it shows:

COMICS CAN LEAD KIDS TO MORE CHALLENGING READING

In this study, the results came from two sample groups of seventh graders from totally different economic levels—one upper class and suburban, one lower class and urban. Subjects were asked to fill out questionnaires on their comic book and general reading habits.

KIDS WERE MORE EXCITED TO LEARN ABOUT SCIENCE USING COMICS

This was a detailed study covering 149 separate teaching sessions with a range of students from high school, middle school, and elementary school, using science comics as part of the lesson plan.

READING COMICS CAN MAKE YOU A BETTER READER

In this study, English as a Second Language readers who read comics were significantly better at understanding complex text than their counterparts who read in non-comics form.

This last study is harder to sum up in a headline, so here's the long version: A group of lower-income elementary school kids in Florida got to pick twelve free books on the last day of school (from lists they made themselves). Three years later, researchers found that students who received the books had "significantly higher" reading scores AND experienced less of a "summer slide" (which means forgetting most of what you learned the year before while you were goofing off all summer) than a group of kids who didn't get the books. What does all this have to do with comics? One of the top books picked by the students was ... *Captain Underpants*, a book series that's basically like a comic. It's ALSO number thirteen of the top twenty-five banned books of the last ten years!

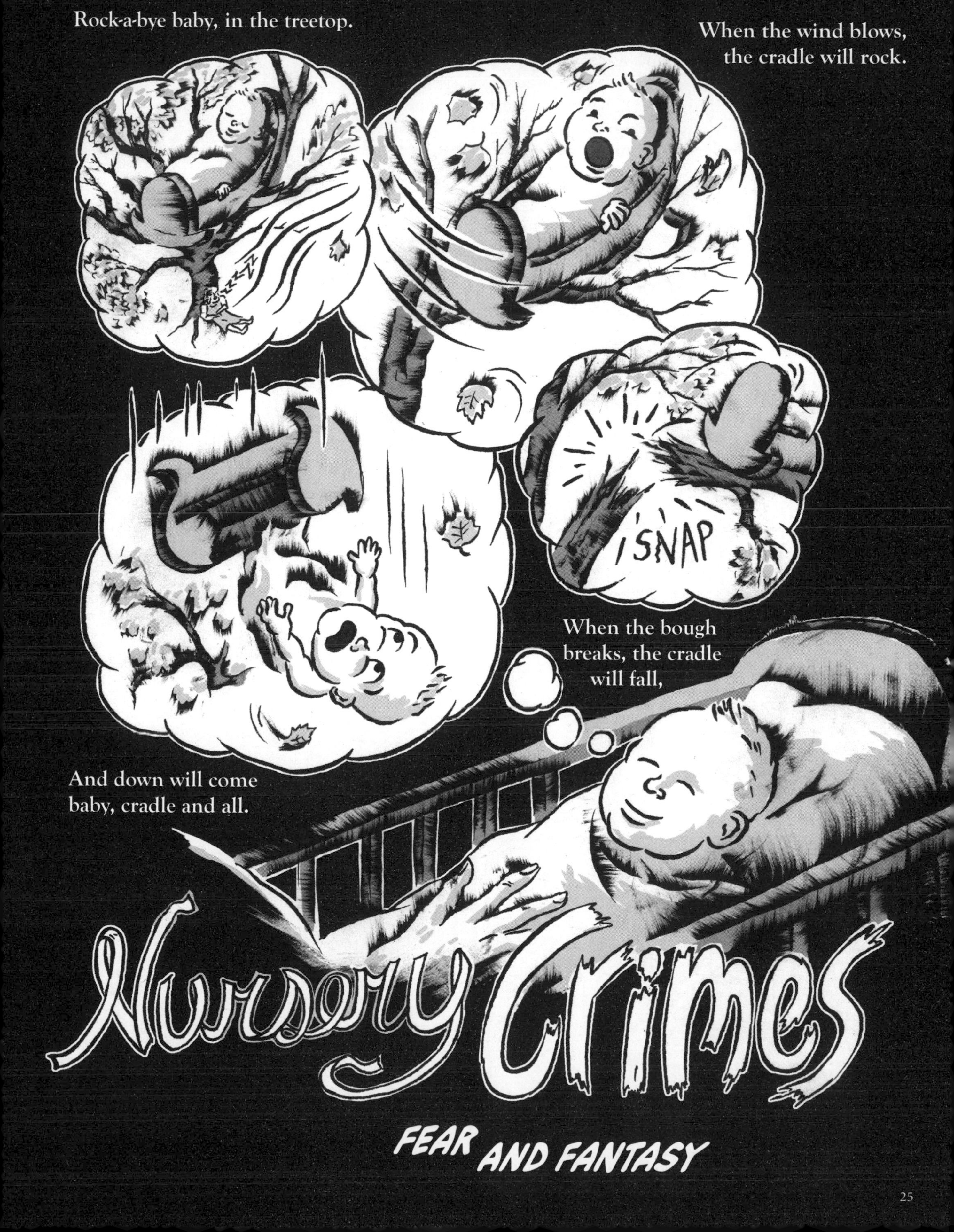
Rock-a-bye baby, in the treetop.
When the wind blows, the cradle will rock.
SNAP
When the bough breaks, the cradle will fall,
And down will come baby, cradle and all.

Nursery Crimes

FEAR AND FANTASY

SOMEWHERE AROUND 380 B.C., THE CLASSICAL GREEK PHILOSOPHER PLATO WROTE,

"Now early life is very impressible, and children ought not to learn what they will have to unlearn when they grow up; we must therefore have a censorship of nursery tales, banishing some and keeping others.

"Some of them are very improper . . . Shall our youth be encouraged to beat their fathers by the example of Zeus . . . The young are incapable of understanding allegory."

INDEED, THESE GREEK MYTHS OF WHICH PLATO WROTE ARE PACKED WITH POORLY BEHAVED GODS AND SCARY MONSTERS.

ONE GREEK MYTH, "CUPID AND PSYCHE," WAS WRITTEN DOWN AROUND A.D. 100. SOME SCHOLARS THINK THIS WAS THE FIRST FAIRY TALE EVER PUBLISHED.

SEVERAL IDEAS IN THE STORY—A JEALOUS GODDESS, EVIL SISTERS, A LOVED ONE WHO CAN'T BE LOOKED UPON, AND A HAPPY ENDING—ARE THE SAME AS IN SOME FAMOUS FAIRY TALES.

IT WAS ALSO VIOLENT AND SCARY, WITH A STABBING, AN ATTEMPTED MURDER, AND A TRIP TO AN UNDERWORLD GUARDED BY A THREE-HEADED DOG.

As already mentioned, these elements aren't so unusual for early fairy tales either.

Scholars believe that fairy tales were originally stories told for entertainment by adults at a time when the line between childhood and adulthood was not so clear. In peasant communities, many children didn't go to school and started working in the fields as early as age eight.

Frenchman Charles Perrault wrote down many of these stories and published them in 1670. They became some of the most popular stories of all time. The collection is best known under its English title: *Tales of Mother Goose.**

*KNOWN IN FRANCE AS *HISTOIRES OU CONTES DU TEMPS PASSÉ* (FAIRY TALES FROM BYGONE ERAS).

Though intended for children, Perrault's stories still contained many grisly elements from the originals.

In 1812, when the Brothers Grimm published their collection of German folktales *Children's and Household Tales,* it was criticized as being unsuitable for children.

Later volumes removed some things, such as cannibalism, and changed Snow White's and Hansel and Gretel's wicked mothers into stepmothers.

In the mid-1800s, known as the Victorian era, the idea of childhood as a time of learning and fun became more common.

One reason for this was that the Industrial Revolution created a larger "middle class"— people who earned more money than before.

Abigail, you'll be late for school!

While most children of the poor worked in factories or on farms, the children of middle-class and wealthy families went to school.

Ahh! I HATE school!

These middle-class parents often spent money on books. Many of these were collections of heavily edited fairy tales that were being published specifically for their children.

As more and more children began to read, some adults became worried. They warned against reading the wrong kind of book, namely novels.

The Guardian; or Youth's Religious Instructor, November 1820

Injurious reading is a source of corrupti... young people. It will be immediately pe... ...ean to reckon that reading which ha... ...ter rather than correct evil pro... ...sons are excessively fond... romances.

Or novels with pictures, which could cause some awful things to happen (that's why the writer warned about "the morality of pictures").

NOVELS AND NOVEL-READING
by the Rev. J. T. Crane* (1869)

The safest rule, in whose application the fewest mistakes will be made, is that of TOTAL ABSTINENCE.

A young man—J. H. W.—committed suicide recently in Indianapolis. He left a letter to his brother, in which he says: "I believe that if I had never read a novel I should now be on the high road to fortune; but, alas! Persuade all persons over whom you have any influence not to read novels."

THE MOTHER'S ASSISTANT

THE MORALITY OF PICTURES
by William A. Alcott

They are as efficient for evil as for good, and perhaps more so. I have no hesitation in saying, that for want of a proper supervision of this matter—by somebody—a flood of evil, more terrible in its consequences than any of the "seven vials" of the Revelator, is at this time about to rush upon our unhappy country.

Reading the wrong material could even cause one to kill a president.

YOUTH'S COMPANION.

Published Weekly, by WILLIS & RAND, at the Office of the Boston Recorder, No. 127, Washington-Street....Price One Dollar a year in advance, or $1, 50, if not paid in advance

No. 33.   May 11, 1865   Vol. IV.

BOOTH AND BAD LITERATURE

The education of John Wilkes Booth had fitted him to act the part of murderer of our President.... Does any young man feel as if he would like to be educated to do as daringly and dexterously as did Booth? Let him keep on, then, reading the bloody tales of the weekly story papers, or the flashy, ten cent, yellow-covered literature sold in almost every book store...

But, young friend, if you have any regard for your character, your future standing in society, the credit of your families, your own peace and the *welfare of your souls*, let such reading alone!

THE ASSASSINATION OF PRESIDENT LINCOLN.
AT FORD'S THEATRE WASHINGTON D.C.APRIL 14TH 1865.

*Father of novelist Stephen Crane, author of the gory classic *The Red Badge of Courage* and the scandalous *Maggie: A Girl of the Streets.*

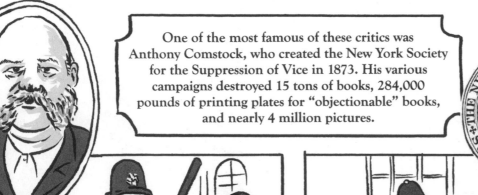

One of the most famous of these critics was Anthony Comstock, who created the New York Society for the Suppression of Vice in 1873. His various campaigns destroyed 15 tons of books, 284,000 pounds of printing plates for "objectionable" books, and nearly 4 million pictures.

Comstock boasted that he was responsible for 4,000 arrests. At the height of his power, he even stopped anatomy textbooks from being delivered to medical students.

In his book, *Traps for the Young*, Comstock wrote, "I unhesitatingly declare, there is at present no more active agent employed by Satan in civilized communities to ruin the human family and subject the nations to himself than EVIL READING."

He railed against the half-dime novels of his time. . . .

"But, above all, at every hazard, rid the home of all of Satan's household traps, and whenever you discover one, burn it to ashes!" Over 120 years later, some people were still taking this advice.

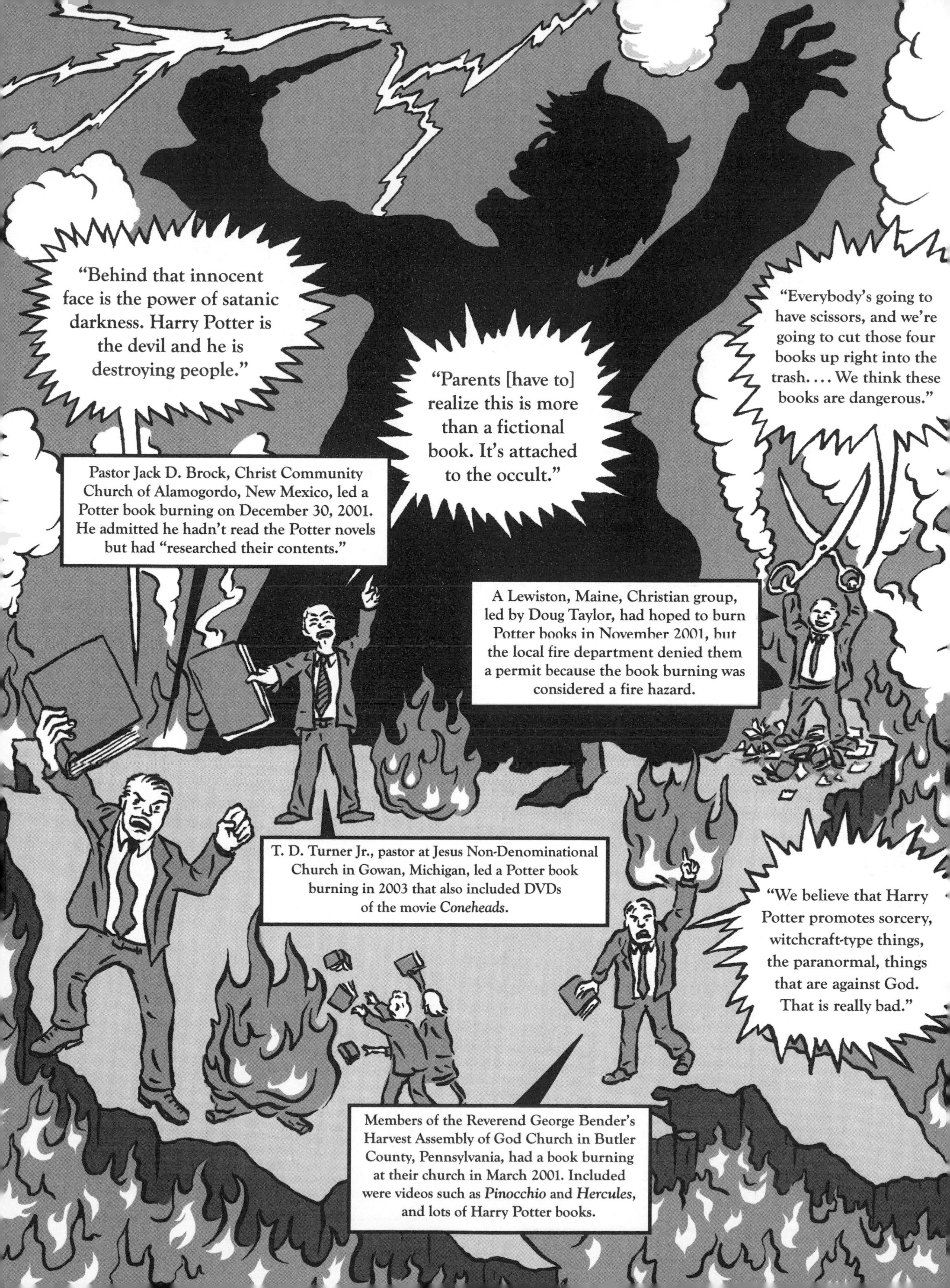
"Behind that innocent face is the power of satanic darkness. Harry Potter is the devil and he is destroying people."
Pastor Jack D. Brock, Christ Community Church of Alamogordo, New Mexico, led a Potter book burning on December 30, 2001. He admitted he hadn't read the Potter novels but had "researched their contents."
"Parents [have to] realize this is more than a fictional book. It's attached to the occult."
T. D. Turner Jr., pastor at Jesus Non-Denominational Church in Gowan, Michigan, led a Potter book burning in 2003 that also included DVDs of the movie *Coneheads*.
"Everybody's going to have scissors, and we're going to cut those four books up right into the trash. . . . We think these books are dangerous."
A Lewiston, Maine, Christian group, led by Doug Taylor, had hoped to burn Potter books in November 2001, but the local fire department denied them a permit because the book burning was considered a fire hazard.
"We believe that Harry Potter promotes sorcery, witchcraft-type things, the paranormal, things that are against God. That is really bad."
Members of the Reverend George Bender's Harvest Assembly of God Church in Butler County, Pennsylvania, had a book burning at their church in March 2001. Included were videos such as *Pinocchio* and *Hercules*, and lots of Harry Potter books.

According to the American Library Association, the Harry Potter books were among the ten most banned or challenged books from 2001 to 2010.

Books are often banned or challenged when parents find something they don't like in a book and complain to the library or school board.*

... SOMETHING CALLED "BUTTER-BEER"!

Books have been challenged for criticizing religion, containing racist language, having gay characters, or dealing with political subjects.

THEY'RE BOTH BOYS!?!

and tango makes three

SO?

Other banned or challenged books include *The Adventures of Huckleberry Finn*, *Bridge to Terabithia*, and the Captain Underpants series.

These are also among the all-time bestselling books for children.

*FOR INSTANCE, ONE GEORGIA MOTHER COMPLAINED THAT POTTER MADE "NO DISTINCTION BETWEEN GOOD AND EVIL." SHE ALSO DISAPPROVED OF THE YOUNG CHARACTERS DRINKING "BUTTERBEER."

MAKE BELIEVE
IT OR NOT!

True Stories about
Fake People

Witchcrap

In all the thousands of Harry Potter fans that author J. K. Rowling has met over the years, not one of them has ever said to her, "I'm so glad I've read these books because now I want to be a witch!" Which is a good thing, since Rowling also says she doesn't believe in magic. Instead, what she believes is that kids who read her books know that the Hogwarts School of Witchcraft and Wizardry is "a fantasy world" and that they "understand that completely." So if young people get the difference between fantasy and reality, then why can't ADULTS?!

Adults, for example, in the fringy religious groups whose websites started popping up—as if by magic—as Rowling's books became big sellers. Web pages like "Harry Potter is of the Devil!" and "The Abomination of Harry Potter!" warned that the characters in the books would cast a REAL spell over the young and weak-willed, ultimatcly converting them to the occult. Despite the predictions, the world has yet to see an increase in child sorcerers. Imagine that!

Which Witch?!

Though back in 2001, it looked like those predictions might be coming true. According to an article in the *World Net Daily*, a popular conservative news site, the First Church of Satan was swamped with applicants that year, and their high priest, Egan, called Potter "an absolute godsend" for his group. Now, if it sounds a little funny to have the high priest in the First Church of Satan using the word "godsend," that's because it's supposed to.

But the humor seemed to have escaped the *World Net Daily* writer Ellen Makkai, as did the fact that she was quoting from a parody newspaper called *The Onion*, which specializes in stories of FICTION! Perhaps her confusion is understandable, in that high priest Egan is a real person (though he did change his name from the less-impressive John Dewey Allee). According to ReligiousTolerance.org, Egan was apparently "in on the joke," though *The Onion* invented all his quotes. And even the "evil" Church of Satan won't take kids under the age of eighteen.

E-Chanted

Roger Lynn began circulating an e-mail that accused Rowling's books of providing "the doorway for children to enter the Dark Side of evil." Potter guided readers to that evil door by "giving . . . examples (even the sources with authors and titles!) of spells, rituals, and demonic powers," Lynn explained. Craig Nowell was one such convert, according to Lynn's e-mail, who joined "the New Satanic Order of the Black Circle" and was said to boast that the Potter books were "cool, cause they teach you all about magic and how you can use it to control people and get revenge on your enemies." The black-hearted Nowell dreamed of the day when he could "learn the Cruciatus Curse, to make my Muggle science teacher suffer for giving me a D." The only problem was that Craig

Nowell was no-well more real than were the quotes from High Priest Egan. Lynn was fooled by THE SAME ARTICLE IN *THE ONION*!!!

Another "Fact"... Another Fiction

The *National Post*, a satirical newspaper similar to *The Onion*, also published a made-up story about Rowling in which she announced, "I worship the Devil, Beelzebub, Satan, Lucifer—in all his unholy forms. And I owe all my success, all my glory, all my power, to my sweet, beautiful Lucifer." Her heartfelt—and totally fictional—declaration to the devil made it into another popular e-mail chain letter that started making the rounds in 2002. It was also written as if the fake story were true.

Real Quotes from Actual People

At least one real-life practicing witch, Christopher Penczak, the high priest of the Temple of Witchcraft,* believes that Potter's magic doesn't extend beyond the reader's imagination. "While J. K. Rowling is writing about witchcraft," High Priest Penczak clarifies, "she isn't writing it from a modern witch's perspective, so don't expect it to be an accurate practice

*Of New Hampshire.

book." Or, as Mike Hertenstein—another full-fledged real person and practicing Christian*—puts it: "Harry Potter is to the 'real occult' what Fred Flintstone is to real anthropology."

No Joke

So, apparently, some adults (not just kids) can tell the difference between fantasy and reality. In 2006, to celebrate the 25th anniversary of Banned Books Week, the American Library Association requested readers to vote for their favorite banned book titles. Guess what—the Harry Potter series finished first in all three age categories: preteen, teen, and ADULT (so most grown-ups get it after all!).

*Practicing it in his article for the Christian magazine *Cornerstone*.

When Fairy was Scary

WHILE WITCHCRAFT IS THE MAIN WORRY OVER POTTER, OTHER BOOK BANS HAVE FOCUSED ON THE "DARK AND VIOLENT" CONTENT IN THE SERIES. FRANKLY, THE STORIES SEEM LIKE FAIRY TALES COMPARED TO . . . WELL, TO THE ORIGINAL VERSIONS OF FAIRY TALES!

SNOW BITE

You'd think it couldn't get much creepier than the Disney version, in which the evil queen demands that Snow White's heart be brought back to her to prove the girl is dead. But you'd be wrong. In both versions the queen hates Snow White because she's the most beautiful in all the land (remember "Mirror, Mirror . . ."?), and the too-humane huntsman can't bring himself to kill the girl. But here's the crucial difference: In the Grimms' original version, after the huntsman gives the queen a boar's heart—lying that it's really Snowy's—the queen then cooks it up (not to mention the boar's lungs and liver) and eats it! By the way, Snow White's only seven in this version.

WICKED STEP BLISTERS

The story everyone knows has Cinderella's wicked stepsisters trying to stuff their big feet into a dainty glass slipper. They struggle, but only Cinderella makes the cut, marries the prince, and lives happily ever after. As a consolation prize, the stepsisters become the brides of two lords. But in the original Grimm Brothers version, when the stepsisters can't scrunch their feet into the shoe, they start hacking off their toes. Luckily, a pair of pigeons see through their trick (literally, since it's now a bloody glass slipper!) and alert the clueless prince. For good measure, the birds peck out the stepsisters' eyes. Blind, and now short a few toes, they stumble through the streets, beggars.

UNBEARABLE

Then there's the tale of Goldilocks. Cute kid, just misunderstood. Ate a little porridge, broke a little chair, messed up a bed. Can you blame her? She was hungry and tired, and in the end, she got what she deserved—scared out of her wits (as well as the house she broke into) when the bear family returned. But back in 1837 when the story originally appeared, Goldilocks was more like Scrawny Old Ladilocks, a homeless woman who wreaks havoc on the bears' bungalow before escaping out the window. In another even earlier version, the bears catch the old lady and try burning her, then drowning her, then impaling her on a church steeple. Finally, she gets the point and dies.

GRANNY GRAVY

You remember the uplifting ending of "Little Red Riding Hood," right? The noble woodsman arrives in the nick of time and splits the wolf open with his ax, thus freeing Little Red's grandma (who had only recently been gulped down by the beast). There are early incarnations of the story with slightly different wrap-ups. In one version, the wolf doesn't swallow ALL of Grandma, but leaves the blood and meat for Little Red to unwittingly cannibalize. Sadly, no woodsman comes along to choke Grandma out of the girl. In other versions, the disguised wolf lures Red into bed and then gobbles her up. The end.

Why are so many stories for kids scary? One theory is that it's because being scared by stories can help kids safely face their fears. That's why fairy tales are full of symbols—things that stand in for the real fears kids experience every day. The idea is that kids can be afraid in the fantasy world of the story and feel stronger afterward, knowing that they survived and they are okay. Fantasy play is thought to function in a similar way. Pretending you're blasting monsters or bad guys with a toy gun or fighting off some fiend with a fake sword or stick can make kids feel stronger and more secure.

It's also kind of fun.

FAIRY TALE SYMBOLISM CONVERTER

Childhood Fear

Fairy Tale Symbol

Darkness = Woods

Strangers = Wolves

Adults = Giants

Abuse = Evil Step-mothers

FANTASY PLAY ACTIVATOR

REAL LIFE

FRUSTRATION

ANGER

FEAR

"CHILDREN CRAVE FANTASY VIOLENCE FOR MANY REASONS, BUT ONE REASON THEY SO OFTEN CRAVE IT RAW, LOUD, AND ANGRY IS THAT THEY NEED IT TO BE STRONG ENOUGH TO MATCH AND MASTER THEIR ANXIETY AND ANGER."

—GERARD JONES, *KILLING MONSTERS: WHY CHILDREN NEED FANTASY, SUPER HEROES, AND MAKE-BELIEVE VIOLENCE*

FANTASY LIFE

STUDIES AT PRESCHOOLS IN ENGLAND HAVE SHOWN THAT, EVEN THOUGH PLAYING WITH TOY GUNS INCREASED THE AGGRESSION DURING KIDS' GAMES IN THE SHORT TERM, "THE ATMOSPHERE IN THE ROOM WAS NOTABLY MORE RELAXED LATER IN THE DAY."

—PENNY HOLLAND, "WAR PLAY IN THE NURSERY," *NEW THERAPIST* (WINTER 2000)

RESEARCHERS AT HARVARD MEDICAL SCHOOL FOUND THAT 62% OF BOYS PLAYED VIDEO GAMES TO "HELP ME RELAX," 48% BECAUSE "IT HELPS ME FORGET MY PROBLEMS," AND 45% BECAUSE "IT HELPS ME GET MY ANGER OUT." CHILDREN'S DESIRE TO "SAFELY MASTER" FEAR, ACCORDING TO ONE OF THE RESEARCHERS, IS AN "IMPORTANT SKILL, PERHAPS EVEN A LIFE-SAVING ONE."

BAD FOR YOU

GAMES

WHILE EXCAVATING THE ANCIENT IRANIAN CITY OF SHAHR-E SUKHTEH, ARCHAEOLOGISTS TURNED UP, ALONG WITH THE OLDEST KNOWN ARTIFICIAL EYE, A PAIR OF DICE ESTIMATED TO BE 5,000 YEARS OLD.

PERHAPS THE MOST ANCIENT OF GAME PIECES, DICE WERE ONCE MADE FROM THE ANKLE BONES OF HOOFED ANIMALS AND WERE ALSO USED BY SOOTHSAYERS TO DIVINE THE FUTURE.

USING DICE TO GAMBLE WAS SO POPULAR AMONG THE ROMANS THAT THE POET HORACE WARNED OF ITS IMPACT ON YOUTH, AND LAWS WERE PASSED THAT LIMITED "DICING" TO THE FESTIVAL OF SATURNALIA.

SIMILARLY, WHEN PLAYING CARDS BECAME POPULAR AFTER THE INVENTION OF THE PRINTING PRESS, ENGLISHMEN COULD PLAY ONLY DURING THE 12 DAYS OF CHRISTMAS.

THE PILGRIMS HAD HOPED TO PREVENT THE EVIL OF DICE AND CARDS FROM FOLLOWING THEM TO AMERICA—BUT THEY FOUND OUT THAT IT WAS ALREADY THERE.

AMERICA, IN FACT, MADE THE DECK OF CARDS ITS OWN BY ADDING THE JOKER IN THE 1860s.

IT'S HARD TO IMAGINE A TIME WHEN GAMES OF DICE AND CARDS WERE FEARED AS TOO "INTOXICATING" FOR YOUNG MINDS. BUT IN THE EARLY 1980s, WHEN A FEW HEADLINE-GRABBING STORIES LINKED TEENS IN CRISIS TO A NEW STYLE OF ROLE-PLAYING GAME, DUNGEONS AND DRAGONS, IT BEGAN A PANIC THAT IS STILL BEING FELT TODAY. . . .

BLAME THE GAME

CREATED IN 1974, DUNGEONS AND DRAGONS (D&D) IS A ROLE-PLAYING GAME (RPG) WHERE PLAYERS CREATE THEIR OWN FICTIONAL CHARACTERS WHO EMBARK UPON IMAGINARY ADVENTURES SET IN FANTASY WORLDS OF THE PLAYERS' CREATION.

D&D GAMES, OR SINGLE ADVENTURES, CAN GO ON FOR MULTIPLE SESSIONS AND CAN BE LINKED INTO EVEN LONGER "CAMPAIGNS."

PLAYERS USE PAPER, PENCIL, AND POLYHEDRAL DICE TO DETERMINE OUTCOMES OF COMPLEX INTERACTIONS. CONCEPTS LIKE EXPERIENCE, ATTRIBUTES, SKILLS, AND DAMAGE, ALL HAVE NUMERICAL VALUE.

WITH ITS COMPLEXITY AND OPEN-ENDED FANTASY STRUCTURE, D&D HAS A POTENTIAL FOR IMAGINATIVE ESCAPISM NOT PREVIOUSLY SEEN IN TRADITIONAL CHILDREN'S BOARD GAMES.

KIDS LIKE CHILD PRODIGY JAMES DALLAS EGBERT III.

D&D IS POPULAR WITH ADOLESCENTS AND YOUNG ADULTS, THE AGE WHEN MANY KIDS ARE EXPECTED TO LEAVE BEHIND FANTASY AND MOVE TOWARD THE ADULT WORLD.

AT AGE 12, DALLAS EGBERT HAD BEEN ASKED BY THE U.S. AIR FORCE TO HELP REPAIR THEIR COMPUTERS. AT AGE 16, HE WAS A COMPUTER SCIENCE MAJOR AT MICHIGAN STATE UNIVERSITY. ON AUGUST 15, 1979, HE DISAPPEARED.

FIVE DAYS LATER, WHEN HIS PARENTS WERE NOTIFIED, THEY HIRED A RENOWNED DETECTIVE, WILLIAM DEAR, TO LOOK INTO THE CASE. DEAR'S INVESTIGATION AND COMMENTS TO THE PRESS PLAYED UP EGBERT'S INTEREST IN DUNGEONS AND DRAGONS.

WHAT WASN'T DISCUSSED SO MUCH WAS THAT EGBERT WAS ALSO VERY DEPRESSED, FEELING ISOLATED, AND MAY HAVE BEEN USING HIS KNOWLEDGE OF CHEMISTRY TO COOK UP MIND-ALTERING DRUGS.

ONE OF DEAR'S MANY THEORIES, WHICH HE PUSHED IN THE MEDIA, WAS THAT EGBERT HAD GOTTEN LOST OR INJURED IN THE STEAM TUNNELS UNDER THE SCHOOL WHILE PLAYING A "LIVE VERSION" OF D&D.

"HE WOULD WANT MORE OF HIS 'FIX,' LIKE A JUNKIE CRAVES THE NEEDLE, UNTIL THE GAME WAS USING HIM, NOT THE OTHER, HEALTHY WAY AROUND.

". . . IN SOME INSTANCES WHEN A PERSON PLAYS THE GAME YOU ACTUALLY LEAVE YOUR BODY AND GO OUT OF YOUR MIND."

DETAILS, LIKE AN APPARENT SUICIDE NOTE AND ARRANGEMENT OF PINS ON A BULLETIN BOARD, WERE PRESENTED AS POSSIBLE PLOYS IN A FANTASY GAME.

ANOTHER THEORY WAS THAT EGBERT ASSOCIATED WITH HIS CHARACTER SO MUCH THAT HE LOST HIS IDENTITY AND HIS CONNECTION TO REALITY.

THE COMBINATION OF A YOUNG "COMPUTER GENIUS," STEAM TUNNELS, AND WHAT THE *NEW YORK TIMES* REFERRED TO AS "AN ELABORATE VERSION OF AN INTELLECTUAL GAME CALLED 'DUNGEONS AND DRAGONS'" PROVED IRRESISTIBLE TO THE MEDIA.

Student Feared Dead in Dungeon

Is Student Victim of Game

STUDENT MAY HAVE LOST LIFE TO INTELLECTUAL FANTASY

THE MEDIA PRINTED STATEMENTS BY SO-CALLED EXPERTS HIGHLIGHTING THE IDEA THAT D&D FULFILLED A "NEED TO ESCAPE FROM THE EVER-MORE UNPLEASANT REALITY"* FOR YOUNG PEOPLE.

A MONTH LATER, EGBERT TURNED HIMSELF OVER TO DEAR IN LOUISIANA. HE MADE DEAR PROMISE NOT TO REVEAL THE DETAILS OF HIS STORY.

AFTER MONTHS OF TALKING TO THE PRESS ABOUT THE D&D CONNECTION, DEAR FINALLY CAME FORWARD AND STATED PUBLICLY THAT THE GAME WAS NOT INVOLVED WITH THE DISAPPEARANCE IN ANY WAY. THIS WAS NOT WIDELY REPORTED.

THAT'S RIGHT.

NO CONNECTION.

IN TRUTH, DALLAS EGBERT WAS STRUGGLING WITH THE PRESSURE TO MEET HIS PARENTS' EXPECTATIONS AND WANTED TO GET AWAY. HAVING STARTED COLLEGE AT 16, HE WAS FEELING ISOLATED FROM HIS CLASSMATES. ALSO, HE MAY HAVE RECENTLY REALIZED HE WAS GAY. TRAGICALLY, LESS THAN A YEAR LATER HE ENDED HIS OWN LIFE.

DEAR ULTIMATELY REVEALED THE DETAILS IN HIS BOOK *THE DUNGEON MASTER*. DALLAS EGBERT HAD GONE DOWN TO THE TUNNELS TO COMMIT SUICIDE. BUT HE COULDN'T GO THROUGH WITH IT AND INSTEAD CHOSE TO DISAPPEAR.

HIS PARENTS ESTABLISHED THE DALLAS EGBERT MEMORIAL FUND, WHICH THEY HOPED WOULD BE ABLE TO HELP OTHER GIFTED YET TROUBLED YOUTH. BUT ANOTHER PARENT, FACING A SIMILAR TRAGEDY, CHOSE A VERY DIFFERENT PATH.

*AMITAI ETZIONI, PROFESSOR OF SOCIOLOGY AT COLUMBIA UNIVERSITY

IN 1982, ANOTHER TROUBLED TEEN AND D&D PLAYER, IRVING "BINK" PULLING JR., USED HIS MOTHER'S HANDGUN TO COMMIT SUICIDE.

PATRICIA PULLING DESCRIBED HER SON AS "A HAPPY, WELL-ADJUSTED KID" AND BLAMED HIS SUICIDE ON "A D&D CURSE [THAT] WAS PLACED ON HIM DURING A GAME CONDUCTED AT HIS LOCAL HIGH SCHOOL."

THE D&D SESSION WAS HELD AS PART OF A GIFTED AND TALENTED PROGRAM. CLASSMATES PRESENT CLAIMED NO SUCH CURSE TOOK PLACE, BUT PATRICIA PULLING SUED THE SCHOOL PRINCIPAL AND TSR, THE MAKER OF THE GAME.

"HE HAD A LOT OF PROBLEMS ANYWAY THAT WEREN'T ASSOCIATED WITH THE GAME."*

*A CLASSMATE OF PULLING ALSO IN THE GIFTED AND TALENTED PROGRAM

THESE PROBLEMS INCLUDED DEPRESSION, SOCIAL ISOLATION, AND VIOLENCE. BINK WAS UNABLE TO FIND A FRIEND TO NOMINATE HIM FOR STUDENT GOVERNMENT, AND JUST THREE WEEKS BEFORE HIS SUICIDE, 19 RABBITS RAISED BY MRS. PULLING WERE FOUND DEAD AND A NEIGHBORHOOD CAT DISEMBOWELED.

YEARS LATER, HIS MOTHER ADMITTED THAT BINK WAS DISPLAYING "LYCANTHROPIC" BEHAVIOR, RUNNING AROUND ON ALL FOURS AND BARKING IN THEIR BACKYARD.

MRS. PULLING'S EARLIER PUBLIC STATEMENTS ABOUT HER SON'S MENTAL STATE AND SURPRISE AT HIS SUICIDE WERE ALSO CONTRADICTED BY THE DETAILS OF HER OWN LAWSUIT, WHICH STATED THAT THE SCHOOL SHOULD HAVE STOPPED HIM PLAYING THE GAME BECAUSE . . .

". . . OF THIS YOUNGSTER UNDERGOING SEVERE EMOTIONAL DISTRESS PRIOR TO HIS ACTUALLY TAKING HIS LIFE."†

†PULLING'S ATTORNEY, W. D. WRIGHT

HER LAWSUITS WERE DISMISSED, BUT PULLING WENT ON TO FORM BADD (BOTHERED ABOUT DUNGEONS AND DRAGONS), AN ORGANIZATION DEVOTED TO EXPOSING THE SATANIC AND SUICIDE DANGERS OF D&D. SHE TEAMED UP WITH PSYCHIATRIST THOMAS RADECKI AND HIS ORGANIZATION, THE NATIONAL COALITION ON TELEVISION VIOLENCE (NCTV).

"THERE IS NO DOUBT IN MY MIND THAT THE GAME DUNGEONS AND DRAGONS IS CAUSING YOUNG MEN TO KILL THEMSELVES AND OTHERS."

TOGETHER THEY FILED A PETITION DEMANDING THAT WARNING LABELS BE REQUIRED ON THE GAMES STATING THAT THEY COULD CAUSE SUICIDE. IT WAS REJECTED.

THEY PRODUCED A LIST OF 128 INSTANCES OF PEOPLE HARMED BY D&D. FEWER THAN 25 ITEMS ON THE LIST WERE COMPLETE, WITH NAMES, DATES, AND LOCATIONS. UPON INVESTIGATION, MANY WERE REVEALED TO BE HEARSAY.

BADD/NCTV ALSO EDITED AND REPRODUCED MAINSTREAM MEDIA ARTICLES, LEAVING OUT CONTRADICTORY INFORMATION. RADECKI EVEN CITED A FICTITIOUS LETTER FROM THE NOVEL *MAZES AND MONSTERS*, BY RONA JAFFE, AS ACTUAL EVIDENCE.

UNBELIEVABLE!!

DESPITE THESE QUESTIONABLE PRACTICES, PULLING AND RADECKI APPEARED AS GAME EXPERTS ON NUMEROUS NATIONAL TV SHOWS LIKE *THE GERALDO RIVERA SHOW*, *SALLY JESSY*, *DONAHUE*, AND *60 MINUTES*.

PUBLIC ENEMY NUMBER 1

THE COMBINATION OF SUICIDE AND SATAN WAS IRRESISTIBLE TO THE MEDIA. BETWEEN 1979 AND 1992, SOME 111 NEWS STORIES APPEARED ON ROLE-PLAYING GAMES. ALMOST ALL NAMED ONLY DUNGEONS AND DRAGONS. OF ALL THE STORIES, 80 WERE ANTI-GAME AND 3 WERE PRO-GAME.

D&D WAS SOON BEING BANNED FROM SCHOOLS, CHURCHES, COMMUNITY CENTERS, AND LIBRARIES AROUND THE COUNTRY.

"MY SISTER TRIED TO START UP THE FIRST RPG CLUB IN THE SCHOOL. THE ANNOUNCEMENT . . . WAS UP FOR TWO DAYS BEFORE ENOUGH PARENTS CALLED UP FOR THE SCHOOL TO BAN IT. WE DECIDED TO USE THE LOCAL LIBRARY AND GOT THEIR PERMISSION. WE HAD A CHANCE TO GET TOGETHER TWICE BEFORE THE LOCAL LIBRARY ASKED US TO LEAVE."

ANYTOWN HIGH SCHOOL

"YOU HAVE AUTHORIZED RUSSIAN ROULETTE! OVER THE MONTHS TO COME THERE WILL BE MANY THRILLING AND HARMLESS CLICKS OF THE GUN AS DUNGEONS AND DRAGONS IS HELD TO THE HEADS OF OUR YOUNG PEOPLE. BUT ANOTHER DEADLY EXPLOSION WILL COME."*

*REV. ROBERT O. BAKKE

BUT GAMERS STARTED TO ORGANIZE AND PUSH BACK AGAINST THE OUTRAGEOUS CLAIMS WHILE SOCIAL SCIENTISTS BEGAN TO EXAMINE THE FACTS ABOUT TEEN SUICIDE.

BY 1991, THE AMERICAN ASSOCIATION OF SUICIDOLOGY, THE U.S. CENTERS FOR DISEASE CONTROL AND PREVENTION, AND HEALTH & WELFARE (CANADA) ALL CONCLUDED THAT THERE IS NO CAUSAL LINK BETWEEN FANTASY GAMING AND SUICIDE. PAUL CARDWELL JR., WRITING FOR THE *SKEPTICAL INQUIRER*, ALSO TOOK A CLOSE LOOK AT 1988 SUICIDE FIGURES FROM THE NATIONAL SAFETY COUNCIL. HE CONCLUDED THAT IF SUICIDES AMONG TEEN GAMERS FOLLOWED IN LINE WITH THE NATIONAL AVERAGE, 1,060 SUICIDES OUT OF THE TOTAL 5,300 SUICIDES WOULD HAVE BEEN GAMERS.

THIS IS ACTUALLY MUCH MORE THAN THE NCTV CLAIMED. WHEN RADECKI AND NCTV CITED STATISTICS TO SHOW THE NUMBER OF SUICIDES, MURDERS, AND ROBBERIES CAUSED BY ROLE-PLAYING GAMES, THEY CLAIMED THERE WAS A TOTAL OF 128. AND THAT NUMBER COVERED THE ENTIRE TIME SINCE D&D STARTED!

PERCENTAGE OF D&D SUICIDES IF THE RATE FOLLOWED THE NATIONAL AVERAGE

PERCENTAGE OF D&D-RELATED SUICIDES, MURDERS, AND ROBBERIES ACCORDING TO BADD AND NCTV STATISTICS

THE ASSOCIATION OF GIFTED-CREATIVE CHILDREN OF CALIFORNIA ENDORSES D&D FOR ITS EDUCATIONAL VALUE. AFTER A STUDY OF ADOLESCENT SUICIDES, THEY TOO FOUND NO LINKS TO D&D.

ALL RIGHT. I'M SORRY, KIDS, BUT WE NEED TO WIND THIS DOWN.

AAAAAHHHH!!!!

NO!

TODAY, MANY SCHOOLS AGAIN OFFER GIFTED AND TALENTED STUDENTS THE CHANCE TO PLAY D&D. AS A STUDENT AT OAKLAND UNIVERSITY SAYS,

"IT ALLOWS YOU TO WORK OUT THE FRUSTRATIONS AND THE DOLDRUMS OF CLASSES. YOU CAN DO ANYTHING YOUR WILDEST IMAGINATION WILL PERMIT. BUT IT'S NOT DANGEROUS."

CHECK-HATE

Think D&D was the first game ever to have nerdy kids across the nation obsessing over playing in a fantasy world? Nope. Way before anyone ever rolled a pair of eight-sided dice, kids were busy "gaming" in another medieval world of battling knights, crafty queens, and powerful kings. And, like D&D itself, this game was accused of having the ability to possess its players' imagination and sap their precious brain juice! At least, that's what the magazine *Scientific American* once warned.

"A pernicious excitement to learn and play CHESS has spread all over the country," *Scientific American* snarled way back in 1859. "Why should we regret this?" Well, they claimed chess was "a mere amusement of a very inferior character, which robs the mind of valuable time that might be devoted to nobler acquirements." Not only did *Scientific American* think chess was distracting kids from all those "nobler acquirements," it was also keeping them from their jumping jacks—since it offered "no benefit whatever to the body." Guess that's why the magazine recommended "out-door exercises" instead of practicing "this . . . mental gladiatorship."

BAD SPORT

But what about "gladiatorship" of the outdoor variety (otherwise known as SPORTS)? Well, the past offers plenty of famous examples of athletics-haters too. For instance, during the fourteenth century, a succession of English monarchs tried—and failed—to ban football (known as SOCCER in the States). It seems that the popular sport had a way of distracting the king's subjects from the more important things in life, such as farming the king's land, fighting the king's wars, and training for fighting the king's wars (especially practicing archery, which, of course, is now considered . . . a SPORT!). In 1366, Edward III was more successful at outlawing BOWLING (who would ever find that distracting?). CRICKET—the game, not the bug—also came in for a beating at the hands of Oliver Cromwell, who was first denounced for playing the "disreputable" sport in 1620 and then banned it when he became the leader of England and Ireland. Not long after that, on the other side of the Atlantic, the state of Connecticut proved you didn't need a king to shut down SHUFFLEBOARD. They prohibited it "in howses of Common Interteinment" (yeah, that's how they spelled back then) because it was "unfruitfully" wasting the settlers' "precious time."

BAD SPORT (ROUND TWO)

BET you don't know one of the biggest reasons for banning games (but ODDS are you can guess it, if you've noticed the hints). It's . . . GAMBLING! Betting on games was the main motive for Boston's Reverend Skinner to outlaw "the immoral practice of CROQUET" back in the 1870s (well, gambling . . . and the fact that croquet could be played by girls and boys—gulp—together!). Thirty years before that banning, Connecticut named another sport a no-no because of wagering on ninepins (yep—it was BOWLING again). Speaking of pins . . . public playing of PINBALL was suppressed in New York from the 1940s until 1976 because if you won a free game, it was considered gambling! That sounds FLIPPIN' crazy! But crazier still is a state law in South Carolina—still on the books—that makes it illegal to play ANY game using cards or dice . . . even if it's in your own home! So if you play a game like Monopoly: Do not pass Go. Do not collect $200. Really GO TO JAIL! Wow—that would definitely cut down on a kid's "out-door exercises." Guess in this case, *Scientific American* was right.

MORAL PANIC MEDIA CYCLE

In 1972, professor of sociology Stanley Cohen coined the phrase "moral panic" to describe how the media overreacts to new behavior and ends up defining (and distorting) how people understand it. For instance, when a new technology becomes popular, especially among youth, it is often greeted with suspicion by the older generation. That suspicion is then amplified by the media to draw more attention—often negative—to the behavior. It happens all the time, actually.

For instance, in the example below, watch how the "moral panic" over video games can turn a simple research paper about a little rise in vitamin D deficiency into . . .

THE RACKET OVER RICKETS.

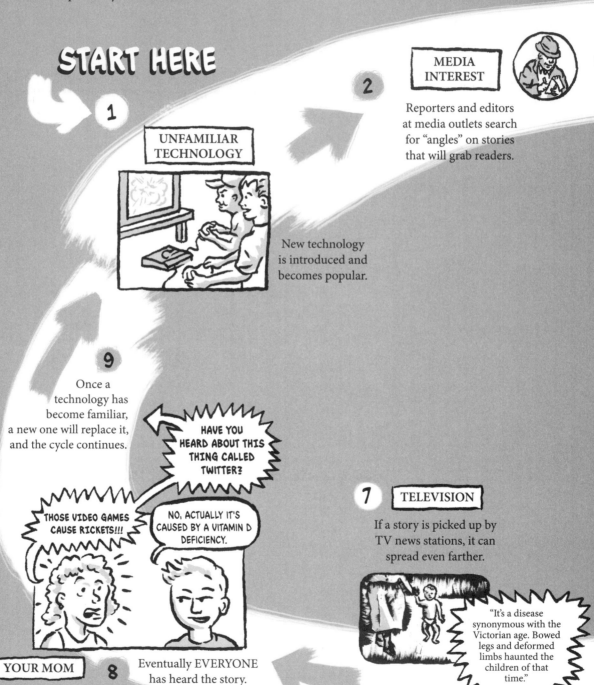

START HERE

1 UNFAMILIAR TECHNOLOGY

New technology is introduced and becomes popular.

2 MEDIA INTEREST

Reporters and editors at media outlets search for "angles" on stories that will grab readers.

9 Once a technology has become familiar, a new one will replace it, and the cycle continues.

HAVE YOU HEARD ABOUT THIS THING CALLED TWITTER?

THOSE VIDEO GAMES CAUSE RICKETS!!!

NO, ACTUALLY IT'S CAUSED BY A VITAMIN D DEFICIENCY.

7 TELEVISION

If a story is picked up by TV news stations, it can spread even farther.

"It's a disease synonymous with the Victorian age. Bowed legs and deformed limbs haunted the children of that time."

YOUR MOM **8** Eventually EVERYONE has heard the story.

50

In England, scientists did a study showing that rickets, a disease caused by a lack of vitamin D, was on the rise. In their report, "Diagnosis and Management of Vitamin D Deficiency," they pointed out lack of sunshine and poor diet as causes. However, the press release for the study had the following quote:

3 PRESS RELEASE

Professor Simon Pearce said, "Kids tend to stay indoors more these days and play on their computers instead of enjoying the fresh air. This means their vitamin D levels are worse than in previous years."

Newcastle University

When a university completes a research study, oftentimes their press office will issue a summary of the study for the media called a "press release."

4 NEWSPAPER STORY

Rickets Warning from Doctors as Vitamin D Deficiency Widens

Sharp Rise in Problem Blamed on Kids Indoors Playing Computers and Parents Using Too Much Sunscreen

A newspaper, trying to grab readers, focuses on the most exciting aspect of the study.

5 MORE NEWS STORIES

The story is picked up by other news outlets, each focusing on the video game angle.

TV and Computer Games Blamed for Return of Rickets

Video Gaming Leads to Surge in Rickets

Rickets Makes Comeback Among Computer Generation

Rickets Reappears Among Kids Hooked on Computers

6 THE INTERNET

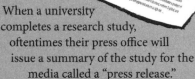

Gaming does NOT cause rickets - official

... so says the writer of the report that last week's headlines seized on

Once the story hits the internet, it is repeated by news outlets but also often debunked by websites devoted to the specific issue addressed.

But the original researchers stated, "We do not say that gaming causes rickets. The average age of a child with rickets is around 20 months old: too young to use a keyboard and mouse!"

FOR INSTANCE, IN 1932, BACK WHEN TALKING PICTURES WERE STILL NEW, A GANGSTER MOVIE, *SCARFACE*, WAS BANNED IN FIVE STATES FOR ITS "GLORIFICATION OF CRIME."

AS THAT TECHNOLOGY BECAME MORE FAMILIAR, THE PANIC OVER IT STARTED TO FADE. IN 1975, NO ONE PROTESTED THE RELEASE OF THE MOVIE *DEATH RACE 2000*, IN WHICH RACERS IN A WEIRD AND TWISTED FUTURE WIN POINTS FOR MOWING DOWN INNOCENT CITIZENS.

"IN THE YEAR 2000, HIT-AND-RUN DRIVING IS NO LONGER A FELONY. IT'S THE NATIONAL SPORT."

THAT LOOKS GREAT!

CAN WE SEE IT, DAD?

BUT A YEAR LATER, WHEN THE VIDEO GAME BASED ON THE MOVIE WAS RELEASED . . . THAT WAS ANOTHER STORY.

IN THE GAME, PLAYERS EARNED POINTS FOR RUNNING OVER PIXILATED "GREMLINS" THAT SCREAMED AND TRANSFORMED INTO GRAVESTONES THAT HAD TO BE AVOIDED.

"WE'VE TAKEN AWAY THEIR GUNS AND HOLSTERS AND COWBOYS AND INDIANS, AND WE'RE NOW GIVING THEM A CARTRIDGE WITH THE SAME KIND OF VIOLENT THEMES.

"THEY'RE NOT LEARNING HOW TO INTERACT WITH THE WORLD AROUND THEM AND THEIR PEERS. WHAT IS THE FUTURE WORLD GOING TO BE LIKE IF OUR CHILDREN CAN'T SPEAK TO EACH OTHER?"

Mrs. RONNIE LAMM
P.T.A. Pres. Long Island, NY

DESPITE ITS TAME GRAPHICS, DEATH RACE CAUSED A HUGE PUBLIC OUTCRY, INSPIRING THE FIRST ORGANIZED PROTESTS AGAINST A VIDEO GAME, LED BY LONG ISLAND PARENT RONNIE LAMM.

LAMM IN 1982, WHEN SHE EXPANDED HER PROTESTS TO INCLUDE VIDEO GAME ARCADES.

DEATH RACE ALSO INSPIRED THE NEWS PROGRAM *60 MINUTES* TO DO THE FIRST TV FEATURE ON THE PSYCHOLOGICAL IMPACT OF VIDEO GAMES.

IN 1981, 15-YEAR-OLD STEVE JURASZEK PLAYED ONE GAME OF DEFENDER FOR 16 HOURS STRAIGHT. IT LANDED HIM ON THE COVER OF *TIME*—AND IN HOT WATER WITH HIS PRINCIPAL WHEN IT WAS REVEALED HE STARTED THE RECORD-SETTING GAME DURING SCHOOL HOURS.

RONNIE LAMM APPEARED ON NATIONAL TALK SHOWS ADVOCATING FOR LAWS LIMITING ARCADES' PROXIMITY TO SCHOOLS AND WHAT HOURS VIDEOS GAMES COULD BE PLAYED BY KIDS.

GALAXY GAMES

NOTHING TO SEE.

MOVE ALONG!

POLICE LINE: DO NOT CROSS

LAMM AND OTHER CRITICS POINTED TO THE LACK OF ADULT SUPERVISION IN ARCADES, PLUS KIDS SKIPPING SCHOOL TO SPEND ALL THEIR CASH TO PLAY.

SPACE INVADERS

IN 1982, SURGEON GENERAL C. EVERETT KOOP WARNED THAT VIOLENT VIDEO GAMES COULD CAUSE "ABERRATIONS IN CHILDHOOD BEHAVIOR." BUT THE UPROAR THAT FOLLOWED FORCED HIM TO ADMIT THAT HIS STATEMENT "WAS NOT BASED ON ANY ACCUMULATED SCIENTIFIC EVIDENCE."

PITTSBURGH, OAKLAND, AND TOWNS ACROSS THE COUNTRY SOUGHT TO BAN OR LIMIT COIN-OPERATED ARCADES. ONE TOWN COUNCIL, IN MARSHFIELD, MASSACHUSETTS, RECENTLY VOTED TO KEEP ITS 29-YEAR-OLD BAN.

MOTION APPROVED! NOW WE MOVE ON TO THIS NUISANCE CALLED THE HORSELESS CARRIAGE!

IN THE LATE 1980s, AS TECHNOLOGY FOR GAME CONSOLES AND HOME COMPUTERS IMPROVED, THE POPULARITY OF VIDEO ARCADES FADED.

WHERE'S YOUR MOM?

PROTESTING AT THE ARCADE.

ONE OF THE MOST POPULAR ARCADE GAMES TO SUCCESSFULLY MAKE THE TRANSITION TO THE HOME MARKET
WAS THE FIGHTING GAME MORTAL KOMBAT. IT WAS ALSO AMONG THE MOST CONTROVERSIAL.

THE GAME INCLUDED "FINISHING MOVES" WHERE THE VICTORIOUS
PLAYER KILLED THE OTHER IN SOME BLOODY, GRUESOME FASHION
SUCH AS PULLING ITS HEAD OFF OR RIPPING OUT ITS HEART.

WHEN SENATOR JOSEPH LIEBERMAN SAW MORTAL KOMBAT,
HE DECIDED TO HOLD THE FIRST CONGRESSIONAL HEARINGS
INVESTIGATING VIOLENT VIDEO GAMES.

"WE'RE NOT TALKING PAC-MAN OR SPACE INVADERS ANYMORE. WE'RE TALKING ABOUT VIDEO GAMES THAT GLORIFY VIOLENCE AND TEACH CHILDREN TO ENJOY INFLICTING THE MOST GRUESOME FORMS OF CRUELTY IMAGINABLE."

EXPERTS FROM ACADEMIA, INDUSTRY, AND CITIZEN GROUPS
TESTIFIED. MANY NOTED THE NEED FOR MORE STUDIES AND
SOME SORT OF REGULATION ON CONTENT.

AT THE CONCLUSION OF THE HEARINGS, VIDEO-GAME
INDUSTRY LEADERS AGREED TO MEET AND CREATE A
RATING SYSTEM, AND IN 1994, THE ENTERTAINMENT
SOFTWARE RATING BOARD (ESRB) WAS ESTABLISHED.

"...CITIZENS, PARENTS, LEGISLATORS, AND EDUCATORS HAVE CAUSE FOR CONSIDERABLE CONCERN AND ALARM."

EUGENE PROVENZO
UNIVERSITY OF MIAMI (FL)

CSPAN
TODAY

BUT ANTI-VIDEO-GAME GROUPS CONTINUED TO ORGANIZE, AND
IN 1998, THE WALMART RETAIL STORE DECIDED TO BAN OVER
50 VIDEO GAMES IT DEEMED TOO VIOLENT FOR MINORS.

THEN SOMETHING HAPPENED THAT WOULD LINK VIDEO GAMES AND VIOLENCE IN THE PUBLIC'S MIND LIKE NOTHING THAT CAME BEFORE IT.

ON A TUESDAY IN 1999, TWO SENIOR HIGH SCHOOL STUDENTS IN COLUMBINE, COLORADO, ENTERED THEIR SCHOOL AND STARTED SHOOTING. WHEN THEY WERE DONE, 12 STUDENTS AND ONE TEACHER WERE DEAD, AND 24 OTHERS WERE WOUNDED.

IN THE AFTERMATH OF THE TRAGEDY, MEDIA AROUND THE WORLD SEARCHED FOR CAUSES. SOME SAID THE ATTACKS WERE REVENGE FOR RELENTLESS BULLYING. OTHERS BLAMED THE MUSIC THE BOYS LISTENED TO.

L 11:57 20-63 AM   04/20/99

ONCE IT WAS DISCOVERED THE KILLERS WERE FREQUENT PLAYERS OF THE VIOLENT GAME DOOM, VIDEO GAMES BECAME A HUGE FOCUS FOR THE MEDIA.

"KILLERS WORSHIPPED ROCK FREAK MANSON"

"OBSESSED WITH THE GAME, THE YOUNG KILLERS CREATED THEIR OWN LAYOUTS BASED ON THEIR SCHOOL."*

* LATER PROVEN UNTRUE.

DOOM WAS ONE OF THE EARLIEST "FIRST PERSON SHOOTER GAME" (FPSG) HITS. AN FPSG PUTS THE PLAYERS IN THE VIEWPOINT OF A SHOOTER ELIMINATING TARGETS.

A FREQUENT GUEST ON NEWS FEATURES HIGHLIGHTING THE VIOLENT VIDEO-GAME ANGLE OF THE STORY WAS LIEUTENANT COLONEL DAVE GROSSMAN. A SELF-NAMED "KILLOLOGIST," HE REFERRED TO FPSGs AS "MURDER SIMULATORS."

"THESE KIDS ARE LOOKING FOR INNOCENT PEOPLE TO GUN DOWN, TO RACK UP THE NEW HIGH SCORE ON THE NATIONAL VIDEO GAME."

47 103% 2 3 4 / 5 6 7 11
AMMO HEALTH ARMS ARMOR

GROSSMAN'S MAIN ASSERTIONS WERE THAT VIOLENT FPSGs DESENSITIZE KIDS TO MURDER AND PROVIDE FIREARMS TRAINING.

HE LINKED FPSGs TO MILITARY BEHAVIORAL TRAINING THAT HELPS SOLDIERS TO OVERCOME A NATURAL HUMAN RELUCTANCE TO KILL.

CRITICS OF GROSSMAN POINTED OUT SEVERAL PROBLEMS WITH HIS UNSUPPORTED THEORIES.

"ONE CAN'T ASSUME THAT HOW SOMEONE ACTS IN A FANTASY WORLD IS HOW THEY WILL ACT IN THE REAL WORLD."

"SOLDIERS AND GAMERS HAVE TOTALLY DIFFERENT GOALS."

"WHAT ABOUT THE MILLIONS OF PEOPLE WHO PLAY DOOM AND DON'T SHOOT ANYONE?"

THESE COUNTERARGUMENTS, HOWEVER, RARELY MADE THE HEADLINES ABOUT THE CONTROVERSY.

Violent Video Game Play Makes More Aggressive Kids, Study Shows

STUDY LINKS VIOLENT VIDEO GAMES, HOSTILITY

The Research Is In: Violent Video Games Can Lead to Violent Behavior

THE VIOLENT SIDE OF VIDEO GAMES

Don't Shoot: Why Video Games Really Are Linked to Violence

SHORTLY AFTER COLUMBINE, THE U.S. GOVERNMENT DID A STUDY THAT FOUND LITTLE EVIDENCE THAT VIOLENT VIDEO GAMES CAUSE VIOLENT BEHAVIOR. AS DAVID SATCHER, THE SURGEON GENERAL AT THE TIME, SAID,

THE U.S. SECRET SERVICE ALSO DID A STUDY THAT FOUND ONLY 12% OF SCHOOL SHOOTERS WERE FANS OF VIOLENT VIDEO GAMES, WHILE 24% READ VIOLENT BOOKS AND 27% WERE VIEWERS OF VIOLENT FILMS.

"WE CLEARLY ASSOCIATE MEDIA VIOLENCE TO AGGRESSIVE BEHAVIOR. BUT THE IMPACT WAS VERY SMALL COMPARED TO OTHER THINGS. SOME MAY NOT BE HAPPY WITH THAT, BUT THAT'S WHERE THE SCIENCE IS."

MY BODY COUNT WAS THROUGH THE ROOF!

THAT'S NOTHIN'— TRY LEVEL SIX!

THEY'RE MAKING A MOVIE. IT'S GOING TO BE SICK!

THIS DID NOT SEEM TO SWAY THE FAMILIES OF THE VICTIMS OF THE COLUMBINE SHOOTING WHO, IN 2001, TRIED TO SUE VIDEO-GAME MAKERS FOR $5 BILLION IN DAMAGES. THEIR CASE WAS DISMISSED.

THEIRS WAS NOT THE FIRST CASE FILED THAT ATTEMPTED TO BLAME VIOLENT BEHAVIOR ON VIDEO GAMES. IN 1999, PARENTS OF VICTIMS OF A SCHOOL SHOOTING IN KENTUCKY TRIED TO SUE VIDEO-GAME MAKERS FOR $33 MILLION. THE CASE WAS ALSO DISMISSED.

THE LAWYER IN THAT CASE WAS JACK THOMPSON, AN ANTI-GAME ACTIVIST WHO WOULD GO ON TO FILE DOZENS OF LAWSUITS AGAINST VIDEO GAME MANUFACTURERS AND PUSH TO GET LAWS PASSED TO RESTRICT VIDEO GAMES.

"WE HAVE A NATION OF *MANCHURIAN CANDIDATE** VIDEO GAMERS OUT THERE WHO ARE READY, WILLING, AND ABLE TO MASSACRE, AND SOME OF THEM WILL.

"YOU JUST WATCH. THERE IS GOING TO BE A COLUMBINE-TIMES-10 INCIDENT, AND EVERY-ONE WILL FINALLY GET IT."

*FAMOUS MOVIE ABOUT A BRAINWASHED SOLDIER PROGRAMMED TO KILL.

IN ADDITION TO HIS ACTIVISM AND LAWSUITS, ALL OF WHICH HE LOST, THOMPSON ALSO TRIED TO INFLUENCE POLICE INVESTIGATIONS, ASKING THAT THEY SEARCH FOR VIOLENT GAMES.

HERE'S SOMETHING CALLED LEGAL ENFORCER.

SOUNDS VIOLENT.

HE WAS OFTEN ACCUSED OF MAKING FALSE STATEMENTS. AFTER THE DEADLIEST MASS SHOOTING IN U.S. HISTORY AT VIRGINIA TECH, HE SAID OF THE KILLER,

"WHEN A KID WHO HAS NEVER KILLED ANYONE IN HIS LIFE GOES ON A RAMPAGE AND LOOKS LIKE THE TERMINATOR, HE'S A VIDEO GAMER."

BUT THE OFFICIAL VIRGINIA STATE PANEL COMMISSIONED TO INVESTIGATE THE SHOOTING DETERMINED THAT THE KILLER "PLAYED VIDEO GAMES LIKE SONIC THE HEDGEHOG," AND THAT "NONE OF THE VIDEO GAMES [HE HAD PLAYED] WERE WAR GAMES OR HAD VIOLENT THEMES."

THOMPSON BECAME SO HATED BY GAMERS THAT ONE CREATED A CUSTOM MORTAL KOMBAT CHARACTER BASED ON HIM AND POSTED A VIDEO OF IT ON YOUTUBE. UNTIL THOMPSON SUED FOR ITS REMOVAL.

IN 2008, THOMPSON WAS PERMANENTLY DISBARRED BY THE FLORIDA SUPREME COURT FOR INAPPROPRIATE CONDUCT. IN 2009, HE ANNOUNCED THAT HE "WAS NEVER DISBARRED" AND VOWED TO CONTINUE TO PRACTICE LAW.

ALMOST A YEAR AFTER THE COLUMBINE SHOOTINGS, THE U.S. SENATE HELD HEARINGS ENTITLED "THE IMPACT OF INTERACTIVE VIOLENCE ON CHILDREN." DR. CRAIG A. ANDERSON, DIRECTOR OF THE PSYCHOLOGY DEPARTMENT AT IOWA STATE UNIVERSITY, WAS AMONG THOSE WHO TESTIFIED.

IN THE 1990s, ANDERSON ESTABLISHED HIMSELF AS THE PREMIER RESEARCHER EXPLORING THIS LINK. HIS RESEARCH IS CITED BY ALMOST EVERY GROUP CONCERNED ABOUT VIDEO-GAME VIOLENCE.

"FACT 2: YOUNG PEOPLE WHO PLAY LOTS OF VIOLENT VIDEO GAMES BEHAVE MORE VIOLENTLY THAN THOSE WHO DO NOT."

Competitive Aggression Without Interaction: Effect of Competitive Versus Cooperative Instructions on Aggressive Behavior in Video Games

Effects of Violent Movies, and Trait of Hostility on Hostile Feelings and Aggressive Thoughts

TO UNDERSTAND HIS RESEARCH, HOWEVER, IT IS NECESSARY TO GO BACK TO THE EARLIEST EXPERIMENTS TRYING TO FIGURE OUT WHETHER KIDS WHO SAW ADULTS ACTING VIOLENTLY WOULD BE MORE LIKELY TO BE VIOLENT THEMSELVES.

IN 1963, SOCIAL SCIENTIST ALBERT BANDURA CONDUCTED AN EXPERIMENT IN WHICH THREE-TO-SIX-YEAR-OLD KIDS WATCHED ADULTS ATTACK A BLOW-UP "BOBO" CLOWN DOLL.

THE CHILDREN WERE THEN PLACED IN A ROOM WITH BOBO TO SEE IF THEY WOULD ATTACK HIM TOO. THEY DID. BANDURA CALLED THIS PROCESS "MODELING."

BOBO

BANDURA'S STUDY WAS VERY INFLUENTIAL, THOUGH SOME SCIENTISTS CRITICIZED ITS ASSUMPTIONS.

A LABORATORY SETTING IS AN ENTIRELY ARTIFICIAL ENVIRONMENT THAT BEARS LITTLE RESEMBLANCE TO REAL LIFE.

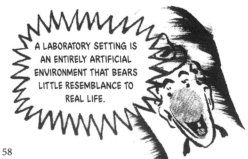

THE CHILDREN MAY HAVE BEEN TRYING TO PLEASE THE ADULT RESEARCHERS.

MEASURING AGGRESSION WITH A CLOWN TOY THAT IS DESIGNED TO BE HIT IS PROBLEMATIC. WHAT ELSE WOULD ONE EXPECT A CHILD TO DO WITH IT?

HITTING BOBO WAS SUPPOSED TO INDICATE THAT THE CHILDREN WERE MADE VIOLENT BY WHAT THEY HAD WITNESSED. THIS IS CALLED A "MEASURE OF AGGRESSION." A MEASURE OF AGGRESSION IS A BEHAVIOR THAT IS THEORIZED TO SHOW A TENDENCY TOWARD VIOLENCE. IT IS AN IMPORTANT CONCEPT FOR ANDERSON'S RESEARCH. FROM 1995 TO 2010, ANDERSON CONDUCTED MANY EXPERIMENTS TRYING OUT A VARIETY OF MEASURES. STUDIES LIKE . . .

"VIDEO GAMES AND AGGRESSIVE THOUGHTS, FEELINGS, AND BEHAVIOR IN THE LABORATORY AND IN LIFE"

IN THIS STUDY, THE SUBJECTS WERE RANDOMLY ASSIGNED TO PLAY EITHER A VIOLENT (CASTLE WOLFENSTEIN) OR A NONVIOLENT (MYST) VIDEO GAME.

CASTLE WOLFENSTEIN 3D PLAYERS "PUNISHED" OPPOSING PLAYERS WITH A NOISE BLAST THAT LASTED 6.81 SECONDS, COMPARED TO MYST PLAYERS, WHO BLASTED OPPONENTS FOR 6.65 SECONDS—A 0.16-SECOND DIFFERENCE.

OTHER ANDERSON STUDIES HAVE USED THE RECOGNITION OF CERTAIN WORDS OR THE ASSIGNING OF DIFFICULT PUZZLES AS "MEASURES OF AGGRESSION" TO SHOW THAT VIOLENT VIDEO GAMES CAUSE VIOLENT BEHAVIOR.

IN THE INTRODUCTION OF THE NOISE BLAST STUDY, ANDERSON POINTS TO THE VIDEO-GAME HABITS OF THE COLUMBINE SHOOTERS. REFERRING TO VIOLENT TV AND MOVIES, HE WROTE, "THERE ARE GOOD THEORETICAL REASONS TO EXPECT THAT VIOLENT VIDEO GAMES WILL HAVE SIMILAR, AND POSSIBLY LARGER, EFFECTS ON AGGRESSION."

THEN THE SUBJECTS PLAYED A COMPETITIVE REACTION-TIME GAME. IF THEIR OPPONENT LOST, THE SUBJECTS WERE TOLD TO "PUNISH" THE LOSER WITH A "NOISE BLAST." HOW LOUD AND LONG THEY SET THIS BLAST WAS HOW THE EXPERIMENTERS MEASURED THE LEVEL OF AGGRESSIVE BEHAVIOR.

SO THAT'S WHAT ANDERSON MEANT BY "INCREASED" WHEN HE WROTE "LABORATORY EXPOSURE TO A GRAPHICALLY VIOLENT VIDEO GAME INCREASED AGGRESSIVE THOUGHTS AND BEHAVIOR." AND WHEN HE TESTIFIED:

BUT DR. CHRISTOPHER J. FERGUSON, A VIOLENCE RESEARCHER AND FREQUENT CRITIC OF ANDERSON, HAD A DIFFERENT TAKE:

"THIS ISN'T REALLY A MEASURE OF VIOLENCE BECAUSE THE NOISE BLASTS OBVIOUSLY AREN'T DAMAGING, BUT HOW DOES IT FUNCTION AS A MEASURE OF AGGRESSION? IT SEEMS INTUITIVE, BUT DESPITE YEARS OF USE, THE MEASURE HAS NEVER BEEN SHOWN TO BE PREDICTIVE OF REAL-WORLD AGGRESSION, LET ALONE VIOLENT CRIME."

ANDERSON AND OTHER VIDEO-GAME CRITICS HAVE COMPARED THE DANGERS OF VIDEO GAMES AND THEIR RELATION TO VIOLENCE TO THAT OF SMOKING AND CANCER.

FOR INSTANCE, ANDERSON ARGUES THAT, EVEN THOUGH A 14-YEAR-OLD MIGHT NOT HAVE KILLED ANYONE, AFTER YEARS OF PLAYING VIOLENT VIDEO GAMES, HIS SITUATION IS COMPARABLE TO THAT OF A 45-YEAR-OLD WITH A TWO-PACK-A-DAY CIGARETTE HABIT. THE TEENAGE GAMER HAS INCREASED HIS RISK FOR VIOLENCE IN THE SAME WAY THAT A MIDDLE-AGED SMOKER HAS INCREASED HIS RISK FOR CANCER.

ANOTHER RESEARCHER, L. ROWELL HUESMANN, USES THE CANCER COMPARISON IN A DIFFERENT WAY:

"THE ONLY EFFECT SLIGHTLY LARGER THAN THE EFFECT OF MEDIA VIOLENCE ON AGGRESSION IS THAT OF CIGARETTE SMOKING ON LUNG CANCER."

BUT IS THIS CIGARETTE-LUNG CANCER COMPARISON A FAIR ONE? CIGARETTE SMOKING HAS BEEN SHOWN TO BE A CONTRIBUTING FACTOR IN CAUSING LUNG CANCER.

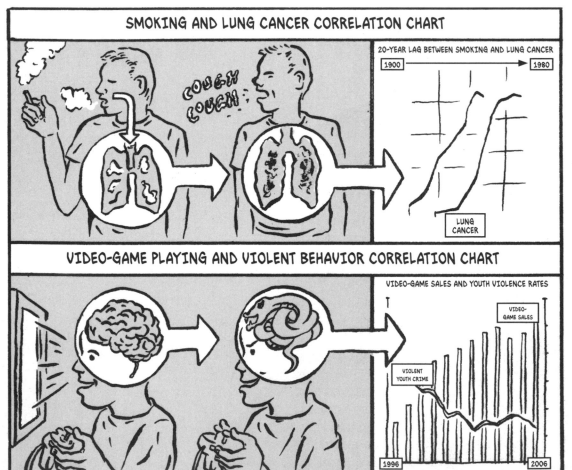

SMOKING AND LUNG CANCER CORRELATION CHART

COUGH COUGH

20-YEAR LAG BETWEEN SMOKING AND LUNG CANCER

1900 → 1980

LUNG CANCER

VIDEO-GAME PLAYING AND VIOLENT BEHAVIOR CORRELATION CHART

VIDEO-GAME SALES AND YOUTH VIOLENCE RATES

VIDEO-GAME SALES

VIOLENT YOUTH CRIME

1996   2006

THE RATES OF LUNG CANCER INCREASED OVER THE YEARS WHEN THE NUMBER OF PEOPLE SMOKING INCREASED. BUT WHEN MORE KIDS STARTED PLAYING VIOLENT VIDEO GAMES, YOUTH CRIME WENT DOWN.

MAJOR STUDIES EXAMINING RESEARCH LIKE ANDERSON'S BY THE HARVARD MEDICAL SCHOOL CENTER FOR MENTAL HEALTH, THE *JOURNAL OF ADOLESCENT HEALTH*, AND OTHERS FOUND NO CONCLUSIVE LINK BETWEEN VIDEO-GAME PLAYING AND VIOLENT BEHAVIOR.

DID FLUFFY SEE ME VAPORIZE THOSE ZOMBIES?

ONE ANALYSIS NOTED THAT ANDERSON AND COLLEAGUES LEFT OUT RESULTS THAT DIDN'T SUPPORT THEIR CASE. ANOTHER CLAIMED DATA WAS IMPROPERLY CALCULATED AND PRODUCED FALSE RESULTS. IN AN ILLINOIS COURT CASE, A RESTRICTIVE VIDEO-GAME LAW WAS THROWN OUT. THE JUDGE CONCLUDED . . .

"DR. ANDERSON ALSO HAS NOT PROVIDED EVIDENCE TO SHOW THAT THE PURPORTED RELATIONSHIP BETWEEN VIOLENT VIDEO-GAME EXPOSURE AND AGGRESSIVE THOUGHTS OR BEHAVIOR IS ANY GREATER THAN WITH OTHER TYPES OF MEDIA VIOLENCE, SUCH AS TELEVISION OR MOVIES."

AT LEAST NINE VIDEO-GAME CENSORSHIP LAWS HAVE BEEN CHALLENGED IN COURTS; IN EACH CASE THE PROPOSED LAWS WERE STRUCK DOWN ON BOTH CONSTITUTIONAL AND SCIENTIFIC GROUNDS.

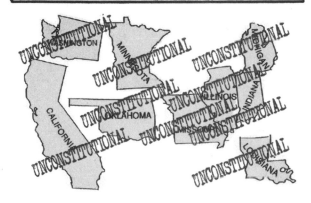

MOST RECENTLY CALIFORNIA, WITH ITS THEN ACTION STAR TURNED GOVERNOR ARNOLD SCHWARZENEGGER, PASSED A LAW MAKING IT ILLEGAL FOR ANYONE TO SELL A VIDEO GAME DEEMED "VIOLENT" TO A MINOR.

WE WILL TERMINATE VIOLENT VIDEO-GAME SALES TO MINORS!

THE CASE ENDED UP IN THE SUPREME COURT, WHERE IT WAS DECIDED THAT THE LAW WAS UNCONSTITUTIONAL ON FREE-SPEECH GROUNDS. WATCHERS OF THE COURT NOTED HOW THE DECISION WAS SUPPORTED BY BOTH LIBERAL AND CONSERVATIVE MEMBERS.

"LIKE THE PROTECTED BOOKS, PLAYS AND MOVIES, VIDEO GAMES COMMUNICATE IDEAS. . . . THAT SUFFICES TO CONFER FIRST AMENDMENT PROTECTION.

"THIS COUNTRY HAS NO TRADITION OF SPECIALLY RESTRICTING CHILDREN'S ACCESS TO DEPICTIONS OF VIOLENCE. . . . GRIMMS' FAIRY TALES, FOR EXAMPLE, ARE GRIM INDEED."

"I MEAN, IF YOU ARE SUPPOSING A CATEGORY OF VIOLENT MATERIALS DANGEROUS TO CHILDREN, THEN HOW DO YOU CUT IT OFF AT VIDEO GAMES? WHAT ABOUT FILMS? WHAT ABOUT COMIC BOOKS?"

DON'T LOOK NOW!

OVERKILL

Protesters who accuse video games of "overkill" are guilty of the same thing when they exaggerate their claims against the games. But "overkill" is a surefire way to grab headlines, which is part of what the protest is all about. The problem is . . . sometimes the surefire can backfire! All of the "negative" publicity that video-game protests produce actually can HELP a game become a HIT!

STUBBS GRUB HUBBUB

Wideload was just a little company when it released its first game, which starred a zombie hero named Stubbs. Early on, the game didn't make much of a (bloody) splash . . . until Stubbs was launched into the news as a promoter of childhood CANNIBALISM! And who did Stubbs (and Wideload) have to thank for all that free publicity? Why, it was Senator Joe Lieberman, who, twelve years after forming his congressional committee to condemn video games, was still at it. But while the game's full title, Stubbs the Zombie in Rebel Without a Pulse, might signal to some people that it was all meant as a joke (and they'd be right), Senator Joe was DEAD serious when he asked the public to chew over the cannibalism charges. During a press conference to announce that the game was one of 2005's "12 to Avoid" for parents, Lieberman lamented that Stubbs sent "just the worst kind of message to kids." But was it the senator who got the message wrong? Wideload sure thought so: "Stubbs, they say, is a cannibal. This is nonsense, as anyone with a working knowledge of cannibals can tell you. Stubbs is a zombie!" After all, Wideload pointed out, someone has to be alive to be a cannibal. That was why the company comically called the cannibalism story "insulting as well as injurious!" But it wasn't "injurious" to their business, as Stubbs became "a huge success" for Wideload. Instead of BITING the dust, as Lieberman hoped would happen, the flesh-munching Stubbs was picked as an Xbox "Classic" in 2008, and the company that created him is now a part of Disney. Turns out that Stubbs is a zombie with nine lives.

CLAP "TRAP"

While we're talking Lieberman, let's note that his biggest attack during his original 1993 committee was aimed at a video game about vampires called Night Trap. According to the committee's "expert" panelists, the game had a kid-corrupting goal of murdering women. But had the "experts" ever PLAYED? Or were they merely engaging in "overkill"—considering that the game's goal was to try to SAVE the women! Speaking of SAVE—that's exactly what the controversy did for the vampire-trapping game (sales had SUCKED until then). By the time Senator Lieberman's second set of hearings started in March 1994, Night Trap was a bestseller! Mortal Kombat experienced a similar boost in business. Even though the game was a rip-off of the more popular Street Fighter II, Kombat had something Street Fighter didn't—a splash of animated blood. At the time of the hearings, the congressmen praised Nintendo for cutting the gore in their version of Kombat (the blood was replaced by giant puddles of sweat—YEECH!) but attacked Sega, who released an uncensored version of the same game. Sega argued that the MA-13 "mature" rating they stamped on their Kombat made them just as "responsible" as Nintendo. It also made them richer. Sega's bloodier version ended up outselling Nintendo's three to one!

CHEESE VERSUS SLEAZE

Even back when Long Island PTA President Ronnie Lamm led the first charge against a video game, the Death Race public protest turned Exidy, which produced the game, into a success. During the same year as the protest, 1976, they sold over 1,000 of their machines (that was a huge number then for the basically unknown company). "It seemed like the more controversy, the more our sales increased," Exidy president Pete Kauffman affirmed. In fact, across the board, arcade-game sales improved that year. But perhaps the biggest backfire of all came from the campaign to keep kids out of arcades completely, blocking the unsupervised mixing of adults and children in the establishments. Atari, one of the biggest companies in video games at the time, agreed with the idea and decided to launch a series of family-friendly arcades that would also serve cheap snacks. Originally the restaurant chain was called Pizza Time Theater, but later it was changed to Chuck E. Cheese's. Instead of stamping out arcades, Lamm's efforts helped to create a super-successful business that brought parents AND kids together to play video games (while chomping on pizza, surrounded by large, animatronic mice).

SICKEST GAME OF ALL?

Attorney Jack Thompson proposed his OWN gory game as a public protest in 2005, and then challenged the video-game industry to actually produce it. Described in disgusting detail, Thompson's game revolves around a father avenging the death of his son, who died at the hands (and baseball bat) of a crazed high-school gamer. At one point, Thompson has the deadly daddy shoot down a Walmart clerk who sold the murder-inducing game. The father kills the clerk and then angrily shouts, "You should have checked kids' IDs!" But maybe Jack should have first checked facts: According to a Federal Trade Commission report, the video game industry's rating systems worked better than BOTH the movie and music industries' systems when it came to limiting sales of M-rated games to underage kids. The FTC also found that 83 percent of game purchases for underage consumers were made by—you guessed it—the parents themselves. So, if you want kids to stop playing M-rated games, you know who to aim for next time, Mr. Thompson.(That's right . . . DADDY!) Or maybe anti-game crusaders should just learn to keep quiet, as it seems the less attention they bring to the violent games, the fewer people will buy them.

GOOD FOR YOU

PLAYING VIDEO GAMES!

So, which wild-eyed youth group of assassins-in-training actually gives AWARDS for kids playing video games? Try the BOY SCOUTS!* Guess those do-GOODers must know something about video games that Senator Lieberman, Dr. Anderson, and attorney Thompson don't (or maybe don't want to acknowledge). Below . . . the video game headlines you RARELY see.

VIDEO GAMES CAN HELP!

Video games are used for pain management in some children's hospitals to distract kids from their discomfort; Foldit turns gamers' virtual world into a real-life viral one, helping in AIDS-related research. And Food Force, sponsored by the U.N. World Food Program, simulates delivering aid to people affected by large-scale humanitarian crises.

BRAINS GAIN FROM GAMES!

Shooter-style games sharpen sensory skills in the brain, as well as the speed of processing information to make faster decisions, according to a 2007 study. Other studies show gaming, with its interactive, exploratory, and discover-the-rules-as-you-go-along structure, "stimulates learning of facts and skills such as strategic thinking, creativity, cooperation, and innovative thinking."

GAMING IS HEALTHY!

Action games improved eye-hand skills in a study of surgeons who played regularly; other studies show general vision enhanced and "lazy eye" improved. Non-violent puzzle and word video games calm people and might one day be used therapeutically for treating high blood pressure. Nintendo's Wii system is physically interactive, providing a good work-out—and if you play sports computer games, you're more likely to play REAL sports, too!

*Cub Scouts, Tiger Scouts, and Webelos Scouts can earn the award by helping an old lady across a "virtual" street, so to speak (that is, teaching a grown-up how to play a video game, along with other tasks).

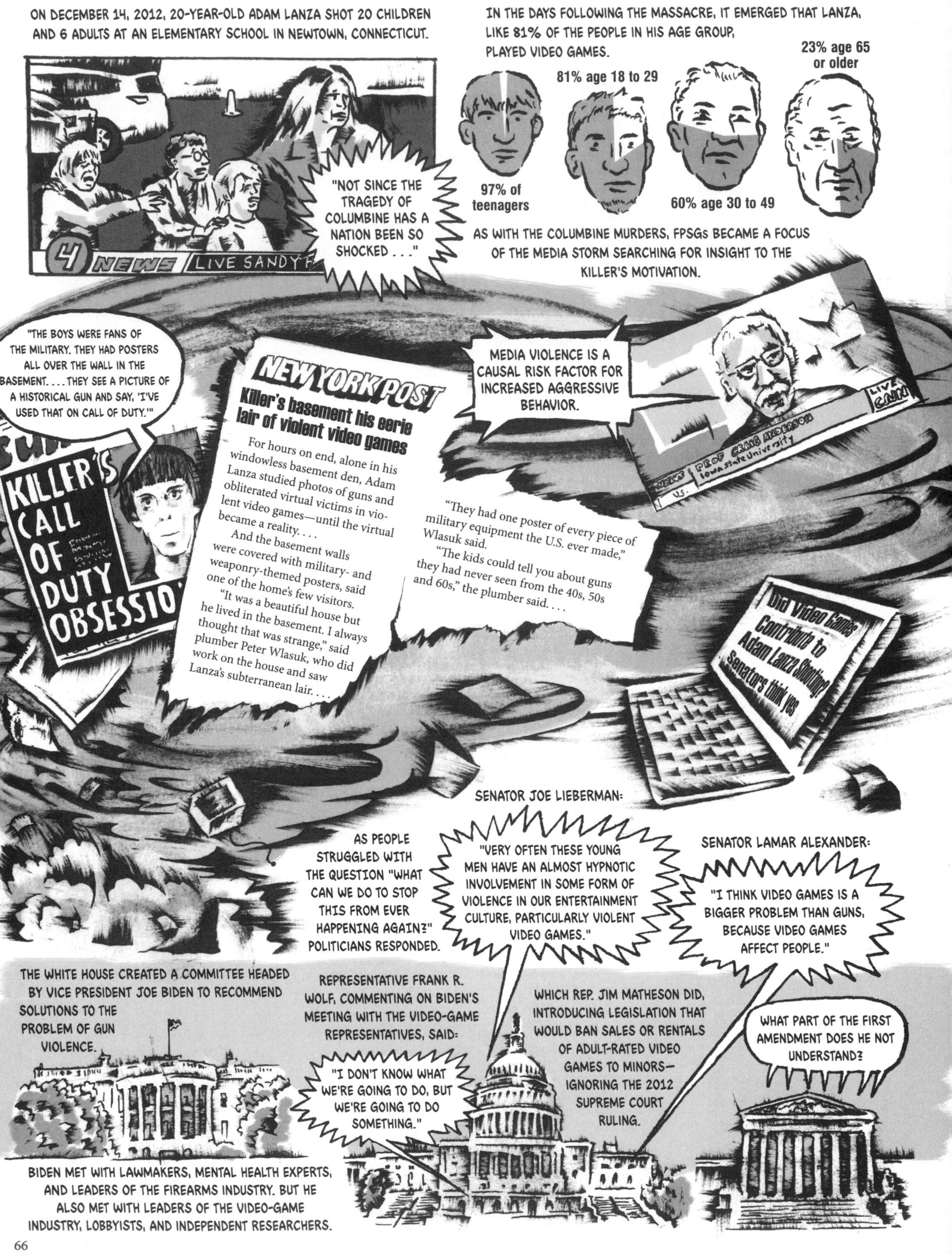

ON DECEMBER 14, 2012, 20-YEAR-OLD ADAM LANZA SHOT 20 CHILDREN AND 6 ADULTS AT AN ELEMENTARY SCHOOL IN NEWTOWN, CONNECTICUT.
4 NEWS LIVE SANDY H
"NOT SINCE THE TRAGEDY OF COLUMBINE HAS A NATION BEEN SO SHOCKED . . ."
IN THE DAYS FOLLOWING THE MASSACRE, IT EMERGED THAT LANZA, LIKE 81% OF THE PEOPLE IN HIS AGE GROUP, PLAYED VIDEO GAMES.
97% of teenagers
81% age 18 to 29
60% age 30 to 49
23% age 65 or older
AS WITH THE COLUMBINE MURDERS, FPSGs BECAME A FOCUS OF THE MEDIA STORM SEARCHING FOR INSIGHT TO THE KILLER'S MOTIVATION.
"THE BOYS WERE FANS OF THE MILITARY. THEY HAD POSTERS ALL OVER THE WALL IN THE BASEMENT. . . . THEY SEE A PICTURE OF A HISTORICAL GUN AND SAY, 'I'VE USED THAT ON CALL OF DUTY.'"
KILLER'S CALL OF DUTY OBSESSIO
NEW YORK POST
Killer's basement his eerie lair of violent video games
For hours on end, alone in his windowless basement den, Adam Lanza studied photos of guns and obliterated virtual victims in violent video games—until the virtual became a reality. . . .
And the basement walls were covered with military- and weaponry-themed posters, said one of the home's few visitors.
"It was a beautiful house but he lived in the basement. I always thought that was strange," said plumber Peter Wlasuk, who did work on the house and saw Lanza's subterranean lair. . . .
"They had one poster of every piece of military equipment the U.S. ever made," Wlasuk said.
"The kids could tell you about guns they had never seen from the 40s, 50s and 60s," the plumber said. . . .
MEDIA VIOLENCE IS A CAUSAL RISK FACTOR FOR INCREASED AGGRESSIVE BEHAVIOR.
LIVE
NEWS PROF CRAIG ANDERSON Iowa State University
Did Video Games Contribute to Adam Lanza Shooting? Senators think yes
SENATOR JOE LIEBERMAN:
AS PEOPLE STRUGGLED WITH THE QUESTION "WHAT CAN WE DO TO STOP THIS FROM EVER HAPPENING AGAIN?" POLITICIANS RESPONDED.
"VERY OFTEN THESE YOUNG MEN HAVE AN ALMOST HYPNOTIC INVOLVEMENT IN SOME FORM OF VIOLENCE IN OUR ENTERTAINMENT CULTURE, PARTICULARLY VIOLENT VIDEO GAMES."
SENATOR LAMAR ALEXANDER:
"I THINK VIDEO GAMES IS A BIGGER PROBLEM THAN GUNS, BECAUSE VIDEO GAMES AFFECT PEOPLE."
THE WHITE HOUSE CREATED A COMMITTEE HEADED BY VICE PRESIDENT JOE BIDEN TO RECOMMEND SOLUTIONS TO THE PROBLEM OF GUN VIOLENCE.
REPRESENTATIVE FRANK R. WOLF, COMMENTING ON BIDEN'S MEETING WITH THE VIDEO-GAME REPRESENTATIVES, SAID:
"I DON'T KNOW WHAT WE'RE GOING TO DO, BUT WE'RE GOING TO DO SOMETHING."
WHICH REP. JIM MATHESON DID, INTRODUCING LEGISLATION THAT WOULD BAN SALES OR RENTALS OF ADULT-RATED VIDEO GAMES TO MINORS—IGNORING THE 2012 SUPREME COURT RULING.
WHAT PART OF THE FIRST AMENDMENT DOES HE NOT UNDERSTAND?
BIDEN MET WITH LAWMAKERS, MENTAL HEALTH EXPERTS, AND LEADERS OF THE FIREARMS INDUSTRY. BUT HE ALSO MET WITH LEADERS OF THE VIDEO-GAME INDUSTRY, LOBBYISTS, AND INDEPENDENT RESEARCHERS.

IN CONNECTICUT, A COMMUNITY GROUP LAUNCHED A VIOLENT VIDEO-GAME BUY-BACK PROGRAM. A GIFT CERTIFICATE PROVIDED BY LOCAL MERCHANTS WAS TO BE GIVEN TO PEOPLE WHO TURNED IN THEIR VIOLENT GAMES.

HOPE THEY'RE GAMESTOP CARDS.

I ALREADY BEAT THIS GAME, AND THE NEW VERSION JUST CAME OUT.

IT WAS REPORTED THAT THE GAMES WOULD BE BURNED, AS HAS BEEN DONE WITH OFFENDING COMICS, RECORDS, BOOKS, AND DVDS. TOWN OFFICIALS, HOWEVER, WERE VAGUE ON THIS POINT.

AFTER MUCH MEDIA ATTENTION, THEY DECIDED NOT TO GO AHEAD WITH THE BUY-BACK. THEY SAID THEY HAD ALREADY MET THEIR GOAL OF RAISING PUBLIC AWARENESS.

POOF!

ACTIVIST JACK THOMPSON SURFACED, SENDING E-MAILS TO GAMING SITES LIKE JOYSTIQ.COM SAYING "BLOOD IS ON YOUR HANDS" AND LEAVING A MESSAGE FOR THE PRESIDENT OF THE ENTERTAINMENT CONSUMERS ASSOCIATION, WHOSE OFFICES ARE NEAR NEWTOWN.

"SO MAYBE NOW YOU'LL GET IT, HAL. MAYBE NOW YOU'LL GET IT . . . THOUGH SOMEHOW I DOUBT IT."

THIS TIME, A NEW VOICE EMERGED, STRONGLY LAYING THE BLAME FOR THE SHOOTINGS ON VIDEO GAMES: THE NATIONAL RIFLE ASSOCIATION (NRA).

"A CALLOUS, CORRUPT, AND CORRUPTING SHADOW INDUSTRY THAT SELLS AND SOWS VIOLENCE AGAINST ITS OWN PEOPLE. THROUGH VICIOUS, VIOLENT VIDEO GAMES WITH NAMES LIKE BULLET STORM, GRAND THEFT AUTO, MORTAL KOMBAT, AND SPLATTERHOUSE."

THE NRA IS AN ADVOCACY GROUP WITH CLOSE TIES TO THE $12-BILLION-A-YEAR GUN INDUSTRY THEY PUSH FOR THE RIGHTS OF GUN OWNERS AND EDUCATE THE PUBLIC ON GUN SAFETY.

IN 2004, THE NRA FOUGHT HARD—AND SUCCESSFULLY—TO DEFEAT THE RENEWAL OF A FEDERAL BAN ON ASSAULT WEAPONS.

BANG

RAT A TAT

BANG

IT HAS BEEN REPORTED THAT LANZA USED A SEMIAUTOMATIC ASSAULT RIFLE IN THE MASSACRE, AND POLICE FOUND TWO HANDGUNS AND A SHOTGUN AT THE SCENE. THE GUNS, AND THREE RIFLES FOUND IN HIS HOME, HAD BEEN PURCHASED BY HIS MOTHER. LANZA HAD MURDERED HER BEFORE HIS RAMPAGE.

ASTER

SIG SAUER

GLOCK

A GUN ENTHUSIAST, SHE TAUGHT HER BOYS HOW TO SHOOT.

SUPPORTERS OF VIDEO GAMES COUNTERED AND QUESTIONED THE NRA'S MOTIVES. RESEARCHER CHRISTOPHER J. FERGUSON CAUTIONED AGAINST BEING DISTRACTED BY "SOMETHING THAT IS NOT GOING TO BE VERY HELPFUL, WHETHER IT'S VIDEO GAMES OR MOVIES OR WHATEVER ELSE."

WRITING IN HIS "INSERT COIN" COLUMN FOR FORBES, PAUL TASSI WAS MORE DIRECT: "THE MESSAGE HERE WAS CLEAR, BLAME EVERYTHING BUT GUNS. WHY BOTHER CONSIDERING THAT VIOLENT VIDEO GAMES ARE PLAYED IN ALL CORNERS OF THE WORLD, YET SOMEHOW IT'S ONLY THE U.S. WITH ITS LAX GUN LAWS WHERE TRAGEDIES LIKE THIS HAPPEN WITH THIS FREQUENCY?"

CRITICS ALSO POINT TO THE AVAILABILITY OF GUNS AS A MORE LIKELY CULPRIT THAN VIOLENT VIDEO GAMES. AMERICA HAS ALMOST 89 GUNS PER 100 PEOPLE; IN OTHER COUNTRIES WHERE VIDEO GAMES ARE JUST AS POPULAR, THERE ARE CLOSER TO 30 GUNS PER 100—EXCEPT JAPAN, WHERE IT'S ABOUT HALF A GUN.

HEY! WHO'S GOT THE HALF A GUN?

BUT IN THE U.S. THOSE NUMBERS MAY BE CHANGING. IN 2012, VIDEO-GAME SALES DROPPED BY 20%. MEANWHILE, GUN DEALERS HAVE REPORTED A HUGE INCREASE IN GUN SALES, ESPECIALLY AUTOMATIC-STYLE WEAPONS. BUYERS MAY FEAR A NEW ASSAULT GUN BAN.

"THIS TIME AROUND— IF THEY PASS ONE—IT MAY NEVER EXPIRE."

ON JANUARY 16, 2013, PRESIDENT BARACK OBAMA ANNOUNCED THE PROPOSALS THE WHITE HOUSE COMMISSION CAME UP WITH, WHICH INCLUDED SETTING ASIDE $10 MILLION TO . . .

"FUND RESEARCH INTO THE EFFECTS THAT VIOLENT VIDEO GAMES HAVE ON YOUNG MINDS."

HE ALSO DIRECTED THE CENTERS FOR DISEASE CONTROL (CDC), THE GOVERNMENT AGENCY WORKING TO PROTECT PUBLIC HEALTH AND SAFETY, TO INVEST $20 MILLION TO EXPAND CURRENT GUN DATA COLLECTION, AND TO RESTART THEIR RESEARCH INTO THE ROOT CAUSES OF GUN VIOLENCE.

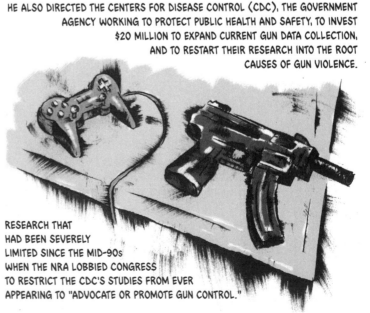

RESEARCH THAT HAD BEEN SEVERELY LIMITED SINCE THE MID-90s WHEN THE NRA LOBBIED CONGRESS TO RESTRICT THE CDC'S STUDIES FROM EVER APPEARING TO "ADVOCATE OR PROMOTE GUN CONTROL."

TECHNOLOGY

HOW LONG HAVE CHILDREN BEEN DOMINATED AND OPPRESSED
BECAUSE OF FEAR OVER THEIR USE OF NEW TECHNOLOGY?
IT GOES BACK A LONG WAY INTO THE DISTANT PAST.
THE OPERATIVE WORD HERE BEING "DISTANT."

REMOTE CONTROL

IN THE LATE 1700s, SOME REPORTS SAY THE CHAPPE BROTHERS, FRENCH TEENAGERS,
EXPLORED A NEW LONG-DISTANCE COMMUNICATION SYSTEM AS A WAY TO SEND MESSAGES
TO ONE ANOTHER WHILE AT DIFFERENT SCHOOLS. WHAT IS KNOWN FOR SURE IS THAT OLDER
BROTHER CLAUDE IS CREDITED WITH THE INVENTION OF THE SEMAPHORE. IT WAS
THE FIRST TELECOMMUNICATIONS SYSTEM OF THE INDUSTRIAL AGE.

DURING THE FRENCH REVOLUTION, WHILE TRYING TO PERFECT THEIR "MECHANICAL INTERNET,"
THEIR APPARATUS WAS TWICE DESTROYED BY MOBS WHO FEARED IT WAS BEING USED TO
COMMUNICATE WITH THE ENEMY. IT IS SAID THAT THE BROTHERS BARELY ESCAPED WITH THEIR LIVES.

NAPOLEON AND OTHERS SAW THE MILITARY
POTENTIAL, AND SOON THE SYSTEM SPREAD
THROUGHOUT EUROPE.

THEN IN 1844, SAMUEL F. B. MORSE DEMONSTRATED HIS TELEGRAPH BY
TRANSMITTING A PHRASE FROM BALTIMORE TO WASHINGTON, D.C.

APPARENTLY OTHERS SHARED THE FEELING REFLECTED IN MORSE'S WORDS.
MEN ADVISED THAT THE SYSTEM BE RESERVED FOR BUSINESS. THIS WAS
TRUE OF THE TELEPHONE AS WELL, WHICH WAS NOT TO BE USED BY. . .

It reads: "What hath God wrought?"

Indeed!

Hear! Hear!

I don't get it.

". . . talkative women with their frivolous electrical conversations about inconsequential personal subjects."

AT LEAST TWO DOZEN NOVELS WERE PUBLISHED TELLING STORIES OF YOUNG WOMEN WHO WORKED AS TELEGRAPH OPERATORS MEETING UNSAVORY CHARACTERS OF DUBIOUS BACKGROUNDS.

WOMEN WERE DEPICTED AS NEEDING TO BE RESCUED OR PROTECTED FROM THE NEW TECHNOLOGY. THE MORAL WAS THAT NO GOOD COULD COME FROM WOMEN USING MEN'S TECHNOLOGY.

WIRED LOVE*
A ROMANCE IN DOTS AND DASHES
AUTHOR Ella Cheever Thayer

*ACTUAL TITLE.

IN THE LATE 1800s, THESE FEARS AND A FEW NEW ONES TRANSFERRED TO THE TELEPHONE.

"THE DOORS MAY BE BARRED AND A REJECTED SUITOR KEPT OUT, BUT HOW IS THE TELEPHONE TO BE GUARDED?"

"DOES THE TELEPHONE MAKE MEN MORE ACTIVE OR MORE LAZY?"

"DOES THE TELEPHONE BREAK UP HOME LIFE AND THE OLD PRACTICE OF VISITING FRIENDS?"

SOME WERE OUTRAGED AND DISGUSTED THAT SWEETHEARTS WERE ACTUALLY MAKING KISSING NOISES OVER THE PHONE.

AND IN THE EARLY DAYS, TELEPHONE COMPANIES COULD LISTEN IN ON CONVERSATIONS AND DISCONNECT OR INTERRUPT CUSTOMERS WHO USED OFFENSIVE LANGUAGE.

BUT I WAS JUST TALKING ABOUT KISSING MY SWEET DONKEY!

AS THE TELEPHONE BECAME A PART OF EVERY HOUSEHOLD, MOST OF THE EARLY FEARS FELL AWAY.

BUT PARENTS CONTINUED TO HAVE FEARS ABOUT THEIR CHILDREN'S USE OF THE TELEPHONE . . .

AND WHO THEY USED IT WITH.

ARE YOU EXPECTING A CALL?

JUST ANSWER IT!

IT'S FOR ME!

WHO WAS THAT?

FRED FRISBEE.

WHO!?

HE LIVES IN CLINTON.

CLINTON!? THAT'S THREE TOWNS AWAY!

WITH THE ADVENT OF CELL PHONES AND THE INTERNET, THE TECHNOLOGY HAS CHANGED, BUT THE BASIC CONCERNS OF PARENTS HAVE NOT.

THOUGH, AS WITH EVERY NEW TECHNOLOGY, OTHER FEARS HAVE ARISEN.

YOU'RE TEXTING SOMEONE IN THE UKRAINE!?

I CAN'T IMAGINE THE CHARGES!

IRELAND'S TEXT-MAD YOUTH LOSING WRITING ABILITIES

IS TEXTING DESTROYING OUR LANGUAGE?

TEXTING REPLACES SPEECH FOR COMMUNICATION AMONG TEENS

TEXTING KEEPS TEENS FROM SLEEPING

IRELAND'S EDUCATIONAL DEPARTMENT ISSUED A REPORT RAISING FEARS THAT "TEXT MESSAGING, WITH ITS USE OF PHONETIC SPELLING AND LITTLE OR NO PUNCTUATION, SEEMS TO POSE A THREAT TO TRADITIONAL CONVENTIONS IN WRITING."

OMG, I BLU THT X-AM.

I DIDNT DO 2 GR8 EITHER.

SOME OPINION WRITERS AND MEDIA OUTLETS HAVE ECHOED AND AMPLIFIED THESE FEARS.

"IT IS THE RELENTLESS ONWARD MARCH OF THE TEXTERS, THE SMS (SHORT MESSAGE SERVICE) VANDALS WHO ARE DOING TO OUR LANGUAGE WHAT GENGHIS KHAN DID TO HIS NEIGHBORS EIGHT HUNDRED YEARS AGO. THEY ARE DESTROYING IT: PILLAGING OUR PUNCTUATION; SAVAGING OUR SENTENCES . . ."* AHHHHHHH!

*JOHN HUMPHRYS, WRITING FOR *THE DAILY MAIL*

AT LEAST ONE SCHOLAR, CRISPIN THURLOW, A LINGUIST AT THE UNIVERSITY OF WASHINGTON, BELIEVES THAT THESE FEARS HAVE REACHED THE LEVEL OF A MORAL PANIC.

"THESE POPULAR BUT INFLUENTIAL (MIS)REPRESENTATIONS TYPICALLY EXAGGERATE THE DIFFERENCE BETWEEN CMD [COMPUTER-MEDIATED DISCOURSE] AND NON-MEDIATED DISCOURSE . . ."

2moR®ow's ©lass @5$1GNMen|-

WTH?

RESEARCHERS AT THE UNIVERSITY OF TORONTO FOUND THAT TEENS COULD SWITCH EASILY BETWEEN TEXTING AND FORMAL WRITING: "TEENS' MESSAGING SHOWS THEM EXPRESSING THEMSELVES FLEXIBLY THROUGH ALL REGISTERS. THEY ACTUALLY SHOW AN EXTREMELY LUCID COMMAND OF THE LANGUAGE."

BELLATRX LS KILLED DA B !!

"THEY CAN TEXT 'IMHO' ON THEIR CELL PHONES, WRITE 'MY OWN OPINION IS' IN A SCHOOL ESSAY, AND READ 'IT IS MY BELIEF THAT YOUR SCAR HURTS WHEN LORD VOLDEMORT IS NEAR YOU' WITHOUT GETTING DISCOMBOBULATED," SAYS ERIC PAULSON, ASSOCIATE PROFESSOR OF LITERARY EDUCATION AT THE UNIVERSITY OF CINCINNATI.

AND SOME SCIENTIFIC RESEARCH SHOWS THE FEARS TO BE UNFOUNDED. A 2009 STUDY DONE BY THE BRITISH *JOURNAL OF DEVELOPMENTAL PSYCHOLOGY* FOUND THAT KIDS WHO USED "TEXTISMS" HAD A LARGER VOCABULARY AND COULD OFTEN UNDERSTAND SPELLING AND GRAMMAR BETTER THAN NONTEXTERS.

INDUBITABLY.

NOBTLY

"WITH SO MUCH WRITTEN CHATTER, BEING ABLE TO READ AND WRITE HAVE BECOME DEFINITE SOCIAL ADVANTAGES," NOTES TIMOTHY SHANAHAN, HEAD OF THE INTERNATIONAL READING ASSOCIATION.

LOL, CHCK THIS VID. SCK!

OMG

OMG

ORGA

YYSSW, GRAN

HTML/.X3

IT WAS A DARK AND

LAST NIGHT'S ASSIGNMENT

WHICH BRINGS UP ANOTHER POPULAR FEAR— THAT KIDS ENGAGE IN TOO MANY FORMS OF MEDIA.

ARTICLES IN MAJOR MEDIA OUTLETS WITH TITLES LIKE "GENERATION WIRED" AND "WIRED KIDS, NEGLIGENT PARENTS?" TALK ABOUT A VARIETY OF FEARS ABOUT THE EFFECTS OF DIGITAL TECHNOLOGY ON THE DEVELOPING BRAINS OF YOUTH.

FRAGMENTATION
A COMMON CONCERN IS THAT JUGGLING E-MAIL, TEXTING, ELECTRONIC GAMES, AND WEB SURFING FRAGMENTS REALITY INTO DISCONNECTED MOMENTS. "WE ARE . . . ASKING [OUR BRAINS] TO DO THINGS WE WEREN'T NECESSARILY EVOLVED TO DO," CLAIMS NEUROSCIENTIST ADAM GAZZALEY.

ADDICTION
RESEARCHERS THEORIZE THAT DIGITAL MEDIA EXCITES THE BRAIN'S IMPULSE TO RESPOND TO THREATS OR OPPORTUNITIES. THIS EXCITEMENT CAUSES THE BRAIN TO PRODUCE A CHEMICAL CALLED DOPAMINE, WHICH CAN BECOME ADDICTIVE, MAKING LIFE SEEM BORING WITHOUT IT.

DISTRACTION
NEUROSCIENTIST MICHAEL MERZENICH ASSERTS THAT OUR BRAINS ARE BEING "MASSIVELY REMODELED" BY THE DISTRACTIONS AND INTERRUPTIONS OF DIGITAL MEDIA AND WARNS THAT THE LONG-TERM EFFECTS ON OUR THINKING COULD BE "DEADLY."

MIND CHANGE
BRAIN RESEARCHER SUSAN GREENFIELD HAS CLAIMED THAT "MIND CHANGE," THE EFFECT OF OVERUSE OF MODERN TECHNOLOGY ON THE BRAIN, COULD POSE THE GREATEST THREAT TO HUMANITY AFTER CLIMATE CHANGE.

HEALTH RISKS
FEARS OFTEN CITED INCLUDE OVERUSE INJURIES TO THE HAND, OBESITY, MUSCLE AND JOINT PAIN, EYE STRAIN, AND EPILEPTIC SEIZURES.

A STUDY AT STANFORD UNIVERSITY IN FACT SHOWED THAT MOST HEAVY MULTITASKERS DO WORSE AT FILTERING DISTRACTION, JUGGLING PROBLEMS, AND FIGURING OUT WHAT INFORMATION HAS VALUE.

OTHER RESEARCHERS QUESTION WHETHER THIS ACTUALLY SHOWS MEDIA IS THE CAUSE. THEY THEORIZE THAT PERHAPS MULTITASKERS USE A LOT OF MEDIA BECAUSE THEY ARE EASILY DISTRACTED.

ONE AREA THAT MULTITASKERS DO WELL IN IS TRACKING NEW INFORMATION. SCIENTISTS THEORIZE THAT THIS SEARCH FOR THE NEW CAN BE ADDICTIVE.

"WE'VE GOT A LARGE AND GROWING GROUP OF PEOPLE WHO THINK THE SLIGHTEST HINT THAT SOMETHING INTERESTING MIGHT BE GOING ON IS LIKE CATNIP. THEY CAN'T IGNORE IT."*

*CLIFFORD NASS, COMMUNICATIONS PROFESSOR AT STANFORD

ADDICTION IS DEFINED AS "THE STATE OF BEING ENSLAVED TO A HABIT OR PRACTICE THAT IS PSYCHOLOGICALLY OR PHYSICALLY HABIT-FORMING, AS NARCOTICS, TO SUCH AN EXTENT THAT ITS CESSATION CAUSES SEVERE TRAUMA."

WITHOUT MY PHONE, I'LL GO CRAZY. I'LL DIE.

THE TERM "ADDICTION" CAN BE CONTROVERSIAL WHEN APPLIED TO BEHAVIORS LIKE GAMBLING, OVEREATING, OR SHOPPING.

TIME FOR SOME RETAIL THERAPY!

A TEN-YEAR "METASTUDY," MEANING A STUDY OF ALL THE OTHER STUDIES, FOUND THAT MOST RESEARCHERS WORKING IN THIS AREA AVOIDED DEFINING THE TERM "INTERNET ADDICTION."

THE METASTUDY ALSO FOUND PROBLEMS WITH CRITERIA USED. IN MANY CASES, A DETERMINATION OF ADDICTION WAS BASED ON PARTICIPANTS' SURVEY ANSWERS; IN OTHER CASES IT WAS MEASURED BY HOW MUCH TIME THEY SPENT ON THE COMPUTER.

I LOVE ONLINE SURVEYS!!

ALSO, MOST STUDIES WERE DONE WITH ONLY HIGH SCHOOL AND COLLEGE STUDENTS WHO ARE JUST LEARNING IMPULSE CONTROL.

I'M DOING MY HOMEWORK!

HONEY, DON'T YOU THINK YOU'VE BEEN ON—

ULTIMATELY THE METASTUDY CONCLUDED THAT MOST STUDIES SIMPLY MEASURED THE BEHAVIOR AND PERSONALITY OF THE INDIVIDUAL HIGH USERS RATHER THAN DETERMINING IF SUCH A THING AS ACTUAL "ADDICTION" EXISTED.

TIME TO SHOWER, DEAR.

PERHAPS THIS IS ONE OF THE REASONS THE LATEST *DIAGNOSTIC AND STATISTICAL MANUAL OF MENTAL DISORDERS* (WHICH CLASSIFIES ALL MENTAL DISORDERS USED BY HEALTH PROFESSIONALS THROUGHOUT THE U.S.) CHOSE NOT TO INCLUDE "INTERNET ADDICTION" AS A DISEASE.†

943 PAGES! THIS THING'S HEAVY!

WAIT, I'LL LOOK IT UP ONLINE.

†IN THE MANUAL'S APPENDIX, INTERNET ADDICTION IS TAGGED AS NEEDING "FURTHER STUDY." SO CHECK BACK IN TEN YEARS OR SO, SINCE THAT'S ROUGHLY HOW OFTEN THE MANUAL IS UPDATED.

BUT DOES DIGITAL MEDIA, AS SOME SCIENTISTS CLAIM, ACTUALLY CHANGE YOUR BRAIN? ONE OF THE MOST VOCAL PROPONENTS OF THIS IDEA IS SUSAN GREENFIELD, A BRITISH NEUROSCIENTIST AND BARONESS.

"IN A SENSE YOU ARE TURNING YOURSELF INTO A COMPUTER."

SHE POINTS TO A CHINESE STUDY SHOWING THAT SELF-DESCRIBED "INTERNET ADDICTS" WHO USED THE COMPUTER TEN HOURS A DAY, SIX DAYS A WEEK, HAD CHANGES IN THE DENSITY IN PARTS OF THEIR BRAIN.

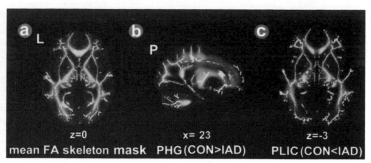

THOUGH THE STUDY HAD NO BEFORE-AND-AFTER COMPARISON, IT STILL CONCLUDED A CAUSE-AND-EFFECT RELATIONSHIP: "IAD (INTERNET ADDICTION DISORDER) RESULTED IN IMPAIRED INDIVIDUAL PSYCHOLOGICAL WELL-BEING, ACADEMIC FAILURE, AND REDUCED WORK PERFORMANCE AMONG ADOLESCENTS."

IN AN ARTICLE CRITICAL OF THE STUDY, KENT ANDERSON REFRAMED THAT SENTENCE: "ADOLESCENTS WITH IMPAIRED PSYCHOLOGICAL WELL-BEING, ACADEMIC FAILURE, AND REDUCED WORK PERFORMANCE RETREATED INTO THE INTERNET." HE WENT ON TO ASK,

"WHICH ONE DO YOU FIND MORE PLAUSIBLE?"

CELLULAR STRUCTURE OF THE HUMAN BRAIN, SCIENTISTS HAVE DISCOVERED, ADAPTS READILY TO THE TOOLS WE USE, INCLUDING THOSE FOR FINDING, STORING, AND SHARING INFORMATION.

SO PERHAPS OUR BRAIN IS CHANGING AND ADAPTING TO OUR DIGITAL CULTURE, JUST AS IT WOULD IF WE WERE SUDDENLY LIVING IN THE WOODS AGAIN. BUT TO CALL THAT "DAMAGE," AS SOME RESEARCHERS HAVE DONE, DOESN'T SEEM CORRECT.

IN FACT, SOME STUDIES, LIKE ONE THAT FOUND VIDEO-GAMING SURGEONS WERE BETTER AT CERTAIN COMPLICATED SURGICAL PROCEDURES, SHOW OUR MINDS AND BODIES ADAPTING IN POSITIVE WAYS.

"THE BOTTOM LINE IS, THE BRAIN IS WIRED TO ADAPT. THERE'S NO QUESTION THAT REWIRING GOES ON ALL THE TIME."*

SWEET MOVE! DOUBLE HEALTH POINTS!

*STEVEN YANTIS, A PROFESSOR OF BRAIN SCIENCES AT JOHNS HOPKINS UNIVERSITY

AS ONE SCIENTIST PUT IT, "ONE CAN NO MORE ASK, 'HOW IS TECHNOLOGY AFFECTING COGNITIVE DEVELOPMENT?' THAN ONE CAN ASK, 'HOW IS FOOD AFFECTING PHYSICAL DEVELOPMENT?' AS WITH FOOD, THE EFFECTS OF TECHNOLOGY WILL DEPEND CRITICALLY ON WHAT TYPE OF TECHNOLOGY IS CONSUMED, HOW MUCH OF IT IS CONSUMED, AND FOR HOW LONG IT IS CONSUMED."

TWITTER, TUMBLR, AND RSS FEEDS

IM AND TEXTING

FACEBOOK, MYSPACE, AND MMORPGS

E-MAIL

WORLD WIDE WEB

BUT HEADLINES ABOUT TECHNOLOGY FEARS IMPLY CAUSE-AND-EFFECT RELATIONSHIPS ALL THE TIME.

TECHNOLOGY BLAMED FOR U.S. OBESITY

Technology Is Cause of Obesity, Say Harvard Economists

VIDEO GAMES, TV DOUBLE CHILDHOOD OBESITY RISK

Video Games, Not TV, Linked to Obesity in Kids

IN THE CASE OF HEALTH RISKS LIKE OBESITY, OVERUSE OF TECHNOLOGY MIGHT BE A HABIT SHARED BY OBESE CHILDREN, BUT OVEREATING UNHEALTHY FOODS AND NOT EXERCISING ARE THE THINGS MAKING THEM FAT.

TOO MUCH OF ANYTHING CAN BE BAD FOR YOU, AFTER ALL. TOO MUCH FOOD . . . OR TOO MUCH TECHNOLOGY. BECAUSE, ISN'T IT REALLY THE **OVERUSE** OF GADGETS THAT CAN MAKE KIDS DISTRACTED?

OR AFFECT THEIR BRAINS?

OR FRAGMENT THEIR THINKING?

OR ISOLATE THEM FROM THE REAL WORLD?

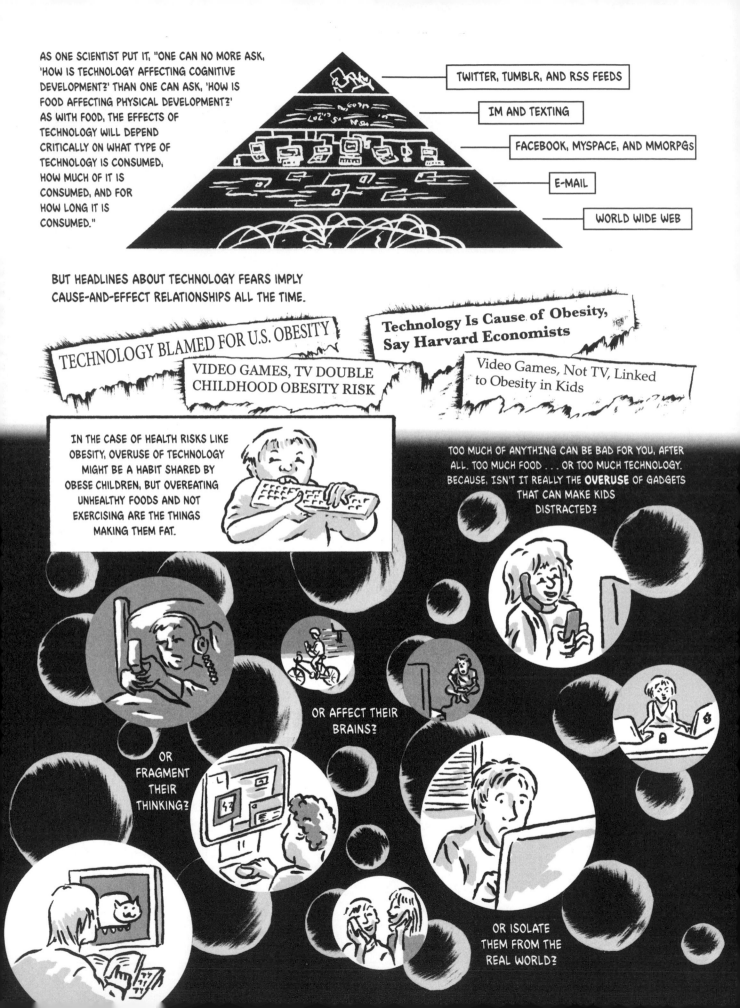

txtN4ever

A Texter's Call to Arms...
(Or at Least Thumbs)

Ytxt?

Remember how the Chappe Brothers may have invented their long-distance communication system—the semaphore—on actual school grounds? Compare that with 69 percent of American high schools that ban the use (or even possession) of today's popular long-distance communication system . . . texting. While no one's suggesting texting during class,* it's still probably one of the more creative things kids could be doing at their desks. That's because of the way texting limits what you can say, forcing you to find new ways to say it. After all, the Chappe boys weren't holding up

*Well, actually somebody is, sort of. The American Association of School Administrators is now calling cell phones "genuine educational tools."

one giant wooden letter at a time to send their messages. (How long would that take? And those wooden letters get heavy real fast.) Instead, those French teens created a movable arm, with additional attachments on the end, and ran it up on a tall pole. By moving these wooden arms into various positions, they developed 192 different signals—a kind of communication shorthand. Texting has a similar history because, with only around twelve to fifteen keys on an old-school cell phone, extra information had to be loaded on those tiny keys to fit a twenty-six-letter alphabet (which is why you had to punch four times to get to Z!). So texters evolved their own techniques to get the message across as quickly and easily as possible (you know . . . ASAP). And symbol writing is only one of many imaginative ways. Hmm, maybe texting isn't so bad4U after all.*

less ƨ mor

Do you ♡ logograms? The Egyptians did, since logograms are the symbolic representation of ideas or words and the basis for their hieroglyphics—as well as a lot of other early forms of written language. While Egyptians are the most famous logogrammers, the Chinese also used it (still do!). And thanks to texters, we all have a twenty-first-century version of hieroglyphics called emoticons :). And OMG—that's just the beginning of all the historical examples that can be connected with texting. There's also initialisms, the technique of taking the first letter of all the words in a phrase and using the initials to stand for the whole thing. The aforementioned OMG dates back to the early 1900s, while LOL was first used in 1960 to mean "little old lady"! One of the oldest known examples of initialism is from 1647, when the Latin term for "after midday" (post meridiem) was shortened to P.M. Another way to shorten the word you're typing is to drop a letter or two (or five). And once again, mister, txtRs weren't the first to employ it (one common case . . . Mr.). Other well-known abbreviations come from the military (Sgt. and Lt.), and weights and measurements (lbs., oz., ft., and kg.). Another form of abbreviation is when whole phrases are condensed. The best example of that is when people say good-bye, which is based on a fairly common farewell from the 1500s, "God be with you." While it might seem a bit of a stretch to turn that phrase into "good-bye," you have to take into account that at the time it was written in a variety of ways, including "God be wy you," "God b'w'y," and "Godbwye"—which, oddly enough, all look like textese!

---

*Now that more kids are upgrading to smartphones, texting shorthand may become a forgotten art.

Do Ive 2 spel it ot 4U?

Wonder why there was such weird spelling in the olden days? Mainly because people spelled any way they liked. You could spell *lady* "lefdi," for instance, which was pretty common—but so were "hlæfdi" and "hlefdige"! Spelling didn't start to become standardized until the invention of the printing press, and even then, a printer would choose spellings "that most pleased his fancy" (or "phansy," as it was often written at the time). Different printers' "house styles" were even influenced by the non-English speakers who worked for them, which explains why our language today is such a mess! But doesn't making up your own spelling show a certain . . . creativity? Look at William Shakespeare—he didn't just spell new versions of words, he made up a whole bunch of new ones (the estimate is that he "invented" 1,700 of 'em!).* It wasn't until the eighteenth century that all those different spellings got folded into a standard system, thanks to the development of dictionaries. But the fact that everyone now agrees how to spell "lady" doesn't stop the flow of new words into our language. Why, only recently the *Oxford English Dictionary* added OMG, TMI, IMHO, and BFF. Kind of makes you want to LOL (another initialism inducted into the . . . *OED*).

*Shakespeare's classic works have now been condensed into SMS text messages by a British company to help kids study for their English exams.

FEAR OF THE NEW

A TECHNO-PANIC TIMELINE

Back in 360 B.C., Plato worried about the (then) relatively new technology of WRITING. He feared young students would rely too much on the written record of a speech and thus weaken their ability to remember it. Plato's complaint may be our first historical record of FEAR OF THE NEW. Of course, the reason people know this is because someone WROTE about it. Which probably makes this the first example of hypocrisy, too—at least when it comes to the topic of techno-panics. But it certainly wasn't the last.

Well-known lecturer on scientific subjects Dionysius Lardner predicts that riding in the recently invented STEAM ENGINE will cause asphyxiation when traveling through train tunnels at a speed of 20 miles per hour. When that doesn't happen, other "experts" warn of "irreversible" shock when passengers rush through tunnels at 30 mph. That doesn't happen either.

1830s

Upon seeing a daguerreotype, an early form of PHOTOGRAPHY, the artist Paul Delaroche declares, "From today, painting is dead!" Except that Delaroche continues to paint, and later calls photography an "admirable discovery."

1839

1854

Author, poet, and philosopher Henry David Thoreau suggests that just because communication is now faster via the TELEGRAPH doesn't mean people have anything important to say. Perhaps Thoreau prefers handwritten letters . . . since his family had a pencil factory (thanks, Conrad Gesner!).

1494

Scribe Johannes Trithemius rails against the invention of the PRINTING PRESS in his treatise "In Praise of Scribes." He believes printing will make books too disposable: "The word written on parchment will last a thousand years. The printed book is on paper. How long will it last?" At least 500 years . . . since HIS book was PRINTED.

1545

One hundred years of the printing press is enough for scientist Conrad Gesner, who worries about an information overload. Too many BOOKS are both "confusing and harmful" to the brain, he claims. But Gesner isn't scared of writing if done with a pencil (which he invents in 1565).

1775

The newly popular NEWSPAPER starts replacing church sermons as the chief way people get their information, according to French statesman Chrétien-Guillaume de Malesherbes. On the positive side, he sees print as a new kind of public speaking that can reach a more "dispersed people." But he also ponders a vision of isolated citizens reading in "sullen silence."

Neurologist George M. Beard charges that both NEWSPAPERS and the TELEGRAPH create "nervous disorders" by exposing people to "the sorrows of individuals everywhere."

1881

Did you hear about the TELEPHONE? It could make you deaf . . . and the electric current might kill you!

1900s

When RADIO becomes popular, one critic declares, "There is now very little danger that Americans will resort to the vice of thinking." The death of conversation is also forecast, to be replaced by "the rattle and bang of incredibly frightful 'jazz.'"

1920s

In *Computer Power and Human Reason*, Joseph Weizenbaum describes COMPUTER programmers as "disheveled" tech-heads, staring at their keyboard buttons with the same obsession as "a gambler's on the rolling dice." Weizenbaum, one of the world's first programmers, may be feeling more regret than fear.

1976

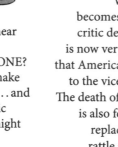

1896

With the invention of MOTION PICTURES, trains are scary once again. One eyewitness describes "cries of terror from the more nervous spectators" in a movie theater, when the "arrival of a train in a station" appears on-screen. Some audience members reportedly leap from their seats when a train, tram, or car seems to bear down on them.

1906

The undisputed leader of marching band music, John Philip Sousa, predicts the PHONOGRAPH will ruin people's ear for the subtleties of live music. "The nightingale's song is delightful because the nightingale herself gives it forth," he warbles. Sousa also foresees that fewer people will learn to play instruments since a record provides folks with "readymade [music] . . . in their cupboards."

1950s

TELEVISION becomes America's new choice for home entertainment and opponents of the latest technology warn that it will "hurt radio, conversation, reading, and the patterns of family living." Where have we heard that before?

2010

Social critic Nicholas Carr compares "the cognitive effects of the INTERNET with those of an earlier information technology, the printed book." Unlike the internet—which he thinks "scatters our attention"—books can focus us. "Unlike the screen," he writes, "the page promotes contemplativeness."*

*But, as you might remember—assuming your memory hasn't been ruined by writing—that was NOT what Conrad Gesner (that old pencil pusher) contemplated back in 1545, when he blamed books for causing the same kind of scattering!

AT THE VERY SAME TIME SOME HAVE EXPRESSED FEARS THAT THE NEW DIGITAL MEDIA IS DISCONNECTING KIDS' THINKING AND ISOLATING THEM FROM REALITY, OTHER CRITICS (AND SOMETIMES THE SAME CRITICS) WARN THAT DIGITAL MEDIA IS . . .

CONNECTING KIDS TO DANGER . . .

MAKING THEM SELF-ABSORBED AND FAME-OBSESSED . . .

WHAT!? ONLY 25 "LIKES" ON MY VIDEO?!

WOW, A POP-UP AD ON JUST THE THING I WANT! I SO KNOW WHAT'S HOT!

ERODING THEIR PRIVACY,

HEY! WHO HACKED MY FACEBOOK PAGE?

HELP ME!

AND PRODUCING A GENERATION OF KIDS INCAPABLE OF IMAGINING OR SYMPATHIZING WITH THE PAIN OF OTHERS. IN EFFECT, CREATING AN . . .

ANTI-SOCIAL NETWORK

THE INVENTION AND POPULAR USE OF THE INTERNET HAS TRANSFORMED THE WORLD IN WAYS NOT YET FULLY UNDERSTOOD.

FOR THE FIRST TIME IN HISTORY, THE TOTAL KNOWLEDGE OF HUMANITY IS AVAILABLE TO ANYONE WITH A COMPUTER AND AN INTERNET CONNECTION.

ACCESS TO THIS KNOWLEDGE AND THE ABILITY TO CONNECT LARGE NUMBERS OF PEOPLE HAVE CONTRIBUTED TO ADVANCES IN SCIENCE AND MEDICINE AND INSPIRED PEOPLE WITHOUT POWER TO GATHER TOGETHER AND STAND UP FOR THEIR RIGHTS.

BUT THE INTERNET HAS ALSO BROKEN DOWN SOME OF THE BARRIERS THAT ONCE STOOD BETWEEN CHILDREN AND MATERIAL THAT THEY COULD FIND DISTURBING IF EXPOSED TO AT TOO EARLY AN AGE.

POLICING THESE BORDERS OF KNOWLEDGE IS OF SPECIAL CONCERN IN PLACES WHERE IT IS DISTRIBUTED: SCHOOLS AND LIBRARIES.

THE CHILD PROTECTION ACT OF 2001 SAYS EVERY SCHOOL THAT GETS CERTAIN FEDERAL FUNDS MUST INSTALL A TECHNOLOGY PROTECTION MEASURE SUCH AS INTERNET BLOCKING SOFTWARE TO BAR ACCESS TO "CONTENT THAT IS HARMFUL TO MINORS."

NEARLY ALL (98%) OF PUBLIC SCHOOL DISTRICTS USE FILTERING SOFTWARE TO BLOCK ACCESS TO INAPPROPRIATE SITES.

"CONTENT-CONTROL," OR FILTERING, SOFTWARE SCANS INCOMING CONTENT TO BLOCK OBJECTIONABLE WORDS OR IMAGES.

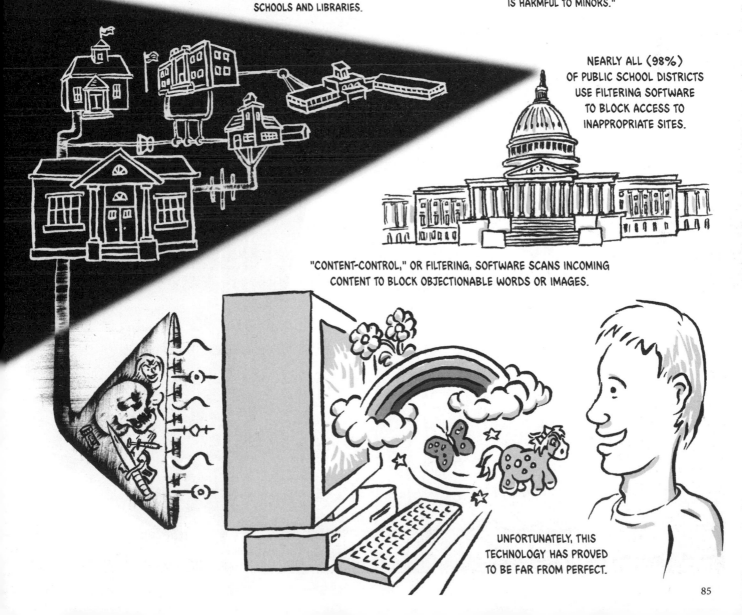

UNFORTUNATELY, THIS TECHNOLOGY HAS PROVED TO BE FAR FROM PERFECT.

TEACHERS HAVE COMPLAINED THAT NUMEROUS POTENTIALLY EDUCATIONAL SITES SUCH AS *NATIONAL GEOGRAPHIC* AND *GLOGSTER* HAVE BEEN BLOCKED.

A TEACHER IN NEW YORK WANTED TO SHOW IMAGES OF ATOMIC TESTING BUT WAS THWARTED BY THE INTERNET FILTER BLOCKING THE LOCATION OF THE TESTS, THE BIKINI ATOLL.

SOME SOFTWARE BLOCKS CONTENT BASED ON WORDS FOUND WITHIN LARGER WORDS. IN APRIL 1998, JEFF GOLD ATTEMPTED TO REGISTER THE DOMAIN NAME SHITAKEMUSHROOMS.COM, BUT WAS BLOCKED BY A FILTER PROHIBITING ONE OF THE "SEVEN DIRTY WORDS."

IN 2011, A WOMAN FROM EFFIN, A TOWN IN IRELAND, FOUND SHE COULD NOT ADD HER VILLAGE NAME TO THE "HOME PLACE" SECTION OF HER FACEBOOK PROFILE.

NO "F"ING WAY

ACTIVIST GROUPS SUCH AS THE CENSORWARE PROJECT HAVE HACKED SOME OF THE SOFTWARE AND DECRYPTED THE BLACKLISTS TO FIND OUT WHAT KINDS OF SITES WERE BLOCKED.

BINGO!

THEY FOUND THAT SOME SOFTWARE REFLECTED THE RELIGIOUS AND POLITICAL LEANINGS OF THE COMPANY OWNERS.

WHAT!

HUH?!

URGH!

BLOCKED SITES INCLUDED THE VATICAN, QUAKERS, THE HERITAGE FOUNDATION, AMNESTY INTERNATIONAL, AND THE NATIONAL ORGANIZATION FOR WOMEN.

ALONG WITH CONTENT, ANOTHER MAJOR FEAR ABOUT CHILDREN WHO USE THE INTERNET IS THE POSSIBILITY OF CONTACT WITH STRANGERS WISHING TO DO THEM HARM. THIS FEAR HAS GROWN WITH THE POPULARITY OF SOCIAL MEDIA SITES WHERE PEOPLE POST PERSONAL INFORMATION LIKE INSTAGRAM AND FACEBOOK.

SURPRISINGLY, THE NUMBER OF SUCH INCIDENTS INVOLVING STRANGERS, EITHER ONLINE OR OFF, HAS ACTUALLY DECREASED SINCE 1994, AND THOSE CONCERNS ARE NOW OVERSHADOWED BY THE FEAR OF A NEW DANGER: CYBERBULLYING.

Add Bogeyman as a friend?

Bogeyman will have to confirm that you are friends.

Add a personal message: Cancel

Thanks for the great comments on my posts.

Add Bogeyman to a Friend List

CYBERBULLYING IS THE USE OF THE INTERNET AND TEXTING TO REPEATEDLY HARASS OR TRY TO CAUSE PSYCHOLOGICAL HARM TO ANOTHER PERSON.

THE TECHNOLOGY CAN ALLOW GOSSIP AND EMBARRASSING OR ALTERED PHOTOS TO SPREAD QUICKLY. IT ALSO GIVES PEOPLE THE ABILITY TO SET UP FAKE IDENTITIES, AND CAN LEAD TO A "PILING ON" EFFECT, WHERE VICTIMS ARE BULLIED BY MANY PEOPLE THEY DON'T KNOW.

LAWMAKERS AND SCHOOLS HAVE TRIED TO ADDRESS THE ISSUE WITH A VARIETY OF MEASURES. IN JUNE OF 2011, THE RHODE ISLAND LEGISLATURE PASSED HB 5941, A LAW THAT, AMONG OTHER THINGS, BANS THE USE OF SOCIAL NETWORKING SITES ON SCHOOL GROUNDS.

SEVERAL CRITICS HAVE POINTED OUT PROBLEMS WITH THE LAW. ADAM GOLDSTEIN, WRITING FOR THE ONLINE NEWS AND CULTURE SITE OF THE *HUFFINGTON POST*, SAID,

THE MEASURE PASSES.

"WHAT IS A 'SOCIAL NETWORKING SITE,' REALLY? THE BILL DOESN'T DEFINE IT. IS THE *HUFFINGTON POST* A SOCIAL NETWORKING SITE? USERS HAVE PROFILES AND WE COMMUNICATE WITH EACH OTHER."

IN FACT, THE STATE LEGISLATURE ACTUALLY HAS ITS OWN FACEBOOK PAGE, WHICH IS NOW ILLEGAL TO ACCESS FROM SCHOOL.

BUT I WAS JUST TRYING TO "LIKE" THE LEGISLATURE.

THE LAW ALSO HAS THE EFFECT OF MAKING IT ILLEGAL FOR TEACHERS TO USE A VERY EFFECTIVE TOOL FOR COMMUNICATING WITH STUDENTS.

WHAT'S IT SAY?

THEY CANCELED LAST WEEK'S CHESS CLUB.

THE STUDENT PRESS LAW CENTER, AN ADVOCATE FOR STUDENT FIRST-AMENDMENT RIGHTS, HAS ANOTHER ARGUMENT AGAINST SUCH LAWS.

SPLC
student press law center
SUPPORT SPLC   LEGAL ASSISTANCE   KNOW YOUR RIGHTS

Cruelty, hate speech and social exclusion did not enter schools with the Internet, nor were any of these behaviors invented by children. Students . . . act hatefully toward each other because they've seen adults do it. We can ban Facebook in schools and congratulate ourselves on having "fixed the problem"— until someone invents a new technology that makes a joke of the law (give that days, tops). We can look in the mirror and start fixing it for real.

BUT ACCORDING TO SOME FEARFUL OF TECHNOLOGY'S EFFECTS, LOOKING INTO THE MIRROR IS PRECISELY THE PROBLEM.

"CURRENT TECHNOLOGY FUELS THE INCREASE IN NARCISSISM. . . . BY ITS VERY NAME, MYSPACE ENCOURAGES ATTENTION-SEEKING, AS DOES YOUTUBE, WHOSE SLOGAN IS 'BROADCAST YOURSELF.'"

JEAN TWENGE, AUTHOR OF *GENERATION ME* AND *THE NARCISSISM EPIDEMIC*

A NUMBER OF AUTHORS AND RESEARCHERS HAVE BEEN WARNING THAT THERE IS A "NARCISSISTIC EPIDEMIC" RUNNING THROUGH THE YOUNGER GENERATION, BROUGHT ON, AMONG OTHER THINGS, BY THE INTERNET.

THEY ASSERT THAT THE LACK OF FACE-TO-FACE CONTACT, THE EMPHASIS ON ACQUIRING "FRIENDS," AND THE SHORT MESSAGES OF THE INTERNET ARE MAKING KIDS SHALLOW AND UNCARING.

"THE EASE OF HAVING 'FRIENDS' ONLINE MIGHT MAKE PEOPLE MORE LIKELY TO JUST TUNE OUT WHEN THEY DON'T FEEL LIKE RESPONDING TO OTHERS' PROBLEMS, A BEHAVIOR THAT COULD CARRY OVER OFFLINE."

OHH! ABBY FRIENDED ME!

WHICH ABBY?

WHO CARES?

THESE RESEARCHERS POINT TO SURVEYS LIKE ONE WHERE 57% OF COLLEGE STUDENTS ADMITTED THAT SOCIAL NETWORKING MADE THEM MORE NARCISSISTIC AND THAT THEIR PEERS USED THESE SITES FOR SELF-PROMOTION AND ATTENTION-SEEKING.

SARA KONRATH, A RESEARCHER AT THE UNIVERSITY OF MICHIGAN'S INSTITUTE FOR SOCIAL RESEARCH, LOOKED AT 72 STUDIES THAT GAUGED EMPATHY AMONG 14,000 COLLEGE STUDENTS IN THE PAST 30 YEARS AND FOUND THAT IT HAS BEEN DECLINING.

SHE CONCLUDED THAT COLLEGE STUDENTS TODAY SHOW 40% LESS EMPATHY THAN STUDENTS IN THE 1980s AND 1990s.

THE SURVEYS ASK QUESTIONS LIKE "I OFTEN HAVE TENDER, CONCERNED FEELINGS FOR PEOPLE LESS FORTUNATE THAN ME" AND "I SOMETIMES TRY TO UNDERSTAND MY FRIENDS BETTER BY IMAGINING HOW THINGS LOOK FROM THEIR PERSPECTIVE."

BUT CRITICS OF KONRATH'S STUDY POINT OUT HOW UNRELIABLE SELF-SURVEYS CAN BE IN MEASURING THINGS LIKE NARCISSISM AND EMPATHY.

FOR INSTANCE, WOULDN'T REAL NARCISSISTS BE MORE LIKELY TO JUDGE THEMSELVES AS EMPATHIC, SINCE THEY MIGHT NOT HAVE THE NECESSARY SELF-AWARENESS TO KNOW IF THEY ARE EMPATHIC OR NOT?

THIS UNRELIABILITY, THE CRITICS CLAIM, IS INCREASED WHEN COMPARING SELF-SURVEYS ACROSS GENERATIONS. ONE POSSIBLE INTERPRETATION OF THE RESULTS MIGHT BE THAT THIS GENERATION IS MORE HONEST IN THEIR ANSWERS OR COMFORTABLE EXPRESSING THEM.

IN FACT, ANOTHER GROUP OF RESEARCHERS LOOKED AT THE SAME SURVEYS AND SOME ADDITIONAL DATA, AND DISCOVERED NO MEANINGFUL DIFFERENCES ACROSS GENERATIONS. THEY THEORIZED:

"WHEN OLDER PEOPLE ARE TOLD THAT YOUNGER PEOPLE ARE GETTING INCREASINGLY NARCISSISTIC, THEY MAY BE PRONE TO AGREE BECAUSE THEY CONFUSE THE CLAIM FOR GENERATIONAL CHANGE WITH THE FACT THAT YOUNGER PEOPLE ARE SIMPLY MORE NARCISSISTIC THAN THEY ARE.

"EVERY GENERATION IS GENERATION ME. THAT IS, UNTIL THEY GROW UP."*

*BRENT ROBERTS, RESEARCHER AT THE UNIVERSITY OF ILLINOIS

WITH THESE STUDIES SUPPORTING CONTRADICTORY IDEAS, PERHAPS IT MAKES SENSE TO LOOK AT SOME OUTSIDE MEASUREMENT OF EMPATHY. SOMETHING LIKE RATES OF VOLUNTEERISM.

THE CORPORATION FOR NATIONAL AND COMMUNITY SERVICE, THE FEDERAL AGENCY THAT OVERSEES AMERICORPS AND OTHER SUCH PROGRAMS, SAYS THE RATE OF VOLUNTEERING AMONG OLDER TEENS NEARLY DOUBLED FROM 1989 TO 2005.

BUT JEAN TWENGE REFERS TO "INVOLUNTARY VOLUNTEERING" REQUIRED BY SCHOOLS AND TEENS WANTING TO IMPROVE THEIR COLLEGE APPLICATIONS AS REASONS FOR THIS INCREASE.

"A LOT OF YOUNG PEOPLE WHO VOLUNTEER SAY 'I WANT TO MAKE A DIFFERENCE.' A GENERATION OR TWO AGO, THE REASON MIGHT HAVE INSTEAD BEEN 'BECAUSE IT'S THE RIGHT THING TO DO.' ALTHOUGH ANY REASON FOR VOLUNTEERING IS A GOOD ONE, 'I WANT TO MAKE A DIFFERENCE' IS STILL AN INDIVIDUALISTIC STATEMENT."

JUDGING FROM THE HEADLINES, PEOPLE WOULD RATHER READ ABOUT TWENGE'S AND KONRATH'S RESEARCH THAN RISING TEEN VOLUNTEER RATES OR CONTRADICTORY STUDIES.

FROM STUDENTS, LESS KINDNESS FOR STRANGERS?
—*New York Times*

ALL ABOUT ME? COLLEGE KIDS LACK EMPATHY
—MSNBC

EMPATHY: COLLEGE STUDENTS DON'T HAVE AS MUCH AS THEY USED TO, STUDY FINDS
—Sciencedaily.com

COLLEGE STUDENTS LOSING THEIR SENSITIVE SIDE
—*Washington Post*

Is the "Me Generation" Less Empathetic?
—*Psychology Today*

TODAY'S COLLEGE STUDENTS LACK EMPATHY
—Livescience.com

"GENERATION ME" TENDS TO BE SELF-CENTERED, COMPETITIVE, U.S. RESEARCH SHOWS
—*U.S. News & World Report*

A RECENT STUDY SUPPORTS THIS IDEA. IN IT, RESEARCHERS SHOWED ADULTS A FAKE ONLINE NEWS SITE AND GAVE THEM A FEW MOMENTS TO BROWSE EITHER NEGATIVE OR POSITIVE VERSIONS OF SEVERAL ARTICLES.

AS IT TURNS OUT, OLDER TEST SUBJECTS TENDED TO PICK NEGATIVE ARTICLES ABOUT YOUNGER PEOPLE AND SHOWED NO INTEREST IN ARTICLES ABOUT PEOPLE THEIR OWN AGE OR OLDER.

THEY BETTER HAVE A LARGE-PRINT VERSION.

BOOK NOOK

TEENS WORSE THAN EVER!

"THE MORE TIME THEY SPENT WITH NEGATIVE NEWS ABOUT YOUNG PEOPLE, THE HIGHER SELF-ESTEEM THEY REPORTED. THEY MAY GET SOME SELF-ESTEEM BOOST OUT OF THIS."*

*STUDY AUTHOR SILVIA KNOBLOCH-WESTERWICK

AS DR. J. J. ARNETT, A DEVELOPMENTAL PSYCHOLOGIST WHO HAS SPENT HIS CAREER STUDYING TEENS, POINTS OUT, "IT'S LIKE A COTTAGE INDUSTRY OF PUTTING THEM DOWN AND COMPLAINING ABOUT THEM AND WHINING ABOUT WHY THEY DON'T GROW UP."

ARNETT, IN A RESPONSE TO RESEARCH THAT SHOWED NO NOTICEABLE DIFFERENCE IN NARCISSISM ACROSS GENERATIONS, THEORIZES THAT LATE TEENS TODAY ARE IN A NEW DEVELOPMENTAL STAGE HE CALLS "EMERGING ADULTHOOD."

"LEADING MANY OLDER PEOPLE TO VIEW THEM AS 'LATE' OR SELFISH, AND THE NEW FEATURES OF THIS NEW LIFE STAGE ARE FREQUENTLY MISUNDERSTOOD AND MISINTERPRETED."

UNLIKE PREVIOUS GENERATIONS, THESE "EMERGING ADULTS" DON'T MOVE INTO MARRIAGE, STABLE WORK, AND PARENTHOOD UNTIL THEIR LATE 20s.

INTERESTINGLY, THIS IDEA OF "LIFE STAGES" MAY ALSO EXPLAIN WHY SO MANY OLDER PEOPLE PREFER TO READ NEGATIVE ARTICLES ABOUT TEENS AND HAVE A COMMON BELIEF THAT THEIR SOCIETY IS IN "MORAL DECLINE."

RECENT STUDIES SUGGEST THAT AS PEOPLE BECOME PARENTS THEIR FOCUS OFTEN SHIFTS FROM SEEKING OUT NEW THINGS TO RECOGNIZING DANGER AND RISK.

FOR INSTANCE, RESEARCHERS FOUND THAT PEOPLE WHO BECAME PARENTS IN THE 1990s THOUGHT CRIME RATES HAD INCREASED IN THAT DECADE WHEN THEY ACTUALLY HAD GONE DOWN.

A STUDY IN 2008 SOUGHT TO REPLICATE THIS EFFECT IN THE LAB. IN IT, PARTICIPANTS PLAYED A CARD GAME WITH A DECK THAT HAD BOTH REWARD AND PENALTY CARDS.

AT THE BEGINNING OF THE GAME, THE PLAYERS WERE TOLD TO MAXIMIZE THEIR POINTS. THESE PLAYERS WERE INTENDED TO REPRESENT A YOUNG ADULT MIND-SET.

BUT LATER IN THE GAME, THEY WERE TOLD THAT THEIR GOAL WAS NOW TO KEEP AS MANY OF THE POINTS THEY'D ALREADY EARNED AS POSSIBLE, A MIND-SET MORE LIKE PARENTHOOD.

CURIOUSLY, AS THE PLAYERS TRIED TO KEEP POINTS, THEY PERCEIVED A LARGE INCREASE IN THE NUMBER OF PENALTY CARDS, EVEN THOUGH THAT NUMBER HADN'T CHANGED.

THIS GROUP WAS COMPARED TO TWO CONTROL GROUPS: ONE WHO PLAYED ONLY TO MAXIMIZE POINTS AND ONE WHO PLAYED ONLY TO KEEP POINTS. NEITHER OF THE CONTROL GROUPS PERCEIVED AN INCREASE IN PENALTY CARDS. TO THE RESEARCHERS CONDUCTING THE STUDY, THESE RESULTS . . .

"SUPPORT OUR HYPOTHESIS THAT THE TENDENCY TO MISTAKE CHANGE IN ONESELF FOR CHANGE IN THE EXTERNAL WORLD IS A SOURCE OF POPULAR BELIEFS IN SOCIAL DECLINE."

AND PERHAPS WHEN IT COMES TO TODAY'S YOUTH, THE OLDER GENERATION SHOULD STOP WORRYING, EMBRACE CHANGE, AND REALIZE . . .

"NOSTALGIA FOR THE GOOD OLD DAYS MAY BE A PHENOMENON ROOTED IN ILLUSION."

YOUTH-A-PHOBIC

FEARING THE YOUNGER GENERATION . . . THROUGH THE GENERATIONS

Ever hear of something called ephebiphobia? The nearly impossible to pronounce word means "fear or loathing of the young," though sociologists and youth advocacy groups like to define it a little differently, calling ephebiphobia the "inaccurate, exaggerated and sensational characterization of young people." Either way you look at it, fear of the young has been around a REALLY long time.

4000 B.C. (estimated)

"We live in a decaying age. Young people no longer respect their parents. They are rude and impatient. They frequently inhabit taverns and have no self-control." Sound familiar? This lament was found inscribed on a 6,000-year-old Egyptian tomb.

1000-600 B.C. (estimated)

Psalms 78:8, 622: "And that they should not be like their fathers, a stubborn and rebellious generation, a generation whose heart was not steadfast, whose spirit was not faithful to

God." Yeah, that one is from the Bible (naturally, the Old Testament).

400 B.C. (estimated)

"What is happening to our young people? They disrespect their elders, they disobey their parents. They ignore the law. They riot in the streets, inflamed with wild notions. Their morals are decaying. What is to become of them?" —Plato, famous Greek philosopher

350 B.C. (estimated)

"[Young people] have exalted notions, because they have not been humbled by life or learned its necessary limitations. . . . They overdo everything—they love too much, hate too much, and the same with everything else." —Aristotle, another Greek philosopher, and a student of Plato (who probably thought Aristotle was disrespectful and inflamed with wild notions)

A.D. 1100 (and it's all A.D. from here)

For the first time, fear of the young and fear of "hoodies" is linked. Teenage apprentice boys in London, who "were away from home for seven years with no parental control," would "riot regularly" while wearing hooded tops—the garment of choice for 12th-century troublemakers (and maybe this time, at least, youth phobia is well-founded; after all, this is the mid-evil period).

1274

"The young people of today think of nothing but themselves. They have no reverence for parents or old age. They are impatient of all restraint. . . . As for the girls, they are forward, immodest, and unladylike in speech, behavior and dress." —Peter the Hermit (Peter the Hermit?! Isn't that like being a hobo?)

1500s

According to Italian writer and political strategist Machiavelli, fear of youth is what prevented the city of Florence from keeping a standing army. (This guy also said "Before all else, be armed.")

1810s

The term "juvenile delinquent" is first coined in America around 1810, according to Jon Savage, author of *Teenage: The Creation of Youth Culture.* Then again, other researchers say the phrase first appears in print in 1816, with the publication the "Report of the Committee for Investigating the Alarming Increases of Juvenile Crime in the Metropolis," a study about spiraling youth crime in London. What's not in question is the fear that the words "juvenile delinquent" inspire in adults.

ju·ve·nile   [joo-vuh-nl, -nahyl]
adjective
1. of, pertaining to, characteristic of, or suitable or intended for young persons: juvenile books.
2. young; youthful: juvenile years.
3. immature; childish; infantile: His juvenile tantrums are not in keeping with his age.

1843

"I think morals are getting much worse. . . . When I was four or five and twenty my mother would have knocked me down if I had spoken improperly to her." —Charlotte Kirkman, whose testimony was part of an investigation by Lord Ashley, the Earl of Shaftesbury, into the bad behavior of English youth

1850

New York City records more than 200 gang wars and blames them on adolescent boys. Teens and preteens running wild in urban America are supposedly "gnawing away at the foundations of society" (you know how hungry kids can get).

1898

The word "hooligan" is used for the first time to describe youth gangs whose "dramatic increase in disorderly behavior" is called by the *London Times* "organized terrorism in the streets." And did you know that if you wear a hoodie it might mean you ARE a hooligan, according to the *Collins English Dictionary*: "Hoodie (informal)—a young person who wears a hooded sweatshirt, regarded by some as a potential hooligan."

1911

Longtime teachers, according to a reporter at the *Atlantic*, worry that the behavior they are witnessing from their current students is "different from anything we have ever seen in the young before" (different in a BAD way, naturally).

1921

"Does Jazz Put the Sin in Syncopation?" asks the *Ladies' Home Journal*. Specifically, the "sin" in society's spawn: "Welfare workers tell us that never in the history of our land have there been such immoral conditions among our young people, and . . . the blame is laid on jazz music and its evil influence on the young people of today."

1938

In the 1930s, jazz music evolves into something called "swing," and bandleader Benny Goodman becomes the anointed king of it. For a performance at New York's Paramount Theatre, more than 3,000 young folks gather in the cold to buy tickets to Benny's show. Panicked by the size of the crowd, theater managers call in police to help them handle the "wild" kids. "It was a savage exhibition," snarls a critic who witnessed the crowd dancing to the music, "as animalistic as a monkey's or an elephant's rhythmic swaying to the beat of a tom-tom [drum]."

1944

There's another concert "riot" at the Paramount Theatre, this one for "teen idol" Frank

Sinatra. One congressman accuses Sinatra of being "the prime instigator of juvenile delinquency in America," and FBI chief J. Edgar Hoover warns that juvenile delinquents are putting America "in deadly peril." This is the year when the term "teenager" first appears in print, in part thanks to the success of a brand-new magazine titled *Seventeen*.

1954

"Let's Face It: Our Teen-Agers Are Out of Hand" —*Newsweek* cover story

1956

"'Voodoo Beat' Blamed for Teen Age Riots Coast to Coast as Music-Maddened Maniacs Maul Many!" is just one example of the media's growing backlash against the latest form of music, rock 'n' roll. In the same article, the success of rock 'n' roll is attributed to the "deadly rhythm of the jungles which sets off a hidden charge within the brain of its hearers and incites them to acts of violence [and] murder." This new musical form "can make a murderer out of the nice kid next door." Former teen idol Frank Sinatra (see 1944) declares that current teen idol Elvis Presley is "deplorable," and his music "fosters almost totally negative and destructive reactions in young people."

1960

Broadway has a new hit musical on its hands called *Bye Bye Birdie,* which spoofs the success of the latest teen idol, Elvis Presley. A portion of the lyrics from one of the show's songs (sung by the parents) goes like this:

1964

A song by the band the Dave Clark Five called "Bits and Pieces" is banned from many concert halls in Britain. The reason: fear that teens "stomping to the beat would damage wooden dance floors."

1977

In its July 11 cover story, *Time* warns of the growing increase in "youth crime."

1993

Time magazine runs another grim cover story: "Big Shots: An Inside Look at the Deadly Love Affair Between America's Kids and Their Guns." This is also the year that three teens are convicted of murder in West Memphis, Arkansas. Even though there was little evidence to connect the teens to the murders, prosecutors suggest that because one of the accused likes "wearing of black clothes, listening to heavy metal music, and reading Stephen King horror books," that is proof of his guilt.*

1996

The government passes the Violent Youth Predator Act, which automatically allows the prosecution of juvenile offenders (kids as young as 14 years old) as adults for specific violent offenses.

1998

During a Crime Prevention Resource Center conference in Fort Worth, Texas, police department representatives from several cities back a plan that calls for "the forced hospitalization of Marilyn Manson fans, and

*Not until 2011 were the Memphis Three, as they came to be called by advocates for their release, finally freed from prison.

recommend[s] the classification of 'Goth rock' fans as street gangs." Luckily for Goth fans, the plan was not enacted.

2000

After a fight breaks out in a Louisiana skating rink, police shut the place down and seize the CDs played as background music for the skaters. The cops claim it was the music that

helped to ignite the violence. Included in the confiscated CDs: "Rudolph the Red-Nosed Reindeer," "The Hokey Pokey," and "Jingle Bells."

2001

Time magazine asks in its August 6 cover story: "Do Kids Have Too Much Power?" Then the magazine answers its own question (also on the cover): "Yes, Say Many Parents. And Now They're Moving to Regain Control."

2002 to the Present

Plenty of recent examples of ephebiphobia already covered in this book (and more to come).

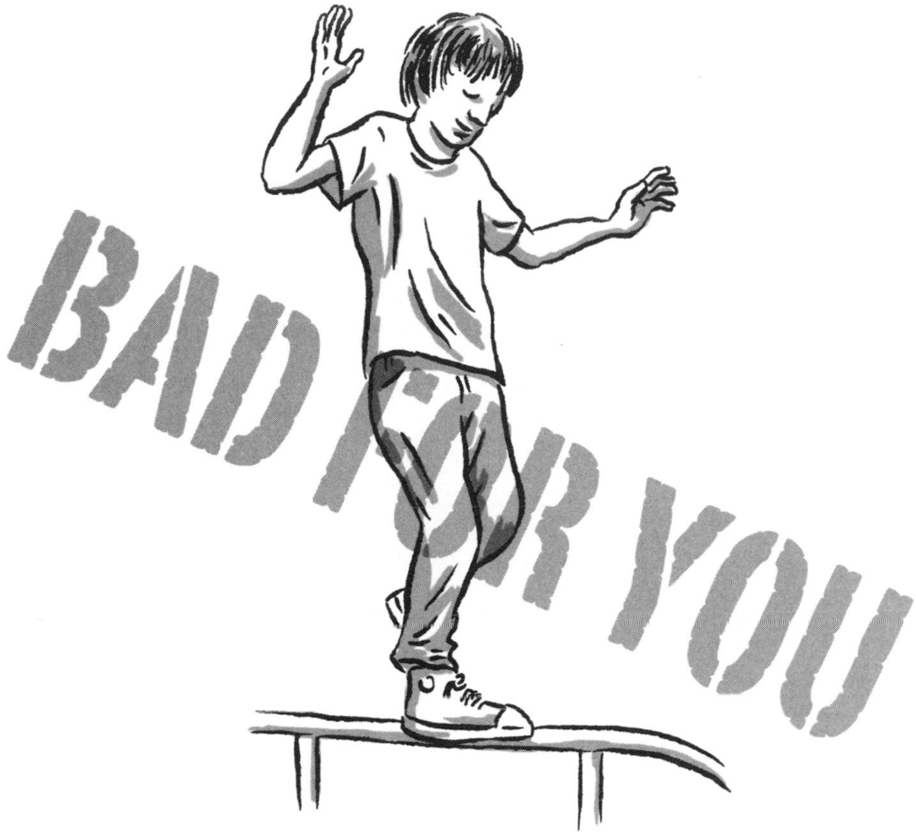
BAD FOR YOU

PLAY

STARTING IN THE LATE 1970s, AMERICA'S PLAYGROUNDS UNDERWENT A TRANSFORMATION. ALL ACROSS THE COUNTRY, UNIQUELY CREATIVE, AND SOME SAID DANGEROUS, PLAYGROUNDS WERE REPLACED BY THE COLORFUL HORIZONTAL LADDERS, WALKWAYS, AND PLASTIC TUBES SO FAMILIAR TO TODAY'S CHILDREN. BUT DID THESE CHANGES MAKE KIDS SAFER OR SIMPLY CREATE A

GRAVEYARD OF FUN?

IN THE MIDDLE AGES, A TIME BEFORE PLAYGROUNDS AND MOTOR VEHICLES, CHILDREN TYPICALLY PLAYED IN THE STREETS OF THEIR VILLAGE OR THE SURROUNDING COUNTRYSIDE. IN THE 1560s, ARTIST PIETER BRUEGEL DEPICTED OVER 250 CHILDREN PLAYING AN ESTIMATED 80 GAMES.

BUT IN 19TH-CENTURY AMERICAN CITIES, THE CHILDREN OF RECENT IMMIGRANTS HAD THE CHOICE OF GARBAGE-STREWN ALLEYS RIFE WITH DISEASE AND RATS OR DANGEROUSLY BUSY CITY STREETS.

101

IN THE SUMMER OF 1885, THE MASSACHUSETTS EMERGENCY AND HYGIENE ASSOCIATION DUMPED A PILE OF SAND IN THE YARD OF THE PARMENTER STREET CHAPEL IN BOSTON. THE PILE WAS CALLED A SAND GARDEN, AND SOON CHILDREN CAME TO DIG, MAKE SAND PIES, SING SONGS, AND HAVE PARADES.

IN 1889, THE FIRST FREE PUBLIC OUTDOOR PLAYGROUND WITH EQUIPMENT OPENED NEAR THE WEST END SLUMS OF BOSTON. CHARLESBANK GYMNASIUM WAS INSTANTLY AND IMMENSELY POPULAR AMONG "A CLASS OF CITIZENS WHO SCARCELY KNOW THE MEANING OF SUMMER VACATION."

MANY OF THE EARLY PLAYGROUNDS WERE BUILT IN WORKING-CLASS URBAN NEIGHBORHOODS ON THE GROUNDS OF SETTLEMENT HOUSES. SETTLEMENT HOUSES FUNCTIONED AS COMMUNITY CENTERS FOR NEW IMMIGRANTS, OFTEN PROVIDING THE ONLY PLACE FOR RECREATION IN THESE AREAS.

IN 1889, HULL HOUSE OPENED ITS PLAYGROUND ON DONATED LAND IN CHICAGO. THE SPOT, BORDERED BY A FACTORY AND BEREFT OF GRASS AND TREES, WAS CLEANED UP, AND SOON NEIGHBORHOOD CHILDREN CAME TO PLAY.

HERE IS ONE OF THE FIRST STRUCTURES BUILT AT THE HULL HOUSE PLAYGROUND. IT WOULD BE FOLLOWED WITHIN A YEAR BY SWINGS, HAMMOCKS, SANDBOXES, AND ROPE LADDERS.

A PLAYGROUND SHELTER WHERE CHILDREN AND INSTRUCTORS COULD GATHER WAS BUILT, AND CHILDREN WERE TAUGHT GROUP GAMES.

"RECREATION IS STRONGER THAN VICE, AND RECREATION ALONE CAN STIFLE THE LUST FOR VICE."*

THE FIRST PLAYGROUND IN NEW YORK CITY WAS OPENED IN 1890 BY UNIVERSITY SETTLEMENT. BY 1900, SOME 14 U.S. CITIES WERE SPONSORING PLAYGROUNDS.

*JANE ADDAMS, FOUNDER OF HULL HOUSE IN *THE SPIRIT OF YOUTH AND THE CITY STREETS* (1909)

BY 1905, 35 AMERICAN CITIES HAD SUPERVISED PLAYGROUNDS, AND THE CITY OF CHICAGO ALONE SPENT $5 MILLION ON 10 NEW PLAYGROUNDS. THE NEXT YEAR, THE PLAYGROUND ASSOCIATION OF AMERICA WAS FORMED AND A MOVEMENT WAS BORN.

BY 1910, THERE WERE 55 CITIES WITH PLAYGROUND PROGRAMS. A SELLING POINT OF THE MOVEMENT WAS THAT PLAYGROUNDS COULD ATTRACT CHILDREN AND THEN TEACH THEM LESSONS IN MANNERS, MORALS, AND SPORTSMANSHIP.

"CITY STREETS ARE UNSATISFACTORY PLAYGROUNDS FOR CHILDREN BECAUSE OF THE DANGER, BECAUSE MOST GOOD GAMES ARE AGAINST THE LAW, BECAUSE THEY ARE TOO HOT IN SUMMER, AND BECAUSE IN CROWDED SECTIONS OF THE CITY THEY ARE APT TO BE SCHOOLS OF CRIME.

"OLDER CHILDREN WHO WOULD PLAY VIGOROUS GAMES MUST HAVE PLACES ESPECIALLY SET ASIDE FOR THEM; AND, SINCE PLAY IS A FUNDAMENTAL NEED, PLAYGROUNDS SHOULD BE PROVIDED FOR EVERY CHILD AS MUCH AS SCHOOLS."
—PRESIDENT THEODORE ROOSEVELT

THROUGHOUT THE 1920s AND 1930s, PLAYGROUNDS WERE RUN BY PUBLIC SCHOOLS AND PARKS DEPARTMENTS AND WERE USUALLY SUPERVISED AND GUIDED BY RULES AND REGULATIONS.

DURING THE DEPRESSION, IN 1934, NEW YORK CITY PARKS COMMISSIONER ROBERT MOSES EMPLOYED 1,800 DESIGNERS AND 70,000 RELIEF WORKERS TO BUILD PLAYGROUNDS ALL ACROSS THE CITY.

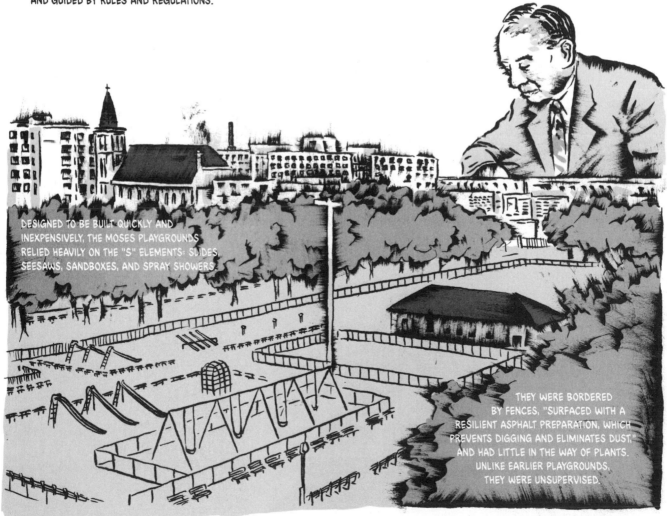

DESIGNED TO BE BUILT QUICKLY AND INEXPENSIVELY, THE MOSES PLAYGROUNDS RELIED HEAVILY ON THE "S" ELEMENTS: SLIDES, SEESAWS, SANDBOXES, AND SPRAY SHOWERS.

THEY WERE BORDERED BY FENCES, "SURFACED WITH A RESILIENT ASPHALT PREPARATION, WHICH PREVENTS DIGGING AND ELIMINATES DUST," AND HAD LITTLE IN THE WAY OF PLANTS. UNLIKE EARLIER PLAYGROUNDS, THEY WERE UNSUPERVISED.

THEN, STARTING IN THE LATE 1950s AND CONTINUING THROUGH THE MID-1970s, THE UNITED STATES ENJOYED A "GOLDEN AGE" OF PLAYGROUNDS. INSPIRED BY THE IDEAS OF CHILD PSYCHOLOGISTS LIKE JEAN PIAGET AND BRUNO BETTELHEIM, ARCHITECTS, LANDSCAPE DESIGNERS, AND ARTISTS DEVISED PLAYGROUNDS THAT WOULD STIMULATE IMAGINATIVE PLAY.

THEY CAME UP WITH ALL SORTS OF CREATIVE FORMS BASED ON . . .

ANIMALS . . .

FAIRY TALES . . .

ROBOTS AND SPACESHIPS...

AND ABSTRACT ART.

THE PLAYGROUNDS WERE DESIGNED TO ENCOURAGE EXPLORATION BY HAVING MANY POSSIBILITIES FOR DIFFERENT TYPES OF PLAY.

THE MOST EXPERIMENTAL OF THESE WERE DUBBED "ADVENTURE PLAYGROUNDS."

INSPIRED BY SPONTANEOUS PLAY SPACES CREATED BY BRITISH CHILDREN AMIDST THE RUBBLE OF WORLD WAR II BOMBING RAIDS, THE PLAYGROUNDS HAD SCULPTED EARTH, MOVABLE ELEMENTS, AND MATERIALS FOR CHILDREN TO BUILD THEIR OWN STRUCTURES WITH. UNFORTUNATELY, THE ADVENTURE WAS NOT TO LAST.

IN THE EARLY 1970s, THE UNITED STATES CONSUMER PRODUCT SAFETY COMMISSION BECAME CONCERNED OVER CHILDREN'S PLAYGROUND INJURIES.

A STUDY IN 1974 SHOWED THAT AROUND 118,000 PEOPLE WENT TO HOSPITAL EMERGENCY ROOMS FOR INJURIES RELATED TO PLAYGROUND EQUIPMENT. MORE THAN THREE-FOURTHS OF THOSE INJURED WERE CHILDREN UNDER TEN.

AFTER A 1978 STUDY INDICATED THAT 59% OF PLAYGROUND INJURIES RESULTED FROM FALLS TO HARD SURFACES LIKE ASPHALT, CONCERNED GROUPS BEGAN TO CALL FOR INCREASED SAFETY STANDARDS AND RULES.

IN 1981, THE COMMISSION PUBLISHED ITS FIRST SET OF PLAYGROUND-SAFETY GUIDELINES. ONCE THOSE STANDARDS WERE ESTABLISHED, PLAYGROUNDS THAT DIDN'T MEET THEM WERE VULNERABLE TO BEING SUED.

"IF THEY ARE NOT COMPLIANT, THEY OPEN THEMSELVES TO CHARGES OF NEGLIGENCE AGAINST THE OWNERS AND TRUSTEES. SIMPLY PUT, YOU CAN'T GET INSURANCE IF YOU DON'T MEET THE STANDARDS."

DONNA THOMPSON, DIRECTOR OF THE NATIONAL PROGRAM FOR PLAYGROUND SAFETY

AS THE OLD CEMENT AND WOOD PLAYGROUNDS BEGAN TO DECAY, CHEAP AND EASILY REPLACEABLE PLASTIC UNITS WERE INSTALLED. THESE NEW UNITS WERE ALSO SUPPOSED TO BE SAFER.

HARD ASPHALT AND PACKED DIRT WERE REPLACED WITH WOOD CHIPS AND RECYCLED RUBBER.

THESE NEW SURFACES ARE MORE EXPENSIVE THOUGH, SO LESS AREA IS PUT ASIDE, RESULTING IN SMALLER EQUIPMENT.

IN FACT, THERE IS A GENERAL TREND TOWARD ALL PLAYGROUNDS HAVING SMALLER EQUIPMENT, WITH MANY ELIMINATING SWINGS.

"YOU NEED ENOUGH SURFACING ON EACH SIDE OF THE SWING SET TO COVER TWICE THE HEIGHT OF THE SWING FRAME, SO THE HORIZONTAL BAR WHERE THE SWING CABLES ARE ATTACHED HAS BEEN LOWERED FROM 12 FEET TO 8."

PEGGY PAYNE, CERTIFIED PLAYGROUND INSPECTOR

"WHEN WE RENOVATED OUR THREE TOWN PLAYGROUNDS RECENTLY, WE BUILT IN A PLAN TO SCALE THEM DOWN IN SIZE. . . ."

"WE WERE CONCERNED ABOUT LITIGATION, LIKE EVERYONE ELSE, AND OUR THOUGHT WAS TO ELIMINATE THE LARGER EQUIPMENT THAT TENDED TO BE MORE RISKY."

ANTHONY T. BRUNETTA, SUPERINTENDENT OF PARKS AND RECREATION FOR ROCKVILLE CENTRE, NEW YORK

UNFORTUNATELY, ALL THESE CHANGES DON'T SEEM TO HAVE SOLVED THE PROBLEM, AND IN SOME CASES HAVE CAUSED NEW ONES. IT HAS RECENTLY BEEN DISCOVERED THAT MANY MATERIALS USED IN SOME NEWER PLAYGROUNDS AREN'T SO SAFE.

ARTIFICIAL TURF FIELDS: SOME TYPES CONTAIN LEAD.

BLACK MATS UNDER JUNGLE GYMS AND SLIDES: REACH TEMPERATURES OF 160° F IN HOT WEATHER.

WOOD RAILROAD TIES: TREATED WITH A TERMITE PESTICIDE THAT CONTAINS ARSENIC.

GROUND-UP SYNTHETIC RUBBER: RELEASES TOXIC CHEMICALS KNOWN AS VOCs.*

*THESE VOLATILE GASES ARE KNOWN TO CAUSE IRRITATION OF NASAL AND RESPIRATORY PASSAGES AND CAN CAUSE CENTRAL NERVOUS SYSTEM DAMAGE, DEPRESSION, NAUSEA, DIZZINESS, HEADACHES, DERMATITIS, EYE DAMAGE, AND KIDNEY DAMAGE.

AND PERHAPS THE EQUIPMENT ISN'T ANY SAFER EITHER. TODAY 215,000 KIDS, ALMOST TWICE THE NUMBER FROM THE 1980s, GO TO EMERGENCY ROOMS EACH YEAR BECAUSE OF PLAYGROUND INJURIES.

THE PLAYGROUND-EQUIPMENT-RELATED INJURY RATE AMONG CHILDREN AGES FIVE AND UNDER HAS DOUBLED SINCE 1980.

SOME PLAYGROUNDS POST RULES AGAINST RUNNING AND IMPROPER USE OF EQUIPMENT.

OTHER SCHOOL PLAYGROUNDS HAVE EVEN GONE SO FAR AS TO OUTLAW TAG.

YET PEOPLE ARE STILL SUING CITIES AND SCHOOLS OVER PLAYGROUNDS. AFTER TWO LAWSUITS IN A YEAR, CABELL COUNTY, WEST VIRGINIA, HAD AN EXTREME RESPONSE TO THE PROBLEM AND IN 2010 DISABLED ALL SWINGS.

BUT THE SWING SETS WERE RETURNED AFTER RUBBER MULCH WAS SPREAD ON THE GROUND. TOO BAD FOR THE KIDS WHO WANTED TO SWING DURING THE TWO YEARS IT TOOK TO RETURN THEM.

KIDS IN FLORIDA WEREN'T SO LUCKY. IN CLEARWATER, THE NEW MAYOR PLEDGED TO BUILD A "HEALTHIER CLEARWATER" AND THEN PROCEEDED TO DEMOLISH NINE PLAYGROUNDS HE SAID WERE TOO EXPENSIVE TO REPAIR.

GIVEN A RECENT STUDY SHOWING THAT KIDS WITHOUT ACCESS TO PLAYGROUNDS HAVE A 20% TO 45% HIGHER CHANCE OF BEING OBESE, THE MAYOR IS UNLIKELY TO FULFILL HIS PLEDGE.

AND ULTIMATELY IT'S HARD TO SAY HOW MUCH MONEY WILL BE SAVED EITHER, WHEN THE CENTERS FOR DISEASE CONTROL ESTIMATES THE COST OF CHILDHOOD OBESITY TO BE $3 BILLION ANNUALLY.

BUT AS TWO COMMITTEES OF THE AMERICAN ACADEMY OF PEDIATRICS HAVE SAID, THE BENEFITS OF PLAY, AND SOME SAY THE BENEFITS OF TAKING RISKS, GO FAR BEYOND THAT OF JUST EXERCISE.

PLAY ALLOWS CHILDREN TO USE THEIR CREATIVITY WHILE DEVELOPING THEIR IMAGINATION, DEXTERITY, AND PHYSICAL, COGNITIVE, AND EMOTIONAL STRENGTH.

PLAY IS IMPORTANT TO BRAIN DEVELOPMENT.

UNDIRECTED PLAY ALLOWS CHILDREN TO LEARN HOW TO WORK IN GROUPS, TO SHARE, TO NEGOTIATE, AND TO RESOLVE CONFLICTS.

PLAY ALLOWS CHILDREN TO CREATE AND EXPLORE A WORLD THEY CAN MASTER, CONQUERING THEIR FEARS WHILE PRACTICING ADULT ROLES.

ABOVE ALL, PLAY IS A SIMPLE JOY THAT IS A CHERISHED PART OF CHILDHOOD.

SUSAN G. SOLOMON, AUTHOR OF *AMERICAN PLAYGROUNDS: REVITALIZING COMMUNITY SPACE*, POINTS OUT THAT TODAY'S "COOKIE CUTTER" PLAYGROUNDS, UNLIKE THE PARKS OF THE PAST, LIMIT KIDS' PLAY OPTIONS.

CALLING IT THE "McDONALD'S MODEL," SHE POINTS OUT THAT KIDS, DUE TO THE DESIGN, MOSTLY HAVE TO "WAIT, GO UP, GO ACROSS, GO DOWN, START ALL OVER AGAIN." NOT UNLIKE WAITING IN LINE FOR A FAST-FOOD MEAL.

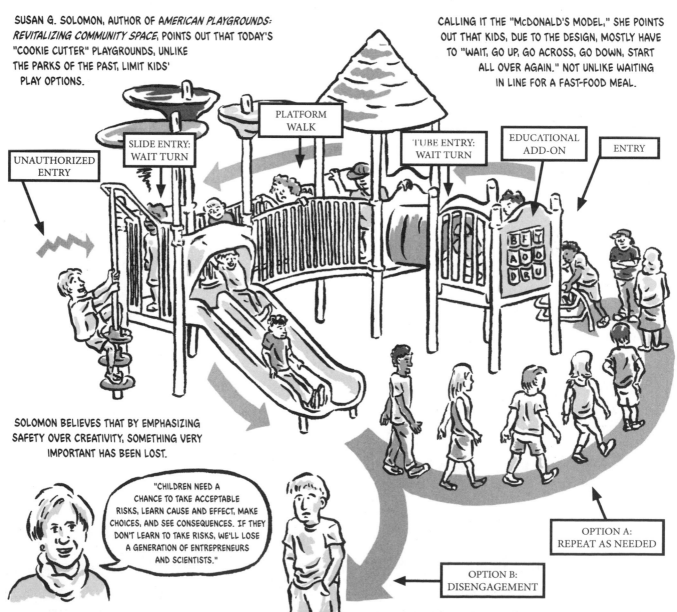

UNAUTHORIZED ENTRY

SLIDE ENTRY: WAIT TURN

PLATFORM WALK

TUBE ENTRY: WAIT TURN

EDUCATIONAL ADD-ON

ENTRY

OPTION A: REPEAT AS NEEDED

OPTION B: DISENGAGEMENT

SOLOMON BELIEVES THAT BY EMPHASIZING SAFETY OVER CREATIVITY, SOMETHING VERY IMPORTANT HAS BEEN LOST.

"CHILDREN NEED A CHANCE TO TAKE ACCEPTABLE RISKS, LEARN CAUSE AND EFFECT, MAKE CHOICES, AND SEE CONSEQUENCES. IF THEY DON'T LEARN TO TAKE RISKS, WE'LL LOSE A GENERATION OF ENTREPRENEURS AND SCIENTISTS."

SOLOMON'S BELIEF MAY BE SUPPORTED BY A STUDY ENTITLED "POPPING THE BUBBLE WRAPS" CARRIED OUT BY AN AUSTRALIAN RESEARCH TEAM AT SYDNEY UNIVERSITY.

IN THE 11-WEEK STUDY, THEY "SPICED UP" THE ROUTINE PLAYGROUND WITH FUN, AND SOME WOULD SAY DANGEROUS, MATERIALS SUCH AS HAY BALES, TIRES, CRATES, WOODEN PLANKS, AND FOAM, MUCH LIKE THE ADVENTURE PLAYGROUNDS OF THE "GOLDEN AGE."

ONE OF THE RESEARCHERS, ANITA BUNDY, THOUGHT THE HIGHER LEVELS OF ENERGY DISPLAYED BY THE KIDS USING THE MODIFIED PLAYGROUND SHOWED THAT HYPER-SAFE EQUIPMENT HAD TAKEN THE FUN OUT OF THE MODERN PLAYGROUND.

"IT SPARKS THEIR IMAGINATION AND THEIR CREATIVITY AND SOCIAL PLAY, AND THE TEACHERS ON THE PLAYGROUND TOLD US KIDS PLAYED WITH KIDS THEY DIDN'T PLAY WITH BEFORE ..."

"WHEN YOU TAKE ALL THE RISK OUT OF ANYTHING, KIDS GET BORED."

AND WHEN KIDS GET BORED, THEY GO ELSEWHERE.

When American educators first visited Communist China to study their schools, they were struck by how differently the kids there played. During recess, the little Communists were always "adult directed, not spontaneous or play-like," and "highly organized" (which kind of makes sense in a place where the government controls everything). Researchers also noticed there were no examples of Chinese kindergartners ever breaking into "dramatic play"...which isn't exactly Shakespeare—it's defined as a kind of make-believe play, which often becomes very active and physical. Dramatic play is considered a GOOD thing for kids to do, and it was something American preschoolers would start doing spontaneously and at a "high frequency." At least, that's what they did back when the original study was published in 1975. These days, some people think kids in the USA have to be trained to play.

RECESSION

"No more goofing off with friends," is how a reporter for the *New York Times* describes the new recess policy at Broadway Elementary School in the Bronx. "No more doing nothing." That's because the school had recently hired a "recess coach," who tells those who won't play by the rules: "There's no choice." Hard to argue with that approach—or with the new program's success: Since Broadway Elementary started using a recess coach to teach kids the techniques of "structured play," the drop in disciplinary actions has been dramatic—a whopping 75 percent! Injuries on the playground are down, too. By the way, "structured play" is just science talk for GAMES, such as the classic "Mother, May I" (although now it's probably called "Recess Coach, May I"). And the company behind the idea, Playworks, is growing, having recently placed their recess coaches in 170 lower-income schools across the country. Of course, Playworks' popularity is directly tied to the increasing demand from American schools to reduce the wrong kind of "dramatic play"—fighting and bullying. But recess coaches don't come cheap, so schools like Broadway Elementary hope for special grants to help, like the one it receives . . . from the nearby Waste Conversion Plant! Florida's Broward County school system went a less expensive route, turning their 140 elementary schools' recess time into "teacher-supervised physical activities" (which is a fancy way to say "gym"). Though organized acts of fitness might mean less trouble on the playground, some critics are worried about their effects on kids in other ways (ways that seem familiar compared with the regimented behavior of certain Commie preschoolers back in '75). Kids should be allowed to invent their own games and "be free to do what they choose to do," according to Dr. Romina Barros (who wrote an important study about it in a big journal— well, big on little kids—called *Pediatrics*). The problem with structured play, Barros explains, is that kids don't have time for their "brain to relax" because they're still "following rules." Relaxed brain or

not, the founder of Playworks sees her coaches as the last hope for any playtime. Sure, she wishes kids could have more freewheeling fun and "figure out how to navigate the world in a way that . . . fosters independence and creative thinking," but often, the only option is "between us and the school that doesn't offer recess." Given those choices, guess a recess coach

doesn't sound so awful after all. Certainly not as awful as, say . . . a friendship coach.

DEFRIENDED

"Parents sometimes say Johnny needs that one special friend," Christine Laycob, director of counseling at the Mary Institute, relates. "We say he doesn't need a best friend" (the "we" Laycob refers to is her colleagues at the Institute . . . not her own BFF). But Laycob is fighting an uphill battle, since according to a recent survey, 94 percent of young people admit to having at least one close friend. While Laycob agrees that kids have a "preference to pair up," that won't stop her from trying to persuade them to "not be so possessive." The counselor is only voicing the concerns some educators have about the exclusiveness of cliques—even cliques of two— because ANY form of exclusion, in theory, could (maybe, somehow . . . eventually) lead to bullying. That's one reason why, at Timber Lake Sleepaway Camp in Phoenicia, New York, when a close bond starts forming between kids, trained "friendship coaches" will swoop into action . . . to try and stop it! The friendship coaches start assigning them to separate sports teams,

then seating them at opposite ends of the dining table, and, in severe cases of friendliness, pairing them up with other kids they don't know. The idea is that it's not "particularly healthy" for children to focus on only one friend. Another reason to split up BFFs is, according to the camp director, to avoid the "devastating" effect a breakup would have (if it were allowed to happen naturally, naturally). But it could be just as "devastating" to never have a close friend. Besides increasing a child's self-esteem and confidence, many psychologists believe "empathy, the ability to listen and console [and] the process of arguing and making up" all grow when negotiating the multilayered world of having a best buddy. Who knew "normal social pain" was good for you?* And, after all, every cloud of "social pain" has a silver lining. At least it can when it's followed by the warm embrace after you and your friend have made up. But be careful, because things could turn cloudy again if you're busted for "extreme hugging."

SQUEEZE PLAY

That's what they call it at Percy Julian Middle School in Oak Park, Illinois—and you can get suspended for it! But ALL hugging has been deemed "extreme" in some schools. In fact, Fossil Hills Middle School in north Texas has declared any PDAs—that stands for "public displays of affection"—as prohibited behavior (that means you two over there, holding hands!). In Fairfax County, Virginia, it's not just affection that's banned, it's ALL physical contact—period! But why is the school getting so touchy about touching? The principal explains: "You get into shades of gray. The kids say, 'If he can high-five, then I can do this.'" "This," in the case of Mascoutah Middle School student Megan Coulter, was a quick hug good-bye to her pals before parting for the weekend. When the 13-year-old got two days' detention (one day per hug) she said it felt "crazy!" But honestly, Megan, aren't you the crazy one for not memorizing your school's personal space policy? If she had, then she would have already known that hugging "reflects poor judgment,

and brings discredit to the school and to the persons involved." For shame, Megan! A student from Autauga County, Alabama, must also hang her head in shame (over her desk while also in detention) for giving a reassuring hug to a male buddy who was feeling sad after his parent had passed away. Anti-hugging is being embraced by many schools as part of a larger movement within the education system called the zero tolerance policy.† Which, in turn, breeds its own special brand of "extreme" behavior . . . from teachers. Like the math instructor who acts as the affection detection coach in the hallways of his St. Louis school, blowing a whistle at anyone in the student body—if they dare bump bodies—while headed for class. Given the amount of encroaching coaching, it's no surprise that a recent ten-year study of middle-class families in Southern California found that parents were raising their kids to become "relatively dependent." The relatively rich dependents of New York City parents can take expensive classes to be coached in basic social skills—or, rather, Socialsklz:-).‡ And why shouldn't they (assuming their mom and dad will pay for it)? If kids need coaching to play, be friends, and hug (or not hug), then maybe it makes sense to fork over $540 for a course in "how to host play dates, talk on the phone, and hold a conversation." One thing to keep in mind, though, as more and more kids get coached on life, is the studies of Stuart Brown, the president of the National Institute for Play. His work on play has shown how most homicidal males, as well as convicted drunk drivers, missed out on typical "rough and tumble" fun when they were young. So what do you want, Coach: a killer . . . a Communist . . . or a normal kid?

---

*Michael Thompson, a psychologist and author of the book *Best Friends, Worst Enemies: Understanding the Social Lives of Children*, did, that's who.

†More about zero tolerance later. A lot more.

‡Yes, it's called Socialsklz:-). And yes, that's a terrible name for a company.

While safety-conscious city planners (and worried parents) dream of future playgrounds built entirely of cushions, the truth is NOTHING can protect children from EVERYTHING out there—especially when kids are "out there." For instance, what about all that dirt lying around on the ground . . . out there? Or the cold germs . . . out there? Or all the candy . . . out there? Maybe here's a better question to ask: Is trying to protect kids from everything that's "out there" driving them OUT of their minds?

FILTHY FACTS ABOUT DIRT!

It might sound SICK to the mom screaming at her crud-caked kid, but according to microbiologist Dr. Mary Ruebush, author of *Why Dirt Is Good*, rolling around in microbe-filled muck will actually help keep you WELL. In the long run, even a little dirt-eating's OK, because it assists in kick-starting a kid's sickness-fighting skills. Early exposure to the gritty world of the playground—emphasis on grit—exercises kids' muscles and their immune systems. It's actually too much cleanliness that's really BAD FOR YOU! Kill too many germs and you weaken the kid—as two new studies indicate, which show a rise in asthma and allergic disease due to increased sanitation.* Overuse of "safer"

antibacterial soaps can also create tougher germs because they kill off the weak bacteria and leave the stronger ones to breed superbugs. And anyway, those fancy soaps don't kill the actual bugs that cause most common illnesses. That's because it's viruses that give you the common cold, fevers, and the runs—NOT BACTERIA!

COMMON SCOLD

At the first sign of frost, kids begin to hear grown-ups' familiar growl: "Button up your

*Paolo M. Matricardi, MD, and colleagues found a link between certain microbial exposure and reduced allergic disease in the U.S. population. A second study found another, similar marker in early exposure to bedding dust in European kids.

coat or you'll catch your DEATH!" But when real scientists, and not parents, check out this claim, the answer isn't so clear. In fact, some studies indicate that kids can bundle up all they want, but it won't stop a cold any more than scrubbing with antibacterial soap does. A series of pretty gross tests, where folks had active viruses shoved up their noses, showed that subjects who were warm got sick just as often as those who were chilled. While there have been other studies, mostly generations ago, that seem to show being cold and getting colds are linked, the only recent study that found a connection had to do with "acute chilling of the feet." Even then, only 10 percent of the subjects experienced cold symptoms. And the authors of *Don't Swallow Your Gum!* (the

book that provides most of the research for this snotty section) question the study's results: "It is very possible these people just reported these symptoms because their feet felt cold." So wear a swimsuit all winter if you want (and if you really feel like playing it safe, wear some socks too).

INTERNAL INJURIES

What if all the worrying that parents do when their precious child is out there actually hurts the kid "in there"—inside their brain? Now,

there's something to worry about! According to a recent study on "helicopter parenting"— so named for the parents' constant "hovering" over the kid—such overprotective behavior can make children "more susceptible to psychiatric disorders, which in turn are associated with defects in part of the prefrontal cortex." Brain scans showed that young people in their twenties with helicopter parents had less gray matter in the spot where abnormalities like schizophrenia seem to lurk. Thanks, Mom and Dad!!! The link the investigators found has to do with the excessive release of cortisol, a stress hormone. Interestingly, the research also found that neglected kids were similarly affected. Too much and too little attention appear to be equally traumatic. Another study at the University of Tennessee found the kids of helicopter parents were more likely to end up medicated for anxiety and/or depression. Bummer! Yet in another study, researchers from Keene State College in New Hampshire found that incoming college freshmen with hovering moms and dads were "more dependent, more neurotic, and less open than their peers." Though these studies are all preliminary and no direct cause and effect can yet be claimed, isn't it enough evidence for helicopter parents to at least try giving less worrying a whirl? They could start small, by dumping this myth: that swallowed gum sticks inside a kid's body for years. They can even dig up the proof . . . in their own kid's poop (just wait a day or two after gum ingestion). The next myth they might try forgetting relates to studies that have shown when parents think their children have had sugar, they claim to see the effect, even though their kids were given sugar-free drinks. What?! Sugar doesn't make kids hyper. Now, that's sweet!

CHILDPROOF!
Real Safety Products for the Panicked Parent

The Thudguard® Infant Safety Hat

What do you do when your child takes those first, scary steps in the house?

It wasn't long ago that nervous parents' only recourse was to duct-tape bubble wrap around their toddlers' tiny heads. But that had its own unfortunate dangers and was eventually declared illegal in 23 states. Thankfully, Thudguard, the top name in skull security systems, stepped in with the Infant Safety Hat. Your little prince or princess can now avoid the hard realities of life, in head-hugging comfort, thanks to this brand-new, all-foam "safety crown." Order it in the next 10 days and get 50% off matching knee pads.

Baby Bottom Fan®

What helicopter parent isn't comforted by the sight of whirling fan blades hovering over a baby's rump? At least once parents know the whirling fan blades are cushy-soft sponges that will both cool and dry the baby's backside with the same motion. Never worry about diaper rash again!

WARNING: Makers of product take no responsibility if later in life child suffers from deep psychological damage—especially should a video of the butt fanning ever be uploaded to YouTube.

Potty Mitts®

Messy public restrooms won't be a problem anymore—even if your kid is a toilet-rim grabber. And later, let them make all the mud pies they want, as long as Mom has an endless supply of these handy disposable mitts around. Use them anytime—or all the time—even in your own disgusting, germ-infested home. With Potty Mitts' patented "Never-Touch" technology, your child never has to touch anything . . . ever . . . again.

NoseFrida®

What overprotective parent isn't willing to suck out their baby's snot?! Anything to ensure that tiny nose hole remains pristine. And now, with the Nosefrida's new, sleek design, you don't have to look totally ridiculous doing it. OK . . . you still look ridiculous, but who cares, it's your precious BABY! Not only stylish, but really keeps the snot flowing. It's up to you to do the rest. Remember our motto:
Parents suck!

Nervous inhaling nasty nasal discharge? Don't worry—thanks to a washable snot filter inside the tube!

O'Pair® Child's Plush and Adult's Sleek Fanny Pack with Connector

Overly attached to your kid? Don't be ashamed. Proudly retie that umbilical cord with the O'Pair Child's Plush and Adult's Sleek Fanny Pack. This innovative fanny pack/child restraint allows for constant monitoring while still giving creative and curious kids all the room they need to explore the world (within the four-foot diameter the "love tether" embraces). Place the fanny pack directly over the stomach and you can almost feel the umbilical cord reattaching (Dad, you're also encouraged to give this a try). It's practical too: You walk your dog, right? So why not walk your kid?

ALL NAMES OF SAFETY DEVICES GUARANTEED TRUE
(descriptions of devices not as guaranteed)

AS PLAYGROUNDS HAVE BEEN MADE TOO DULL FOR ANY KID OVER AGE EIGHT, OLDER KIDS IN SEARCH OF FUN HAVE LOOKED FOR ALTERNATIVES. WHILE MANY HAVE SIMPLY GONE INSIDE OR BEEN ORGANIZED INTO PLANNED ACTIVITIES, THOSE KIDS WHO CRAVE FREEDOM AND ADVENTURE IN THE REAL WORLD ARE RUNNING INTO MORE AND MORE OBSTACLES. AND THEY MAY BE LEFT WONDERING . . .

WHO OWNS THE STREETS?

THERE IS PROBABLY NO LEGAL ACTIVITY THAT KIDS DO IN PUBLIC SPACE THAT HAS ANGERED AND FRIGHTENED ADULTS MORE THAN SKATEBOARDING.

STORE OWNERS CLAIM THAT SKATERS SCARE CUSTOMERS AND DAMAGE PROPERTY. MANY STREET MALLS HAVE BANNED THEM AND INSTALLED ANTI-SKATEBOARDING DEVICES.

IN FACT, IT IS INCREASINGLY DIFFICULT TO EVEN CALL IT A LEGAL ACTIVITY BECAUSE SO MANY CITIES HAVE LAWS BANNING SKATEBOARDING IN MANY LOCATIONS.

LAWS VARY FROM CITY TO CITY, STATE TO STATE. SOME TOWNS REQUIRE ADULT SUPERVISION OR EVEN A LICENSE. OTHERS HAVE TRIED TO BAN SKATEBOARDING COMPLETELY.

THE TOWN COUNCIL OF CAPE MAY, NEW JERSEY, TRIED TO MAKE IT ILLEGAL TO "POSSESS, PARK OR STAND, CARRY OR TRANSPORT" ANY SKATEBOARD IN PUBLIC PLACES. BUT IT WAS FORCED TO SHELVE THE LAW AFTER PUBLIC OUTCRY AND RIDICULE.

117

STREET SKATERS OFTEN EMBRACE THEIR OUTLAW STATUS AND ARE ESPECIALLY ATTRACTED TO UNUSUAL AND CHALLENGING ELEMENTS COMMON IN PUBLIC PLAZAS AND MALLS.

BUT THIS UNAUTHORIZED AND RISKY USE OF PUBLIC SPACE, AS WELL AS THE NUMBER OF KIDS HANGING OUT, HAS LED TO MORE CONFLICTS BETWEEN SKATERS AND POLICE.

IN 2008, A VIDEO WAS POSTED ON YOUTUBE THAT SHOWED BALTIMORE POLICE OFFICER SALVATORE RIVIERI MANHANDLING A 14-YEAR-OLD BOY WHO WAS SKATEBOARDING ILLEGALLY IN A PUBLIC PARK.

RIVIERI WAS ANGRY THAT THE BOY HAD CALLED HIM "DUDE" AND SAID ONE DAY SOMEONE WOULD KILL THE BOY IF HE DIDN'T "LEARN THE MEANING OF RESPECT."

THE VIDEO BECAME INFAMOUS, AND RIVIERI EVENTUALLY LOST HIS JOB.

SINCE THEN, HUNDREDS OF SIMILAR VIDEOS HAVE BEEN POSTED ONLINE SHOWING CONFRONTATIONS WITH POLICE OR SECURITY GUARDS.

THIS IS THE ARREST OF A 13-YEAR-OLD IN HOT SPRINGS, ARKANSAS, ON "GO SKATEBOARD DAY."

MANY OF THE VIDEOS SHOW THAT THE TROUBLE STARTS WHEN GUARDS TRY TO TAKE KIDS' SKATEBOARDS.

OTHERS SHOW SKATERS BEING ARRESTED FOR MOUTHING OFF OR, IN ONE CASE, SMILING.

SKATEBOARDING HAS HAD A BAD REPUTATION RIGHT FROM ITS BEGINNING. INVENTED BY SURFERS IN 1958, IT WAS ONLY A FEW YEARS BEFORE THE AMERICAN MEDICAL ASSOCIATION DECLARED IT "A NEW MEDICAL MENACE," AND HUNDREDS OF COMMUNITIES BANNED IT ENTIRELY.

SKATEBOARDS, OR "SIDEWALK SURFBOARDS," WERE MORE DANGEROUS BACK THEN BECAUSE THE WHEELS WERE MADE OF CLAY, WHICH HAD BAD TRACTION AND COULD BE STOPPED INSTANTLY BY THE SMALLEST OF PEBBLES.

BUT WHEN THE POLYURETHANE WHEEL WAS INVENTED IN THE EARLY 1970s, ITS BETTER GRIP OPENED UP NEW TERRAIN FOR SKATERS.

SKATERS WOULD SNEAK INTO EMPTY POOLS OR CEMENT DRAINAGE DITCHES IN SEARCH OF CHALLENGING, THOUGH OFTEN ILLEGAL, TERRAIN.

AS SKATEBOARDING AND VERTICAL SKATING SURGED IN POPULARITY, SKATE PARKS WERE BUILT AS A LEGAL AND, AT FIRST, MONEY-MAKING ALTERNATIVE. BUT WHEN INSURANCE COMPANIES RAISED THEIR RATES, MANY PARKS HAD TO CLOSE.

SOME SKATERS BUILT RAMPS. OTHERS RETURNED TO THE STREET, JUST AT A TIME WHEN A NEW TRICK, THE OLLIE, OPENED UP NEW POSSIBILITIES.

A 2008 SKATER SURVEY IN LOUDOUN COUNTY, VIRGINIA, THE RICHEST COUNTY IN AMERICA, FOUND:

67% (9,184) OF KIDS SKATE MOSTLY IN SHOPPING PLAZAS, BUSINESS BUILDINGS, AND PUBLIC PARKS (ILLEGAL AREAS).

92% (12,610) SAID THEY ARE TOLD TO LEAVE PUBLIC PROPERTY AT LEAST TWICE A WEEK.

89% (12,199) SAID THEY WOULD STOP GOING TO ILLEGAL SKATE AREAS IF LEGAL SKATE AREAS WERE BUILT.

"THEY BUILD FIELDS FOR SOFTBALL AND BASEBALL AND COURTS FOR TENNIS. WE JUST GET HASSLED. THE CITY IS SAYING, 'PLAY THESE SPORTS OR NOTHING.' I'D LIKE TO BE ABLE TO SKATE WITHOUT FEELING LIKE A CRIMINAL. YOU CAN'T EVEN USE YOUR BOARD AS TRANSPORTATION TO GET FROM ONE PLACE TO ANOTHER."*

*JASON SMITH, GALESBURG, ILLINOIS

STATISTICS COMPILED BY THE INTERNATIONAL ASSOCIATION OF SKATEBOARD COMPANIES SHOW AT LEAST 20 MILLION ACTIVE SKATEBOARDERS IN THE U.S., MORE THAN THE NUMBER OF KIDS IN LITTLE LEAGUE BASEBALL.

AND IN 2004, SKATEBOARDERS HAD 33% FEWER INJURIES THAN BASEBALL PLAYERS AND 86% FEWER THAN BASKETBALL PLAYERS. A 2012 STUDY SHOWED THAT PEOPLE WERE MORE THAN TWICE AS LIKELY TO BE INJURED PLAYING FOOTBALL. BUT NO ONE IS PASSING LAWS LIMITING FOOTBALL.

FOOTBALL

BASKETBALL

SKATEBOARDING

Percentage of Injury per 100 Participants

THIS CALLS INTO QUESTION ONE OF THE MOST OFTEN-CITED REASONS POLICE GIVE FOR AGGRESSIVE ENFORCEMENT.

TWO OTHER STATISTICS, THAT OVER HALF THE SKATER INJURIES COME FROM IRREGULAR SURFACES AND THAT ONLY 5% HAPPEN IN SKATE PARKS, MAY POINT TO A STRATEGY FOR REDUCING INJURIES EVEN MORE.

STOP MOVING OR I'LL HIT YOU.

"THERE IS A DUTY TO PROTECT THESE KIDS FROM BECOMING PARAPLEGICS."†

†ASSISTANT POLICE CHIEF RICHARD W. WADE, AFTER POLICE IN PALM BEACH, FLORIDA, HANDCUFFED AND ARRESTED THREE SKATEBOARDING TEENS, AGES 14, 15, AND 16

BUT PUBLIC SKATE PARKS MAY NOT SOLVE ALL THE PROBLEMS. ANY AREA THAT IS APPROVED BY THE CITY AS AN OK PLACE TO PLAY IGNORES ANOTHER IMPORTANT PART OF WHAT KIDS NATURALLY DO AS THEY DEVELOP INTO ADULTS.

THEY SEEK OUT PLACES THAT AREN'T "OFFICIALLY" SANCTIONED: PLACES WITH AN ELEMENT OF REAL-LIFE RISK.

MANY TOWNS HAVE ABANDONED BUILDINGS, TUNNELS, CEMETERIES, OR BRIDGES WITH GHOST STORIES ATTACHED TO THEM. OFTEN THEY BECOME PLACES WHERE GROUPS OF TEENS GO TO TEST THEIR COURAGE.

THIS ACTIVITY IS SO COMMON THAT SOCIOLOGISTS HAVE GIVEN IT A NAME: LEGEND TRIPPING.

LEGEND TRIPPING USUALLY OCCURS AT NIGHT AND SOMETIMES INVOLVES THE RETELLING OF THE SCARY STORY ATTACHED TO THE LOCATION.

THE TRIP USUALLY ENDS WHEN A "GHOST" IS SIGHTED OR SOMETHING ELSE HAPPENS THAT BOTH SCARES THE WITS OUT OF EVERYONE AND GIVES THEM A GOOD STORY TO TELL.

SOME THINK LEGEND TRIPPING FUNCTIONS AS A WAY FOR TEENS TO FEEL CONFIDENT THAT THEY CAN FACE DANGER OR, ON A DEEPER LEVEL, THE UNKNOWN FUTURE THEY WILL SOON BE LIVING ON THEIR OWN.

SO SEEKING DANGER IS A NECESSARY COMPONENT. ONE JOB OF PARENTS AND AUTHORITIES, OF COURSE, IS TO PROTECT TEENS FROM DANGER.

IN ORDER TO DO THIS, MANY PARENTS SET RULES FOR THEIR TEENS, INCLUDING WHAT TIME THEY NEED TO BE AT HOME. THIS IS CALLED A CURFEW.

IN RECENT YEARS, MANY CITIES AND TOWNS HAVE BEEN INSTITUTING TEEN CURFEWS IN AN ATTEMPT TO CONTROL YOUTH CRIME AND PROTECT TEENS FROM DANGER. CURFEW LAWS MAKE IT ILLEGAL FOR AN UNDERAGE PERSON TO BE OUTSIDE DURING CERTAIN TIMES.

PUNISHMENT VARIES WIDELY FROM STATE TO STATE, TOWN TO TOWN. SOMETIMES POLICE GIVE A WARNING OR MAKE THE YOUTH RETURN HOME; IN OTHER TOWNS, THERE MAY BE A FINE OR JAIL TIME INVOLVED.

TEEN CURFEW LAWS HAVE BEEN INCREASING SINCE THE MID-1980s. IN 2000, 337 CITIES HAD THEM. TODAY THAT NUMBER HAS GROWN TO AROUND 500 CITIES. NO ONE KNOWS HOW MANY TOWNS HAVE TEEN CURFEWS.

PREVIOUSLY, GOVERNMENT-ENFORCED CURFEWS WERE USUALLY INSTITUTED ONLY IN TIMES OF EMERGENCY, LIKE DURING WARTIME OR TO QUELL CIVILIAN RIOTS.

THE RECENT USE OF TEEN CURFEWS AS A COMMON LAW-ENFORCEMENT TOOL HAS BEEN CHALLENGED IN COURT BY CIVIL RIGHTS ORGANIZATIONS.

THIS CURFEW CRIMINALIZES ALL YOUTH, REGARDLESS OF WHETHER THEY ARE BREAKING ANY LAWS OR POSING ANY THREAT.

ONE OBJECTION IS THAT CURFEWS VIOLATE THE CONSTITUTIONAL RIGHT TO ASSEMBLY AND FREEDOM OF SPEECH. MANY COURTS HAVE AGREED WITH THIS AND STRUCK DOWN LAWS THAT DON'T ALLOW FOR PROTESTS.*

*IN WEST PALM BEACH, FLORIDA, KIDS CAN BE OUT AFTER CURFEW, AS LONG AS THEY'RE PROTESTING SOMETHING (LIKE CURFEW LAWS).

SOME COURTS HAVE FOUND THAT CURFEW LAWS VIOLATE THE 14TH AMENDMENT, WHICH SAYS THAT STATES CANNOT PASS LAWS THAT AFFECT SOME CITIZENS AND NOT OTHERS. BUT THIS DOESN'T APPLY TO PRIVATELY OWNED PUBLIC SPACES, LIKE SHOPPING MALLS, WHERE CURFEWS ARE INCREASINGLY COMMON.

JUVENILE CURFEWS HAVE BEEN FOUND TO BE UNCONSTITUTIONAL BY THE SUPREME COURTS OF WASHINGTON, IOWA, AND HAWAII, AND HAVE RECENTLY BEEN STRUCK DOWN BY THE FEDERAL COURT IN SAN DIEGO, CALIFORNIA. HOWEVER, COURTS HAVE UPHELD CURFEWS IN DALLAS, TEXAS; WASHINGTON, D.C.; AND CHARLOTTESVILLE, VIRGINIA.

CRITICS POINT OUT THAT TEEN CURFEWS LUMP ALL TEENS TOGETHER WHEN ONLY 6 PERCENT OF THEM COMMIT TWO-THIRDS OF ALL VIOLENT CRIMES FOR THEIR AGE GROUP.

"THE POLICE ALREADY HAVE THE ABILITY TO ARREST JUVENILE CRIMINALS; THE CURFEW ADDS NOTHING MORE THAN THE DISCRETION TO ARREST THE INNOCENT AS WELL.

"THE PROPER RESPONSE TO JUVENILE CRIME IS TO ARREST THE CRIMINALS, NOT TO PLACE THOUSANDS OF LAW-ABIDING YOUNG PEOPLE UNDER HOUSE ARREST."

LENORA LAPIDUS, AMERICAN CIVIL LIBERTIES UNION (ACLU) OF NEW JERSEY LEGAL DIRECTOR

THE ACLU FILED A SUIT IN WEST NEW YORK, NEW JERSEY, ON BEHALF OF TEENS WHO WERE ARRESTED FOR CURFEW VIOLATIONS. SOME WERE ON THEIR WAY HOME FROM DELIVERING CAKE TO A GRANDPARENT . . .

OR WORKING AT MCDONALD'S . . .

OR EATING IN A RESTAURANT WITH AN ADULT FRIEND.

IN JULY OF 2011, POLICE IN OKLAHOMA CITY, OKLAHOMA, ARRESTED 20 TEENS WHO WERE WAITING FOR RIDES FROM THEIR PARENTS AFTER A MOVIE. PARENTS CLAIMED THE ARRESTS BEGAN BEFORE THE 11 P.M. CURFEW.

WHEN POLICE IN HOUSTON COULDN'T FIND ANYONE TO CATCH IN THEIR CRACKDOWN ON LATE-NIGHT ILLEGAL RACING, THEY INSTEAD ARRESTED 278 PEOPLE (MANY SHOPPING AT A 24-HOUR KMART) ON CHARGES OF TRESPASSING AND CURFEW VIOLATIONS.

INCIDENTS LIKE THESE HAVE CRITICS WONDERING IF ENFORCING CURFEWS CAN ALSO BE A DRAIN ON RESOURCES THAT POLICE SHOULD BE USING TO FIGHT CRIMINAL BEHAVIOR.

A 2003 RESEARCH ARTICLE PRINTED BY THE AMERICAN ACADEMY OF POLITICAL AND SOCIAL SCIENCE LOOKED AT TEN SCIENTIFIC STUDIES ON CURFEWS AND FOUND THAT THEY SHOWED NO EFFECT ON CRIME RATES.

BUT PERHAPS THE BIGGEST CRITICISM AGAINST TEEN CURFEWS IS THAT THEY DON'T DO WHAT THEY ARE SUPPOSED TO: REDUCE TEEN CRIME AND PROTECT TEENAGERS.

AND ACCORDING TO THE FBI, "YOUTH BETWEEN THE AGES OF 12 AND 17 ARE MOST AT RISK OF COMMITTING VIOLENT ACTS AND BEING VICTIMS BETWEEN 2 P.M. AND 8 P.M."—EXACTLY THE TIMES NOT COVERED BY CURFEWS.

IN 2011, PHILADELPHIA INSTITUTED THE MOST RESTRICTIVE CURFEW IN THE NATION IN RESPONSE TO A NEW PHENOMENON INVOLVING TEENS, TECHNOLOGY, AND PUBLIC SPACE: THE FLASH MOB.

A FLASH MOB IS WHEN A GROUP OF PEOPLE, USUALLY YOUNG ADULTS OR TEENS, USE SOCIAL MEDIA OR CELL PHONES TO ORCHESTRATE A GATHERING IN A PUBLIC PLACE. IT ALL STARTED IN 2003, IN NEW YORK CITY, AS A "SOCIAL EXPERIMENT"— OFTEN WITH A PUBLIC PERFORMANCE ASPECT.

"WE HAD A COUPLE—MORE THAN A COUPLE—OF THESE EPISODIC INCIDENTS OF TEENAGE INSANITY."

PHILADELPHIA MAYOR MICHAEL NUTTER

THE TERM "FLASH MOB" IS APPLIED TO A VARIETY OF PUBLIC-SPACE SPECTACLES LIKE MASSIVE PUBLIC PILLOW FIGHTS, CHOREOGRAPHED DANCING, NO-PANTS SUBWAY RIDES, AND ZOMBIE WALKS.

BUT AFTER AN UGLY INCIDENT IN PHILADELPHIA WHERE PARTICIPANTS ATTACKED A BYSTANDER, THE NEWS MEDIA BEGAN CONNECTING FLASH MOBS TO INCIDENTS OF VIOLENCE.

FLASH MOBS: FROM SOCIAL MEDIA TO "TSUNAMI OF KIDS"

WILL FEAR OF FLASH MOBS KEEP YOU AND YOUR KIDS INDOORS?

AFTER FIGHTING AT THE COVENTRY STREET FAIR WAS LABELED BY MEDIA OUTLETS AS A FLASH MOB, CLEVELAND, OHIO, EXPANDED ITS CURFEW AND PASSED A LAW THAT SPECIFICALLY LISTED "ELECTRONIC MEDIA DEVICES" SUCH AS COMPUTERS AND CELL PHONES AS CRIMINAL TOOLS.

BUT A LOCAL NEWSPAPER, THE CLEVELAND *PLAIN DEALER*, INTERVIEWED THOSE ARRESTED AND TRACED THE VIOLENCE TO A STREET GANG, NOT SOCIAL MEDIA. MANY OF THEM HAD NEVER HEARD THE TERM "FLASH MOB."

"I WANTED TO GO MEET SOME OF THOSE HEIGHTS GIRLS AND GET NUMBERS. EVERYBODY GOES TO COVENTRY."

ANOTHER ANTI-FLASH-MOB LAW WAS PROPOSED IN MONTGOMERY COUNTY, PENNSYLVANIA, AFTER A LARGE GROUP OF TEENS RETURNING FROM A STATE FAIR DECIDED TO ROB A CONVENIENCE STORE. LATER IT WAS REVEALED . . .

CRITICS OF ANTI-FLASH-MOB LAWS, LIKE MAYOR FRANK JACKSON OF CLEVELAND, WHO REFUSED TO SIGN THAT CITY'S LAW, POINT OUT THAT THE POLICE HAVE ALL THE TOOLS THEY NEED TO ADDRESS MOB VIOLENCE.

"THIS WAS NOT ORGANIZED BY A TWEET [OR ON] FACEBOOK. IT WAS SOMETHING MORE DYNAMIC AND OCCURRED ON THE WALK FROM THE BUS STATION TO THE 7-ELEVEN."

MONTGOMERY COUNTY STATE'S ATTORNEY JOHN McCARTHY

"THESE ORDINANCES MIRROR STATE LAWS ALREADY IN PLACE."

INDEED, TOWNS LIKE NORFOLK, VIRGINIA, AND SOUTH ORANGE, NEW JERSEY, HAVE CHOSEN TO MONITOR SOCIAL NETWORK SITES RATHER THAN PASS NEW LAWS IN ORDER TO CONTROL THE PHENOMENON.

AFTER FEATHERS FROM A FLASH MOB PILLOW FIGHT CLOGGED UP SEWERS IN SAN FRANCISCO, CITY OFFICIALS SAID FLASH MOBS MAY HAVE TO APPLY FOR PERMITS, PROVIDE SECURITY AND PORTA-POTTIES, AND PAY FOR CLEANUP.

HOLD ON . . . I'VE GOT A TWEET.

"OTHERWISE WE ARE GOING TO HAVE TO FIND A WAY TO SHUT IT DOWN."*

*LISA SEITZ GRUWELL OF THE RECREATION AND PARK DEPARTMENT

WHICH IS WHAT HAPPENED ON HALLOWEEN, 2011, IN DURANGO, COLORADO, WHEN CLOSE TO 1,500 ZOMBIES SHOWED UP FOR THE ANNUAL ZOMBIE MARCH.

22 ZOMBIES WERE ARRESTED, NOT BECAUSE OF VIOLENCE . . .

OR BECAUSE THEY WERE USING TECHNOLOGY . . .

BUT, ACCORDING TO THE POLICE, BECAUSE THE ZOMBIES DIDN'T HAVE A PERMIT.

BRAINS! BRAINS!

BARS! BARS!

YOU HAVE THE RIGHT TO REMAIN UNDEAD . . .

Flash-mob arrests, like teen curfews and anti-loitering laws, expose a certain fear that society feels whenever young people congregate (can you pronounce "ephebiphobia"?). Now, supposedly, the real deal behind kid crowd control is that all-American adolescents need special restrictions . . . for their own safety. If that's true, though, then why was it that when laws were increasing to "protect" kids in the previous decade, so were laws making it easier for minors to be tried in adult courts? If kids' safety is the real concern, then why should society punish them as if they are grown-ups—since the whole idea is that they need extra protection because they're not like grown-ups? Wonder who is protecting who from whom, hmmm? Society, it sure sounds like you're sending kids . . .

MIXED SIGNALS

BUZZ OFF

And a "mixed signal" is literally what the Mosquito sends. It's the British invention for curbing congregating teens, and like the online monitoring of flash mobs, it's another high-tech approach. Only this time, instead of eavesdropping, the Mosquito is ear-splitting. At least it is for kids, who hear the ultrasonic signal as a brain-rattling buzz. But here's the really mixed-up part: When adults are blasted by the same sound,

they hear . . . nothing. Younger ears are sharp enough to pick up the higher frequency the Mosquito emits (a sound likened to "15 or 20 people dragging their nails down a chalkboard"), but grown-ups don't groan because they've grown too deaf. It's a sonic balance that inventor Howard Stapleton perfected by testing the painful frequency on his own children. But, hey, it's also "perfectly safe." Or so says KIDS BE GONE, the catchy-named company that produces an American version of the device.

BUGGED BITE

Catchy-named companies might not be the best source for information, though. According to a 2007 report from the German Federal Institute for Occupational Safety, long-term exposure to the Mosquito can cause: "Disruption of the equilibrium senses, as well as other extra-aural effects. . . . With the sound levels that can be reached by the device, the onset of dizziness, headache, nausea and impairment is to be expected." That's too bad for fifteen-year-old Eddie Holder, whose apartment is in a building with a Mosquito nearby. "It's this screeching sound that you have to get away from or it will drive you crazy," he wails. Unfortunately, the Mosquitos are spreading. A mall in Maryland, a movie theater in Massachusetts, a parking lot in South Carolina—one by one, businesses and municipalities are adding the teen-scattering whine to their crowd-control arsenal. It's becoming the high-tech equivalent of a cop's "Move along, kid." Of course, anyone twenty-six or over can hang around and do all the criminal things they want, since they're around the age when the buzz loses its bite. If your target is teens, though, they'll feel the Mosquito's sting. Just ask school emergency manager Rick McGee. After installing two in the Columbia High parking lot, the kids who used to gather there after hours to "trash talk" and fight now "just get aggravated and leave."

MOSQUITO BE GONE

Sometimes it's the townspeople who get aggravated, though, and then they tell the Mosquito to leave. In Great Barrington, Massachusetts, for instance, the movie theater owner who installed the kid zapper was forced to remove it after citizens protested. When Milford, Connecticut, wanted to place a device in a park, people resisted, so the city upped police patrols instead. Perhaps they are heeding the warning from criminalist James Alan Fox that these kinds of crowd-controlling devices are "dangerous" in the hands of private businesses. Wonder if it's any better in the hands of government, where a souped-up version of the Mosquito, with a higher-decibel output, is exclusively sold. People have been questioning the use of the anti-teen beam right from the start: A UK campaign against the device described it as a "sonic weapon," and civil liberties groups in England, Australia, Scotland, and America have all supported bans. The Assembly of the Council of Europe took another swat at it, declaring the device "degrading and discriminatory" toward young people. Maybe the most ironic tonic for the sonic weapon came when enterprising English teens found a way to mix up the Mosquito's signal even more. They transformed it into the irritating buzz of rebellion by turning the technology on its ear. And it was all so easy, really; they simply made the Mosquito their cell phone tone. Having rendered their rings now inaudible to parents and, more importantly, teachers, British boys and girls could call and text each other in class while Mr. or Ms. Fill-in-the-Blank continued writing on the board, totally deaf to what was happening behind them. Probably not a big surprise, the ring caught on quicker than the actual Mosquito and even acquired its own name, the "Teen Buzz." These days, kids can download it directly off the internet (just don't say you heard about it here).

TAG, YOU'RE AN IT

Another high-tech technique used for kid control is a tracking system that can work on a GLOBAL scale, thanks to the perfectly synchronized orbits of some really expensive U.S. Department of Defense satellites. Their signals can pretty much pinpoint anyone anywhere, if that anyone is carrying a GPS receiver. GPS stands for Global Positioning System, but the technology is commonly referred to as "microchipping" or "tagging," terms first used to describe ways of identifying and tracking animals. A receiver can take many forms—cell phone, PocketFinders—and can be embedded in most anything—shoes, clothing, even backpacks (some of which feature a rip-cord–activated high-decibel alarm and strobe light). So far, no tracking has been directly implanted into children, but hey, they do it with pets (and remember those kid leashes earlier). Other things trackers can do—besides, of course, tracking—include monitoring a kid's heart rate, blood pressure, and body temperature. Some are equipped with cameras that switch on remotely, and even little speakers for Mom and Dad to issue worried warnings through. It all sounds so extreme . . . yet so familiar, like stuff from the CHILDPROOF catalog. Only with GPS, helicopter parents can upgrade to parent "stars" and hover over their kids from space. "Relax—now you can have peace of mind 24 hours a day," assures one of the tracking company ads, "while you and your child are the high-tech envy of the neighborhood!" Less envious were *Scientific American* editors, who warned that society was paying a high price for that peace of mind: "Tagging . . . kids becomes a form of indoctrination into an emerging surveillance society that young minds should be learning to question." Here's a question: Think those young minds are learning about it in their public schools? Sure, especially when their PS is using GPS!

SCHOOL MONITOR

First Dallas, then Midland, then San Antonio plugged into the GPS system, as part of the state of Texas's comprehensive program to reduce high school truancy. Students with a history of skipping school were selected to wear a thick ankle bracelet that tracked their whereabouts 24/7, and they could never take it off through the entire program (which sometimes lasted months). In Santa Fe, a suburb outside Houston, "smart tags" have been issued to the entire student body—whose student bodies can be tracked anywhere on school grounds (the district is trying to wire the buses next). The main claim for the mass tagging is student safety, but that works only up to a point—the point being just 100 feet from the school building (and to think, these "smart tags" cost the district only $150,000). The schools do expect better attendance records from the computer monitoring, but that's assuming students don't give their tags to someone else, or leave them at home, or forget them at a friend's. But no kid would ever do that. The ACLU, which opposes the forced surveillance of children, points out that a similar plan for preschoolers in

Richmond, California, could actually backfire and make it easier for a kidnapper or stalker to track a tagged kid using the SAME technology! But don't freak out—that's a worst-case scenario . . . which, unfortunately, is the same kind of panicked thinking that has led to microchipping kids in the first place.

AMERICA'S WORST MOM

Her name is Lenore Skenazy; google her, and that's what shows up: "America's Worst Mom" (although she's recently been upgraded to "World's Worst Mom" as the host of a TV show). So what did Lenore do to earn the title? Specifically, she put her nine-year-old son on a New York City subway and let him ride it alone. Then she exposed her shocking deed to the world by writing about it in a newspaper column. It turned her into an instant celebrity, as Skenazy had to defend her actions on *The Today Show,* MSNBC, Fox News, National Public Radio, and a slew of other places. That was all back in 2008, but she remains defiant today. "Factually, statistically, and luckily," Skenazy argues, Americans are living in "one of the safest periods for children in the history of the world." And she wants parents, in particular, to act like it, allowing their kids an independence they themselves had when growing up. "'Scary' equals 'fun' for kids," she affirms, and to that end, endlessly promotes her ideas on her website FreeRangeKids.com. One thing she advocates for is an annual "Take Our Children to the Park . . . and Leave Them There Day." She also calls for the revival of the much wimp-ified holiday—Halloween. She asks adults to remember when they were older kids, "trick-or-treating without your parents," and begs them to let their kids today "have that same empowering, en-candying experience." Which, as you can imagine, means she's against Trick-or-Tracker, a new app that, according to the company website, "enables responsible parents to know the exact whereabouts of their trick-or-treating kids." Lenore shouts "Boo" to that!

How did Halloween become a holiday that kids have to be protected from, rather than one they can simply enjoy? Blame it on the stories that sprang up in the 1970s and '80s, describing deadly trick-or-treat candy and fruit embedded with razor blades, needles, drugs, and poison. More parental control and citywide curfews followed; only this time, the moral panic was based on NOTHING! There is absolutely NO statistical evidence of anyone EVER receiving tainted treats from a stranger. Halloween was ruined forever because of rumors—nothing but rumors. Now, just imagine what other "scary" risks are out there that might be put into perspective with a little help from statistics. Or don't imagine it, just look at the charts below and you'll find a few surprises, including what Moms and Dads who keep children from going outdoors should REALLY be worried about (hint: it's a lot closer to home). Danger is all relative, as revealed by the sometimes shocking . . .

GRAPHS OF DEATH!!!*
*and Injury

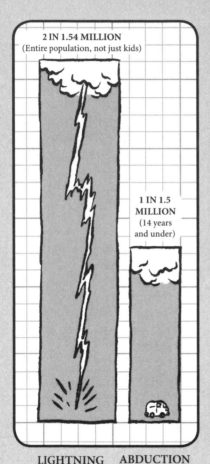

2 IN 1.54 MILLION
(Entire population, not just kids)

1 IN 1.5 MILLION
(14 years and under)

LIGHTNING   ABDUCTION
AND MURDER

ENLIGHTENING STRIKES
One of the major reasons kids no longer wander their neighborhoods freely is fear of abduction and murder. But, statistically speaking, getting picked up by some killer creep in a van is around HALF as likely as being blasted to bits from above (and how many people do *you* know who have been hit by lightning?).

HOME BODY . . . COUNT

That's right, there are, on average, ten more people a year killed by hot tap water than there are at the (dirty) hands of a crazed school shooter! Actually, the statistics are for all violent deaths on school property, so depressed teachers committing suicide are a big part of that too (as well as murders of school employees by their angry lovers). And when it comes to windows . . . you're definitely at more risk when at home, since most windows at schools don't even open.

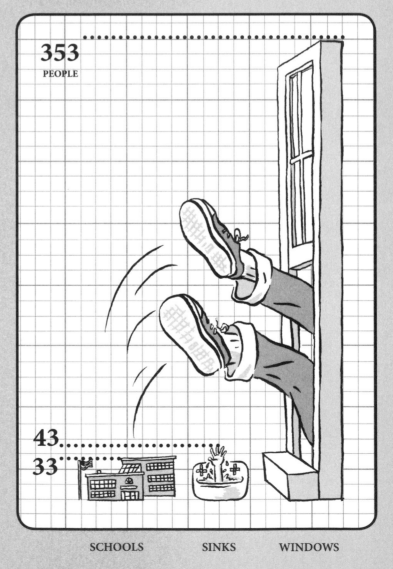

353
PEOPLE

43
33

SCHOOLS   SINKS   WINDOWS

OUT OF STEP

Obviously, with all the potential places you can stub your toe in the kitchen, your home is a fall-friendly death trap. And we didn't even include another home killer of kids . . . FIRE! It's the third-largest cause of fatal home injury. Oh, and did you hear that 70% of the playground deaths in the graph were from HOME playgrounds?! Kids would probably be safer living outside.

95

15

KIDS WHO DIE FROM
PLAYGROUND INJURY
(YEARLY AVERAGE)

KIDS WHO DIE FROM
FALLING AT HOME
(2002)

STREET SMARTS

So maybe the lesson from these numbers is that pedestrians should wear protective equipment when out and about: the "Walking Helmet" suitable for ages 14 and under! Then again, at least one researcher in England noticed that helmets might make drivers less cautious. After he wired his bike with ultrasonic sensors and started riding around town—2,300 times—the researcher discovered that cars, on average, drove 3.35 inches closer to him when he had a helmet on. But when he was bareheaded, drivers gave him more room. Weird! Equally nutty, in Australia, when the number of cyclists doubled between 1982 and 1989, bike fatalities actually dropped! The reason researchers gave was that motorists look out for bikers when there are more bikers to look out for. It also works the opposite way: When helmets became required in 1992, Aussies didn't like wearing them very much, and many stopped biking (the same thing happened in America); with fewer cyclists on the road, drivers got sloppy and . . . WHAMMO! All this illustrates a little principle known as "unintended consequences," which means it's sometimes hard to predict what's coming. For instance, you probably aren't expecting this: YOU STILL SHOULD WEAR A HELMET WHEN YOU BIKE!

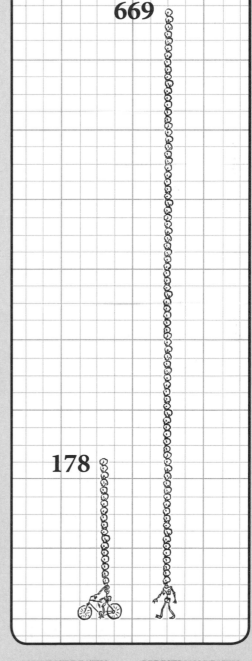

669

178

BICYCLIST DEATHS,
14 OR YOUNGER (2000)

PEDESTRIAN DEATHS,
14 OR YOUNGER (2001)

BAD FOR YOU

THOUGHT

IN PUBLIC SCHOOL IN AMERICA TODAY, RECESS IS SHRINKING OR, IN SOME CASES, DISAPPEARING.

THE SAME IS TRUE FOR ART AND MUSIC CLASSES.

AND HISTORY, SOCIAL STUDIES, AND SCIENCE.

TEACHERS ARE SPENDING MORE TIME ON FEWER SUBJECTS, WITH MATH AND READING TAKING UP MOST OF THE DAY.

MEANWHILE, HOMEWORK LOADS ARE INCREASING.

AND STANDARDIZED TESTS ARE REPLACING CRITICAL THINKING AND CREATIVE LEARNING.

ALL THIS MAY HAVE KIDS FEELING MORE AND MORE LIKE THEY ARE NOT IN A SCHOOL BUT A FACTORY. AND MAYBE THAT'S BECAUSE, IN SOME WAYS, THEY ARE.

WELCOME TO THE MACHINE

THE BIRTH OF PUBLIC SCHOOLS IN AMERICA IS INTERTWINED WITH THE CHANGE FROM A FARMING ECONOMY TO A MANUFACTURING ECONOMY. THIS TRANSITION IS KNOWN AS THE INDUSTRIAL REVOLUTION.

BEFORE THE INDUSTRIAL REVOLUTION, MANY CHILDREN WORKED WITH THEIR FAMILIES AS FARMERS, ARTISANS, OR SHOPKEEPERS. HOW THEY WERE EDUCATED DEPENDED ON WHERE THEY LIVED AND HOW MUCH MONEY THEIR FAMILY HAD.

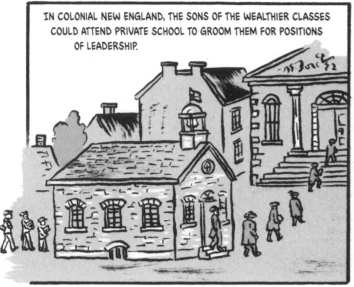

IN COLONIAL NEW ENGLAND, THE SONS OF THE WEALTHIER CLASSES COULD ATTEND PRIVATE SCHOOL TO GROOM THEM FOR POSITIONS OF LEADERSHIP.

THOUGH THE FIRST "FREE SCHOOL" WAS ESTABLISHED IN VIRGINIA IN 1635, MOST CHILDREN IN THE SOUTH WERE TAUGHT AT HOME BY PARENTS OR TUTORS.

ONE OF THE EARLIEST LAWS REQUIRING EDUCATION WAS PASSED IN 1647 IN MASSACHUSETTS. IT WAS KNOWN AS "THE OLD DELUDER SATAN" LAW BECAUSE THE PURITANS WANTED THEIR CHILDREN TO BE ABLE TO READ THE BIBLE.

GET THEE BEHIND ME, SATAN!

THE CHILDREN OF THE URBAN POOR, IF THEY WENT TO SCHOOL AT ALL, WENT TO "CHARITY SCHOOLS" RUN BY RELIGIOUS ORGANIZATIONS OR TOWN COUNCILS WHO SOUGHT PRIMARILY TO IMPART MORAL VALUES.

IN THE MID-1800s, AS THE INDUSTRIAL REVOLUTION TOOK HOLD IN CITIES LIKE NEW YORK AND PHILADELPHIA, THE CHARITY SCHOOLS BECAME LARGE INSTITUTIONS AND BEGAN TO FUNCTION AS UNOFFICIAL PUBLIC SCHOOLS.

BUT MANY CHILDREN AT THIS TIME DIDN'T GO TO SCHOOL. AS THEY HAD WORKED IN THE FIELDS IN EARLIER TIMES, THEY NOW WORKED IN THE FACTORIES.

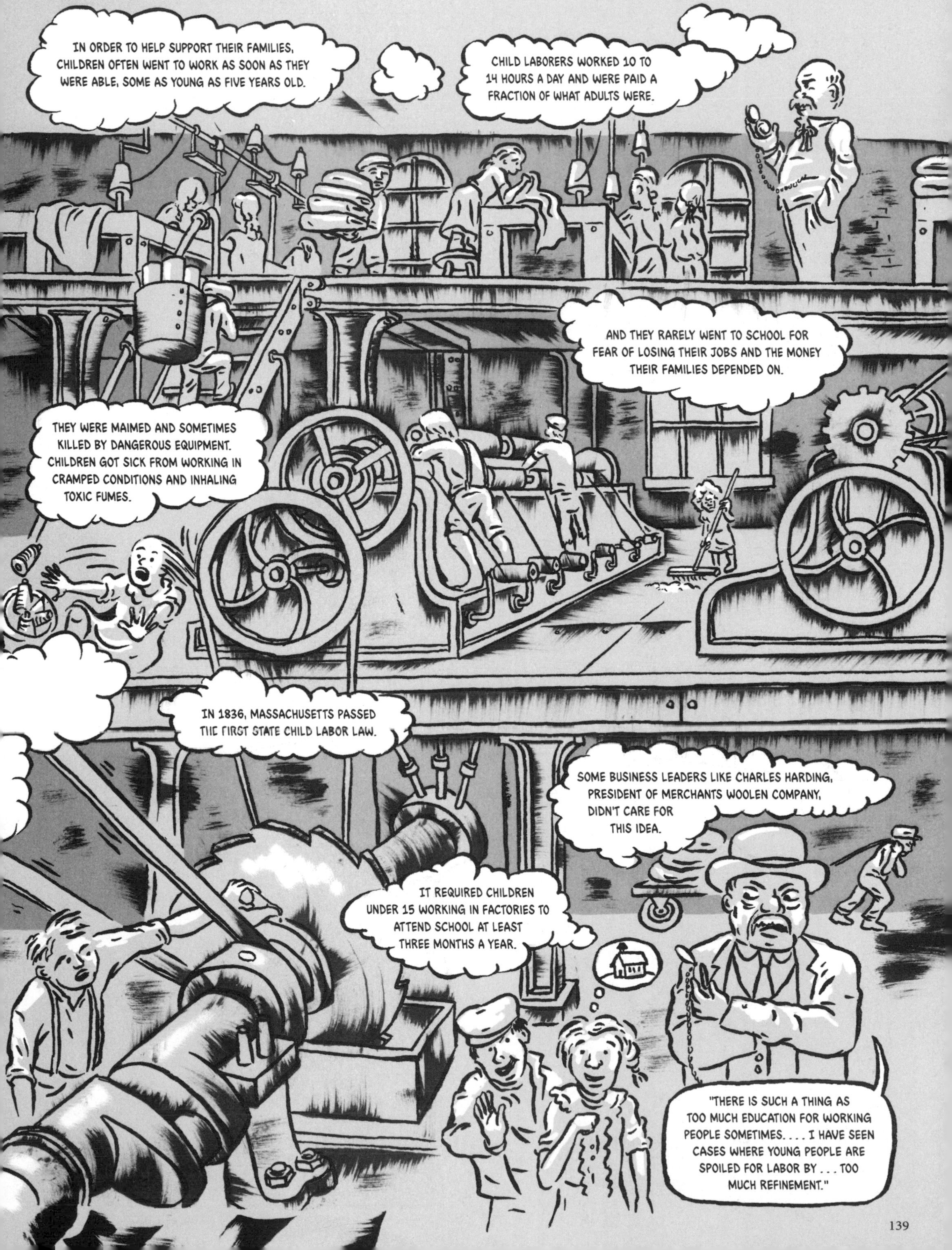
IN ORDER TO HELP SUPPORT THEIR FAMILIES, CHILDREN OFTEN WENT TO WORK AS SOON AS THEY WERE ABLE, SOME AS YOUNG AS FIVE YEARS OLD.
CHILD LABORERS WORKED 10 TO 14 HOURS A DAY AND WERE PAID A FRACTION OF WHAT ADULTS WERE.
AND THEY RARELY WENT TO SCHOOL FOR FEAR OF LOSING THEIR JOBS AND THE MONEY THEIR FAMILIES DEPENDED ON.
THEY WERE MAIMED AND SOMETIMES KILLED BY DANGEROUS EQUIPMENT. CHILDREN GOT SICK FROM WORKING IN CRAMPED CONDITIONS AND INHALING TOXIC FUMES.
IN 1836, MASSACHUSETTS PASSED THE FIRST STATE CHILD LABOR LAW.
SOME BUSINESS LEADERS LIKE CHARLES HARDING, PRESIDENT OF MERCHANTS WOOLEN COMPANY, DIDN'T CARE FOR THIS IDEA.
IT REQUIRED CHILDREN UNDER 15 WORKING IN FACTORIES TO ATTEND SCHOOL AT LEAST THREE MONTHS A YEAR.
"THERE IS SUCH A THING AS TOO MUCH EDUCATION FOR WORKING PEOPLE SOMETIMES. . . . I HAVE SEEN CASES WHERE YOUNG PEOPLE ARE SPOILED FOR LABOR BY . . . TOO MUCH REFINEMENT."

BUT NOT EVERYONE FELT THIS WAY. WHEN THE MASSACHUSETTS STATE BOARD OF EDUCATION WAS FORMED IN 1837, EDMUND DWIGHT, A MAJOR INDUSTRIALIST, OFFERED TO HELP FUND THE AGENCY WITH HIS OWN MONEY.

THE BOARD WAS HEADED BY HORACE MANN, WHO WAS AN ADVOCATE FOR "COMMON" SCHOOLS—FREE AND HIGH-QUALITY PUBLIC EDUCATION FOR EVERYONE.

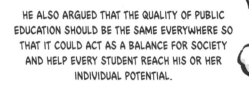

MANN BELIEVED THAT BESIDES TEACHING READING, WRITING, AND ARITHMETIC, SCHOOL COULD INSTILL VALUES SUCH AS OBEDIENCE TO AUTHORITY AND PROMPTNESS IN ATTENDANCE. HE FELT THAT ORGANIZING THE TIME ACCORDING TO BELL-RINGING WOULD HELP STUDENTS PREPARE FOR FUTURE EMPLOYMENT.

HE ALSO ARGUED THAT THE QUALITY OF PUBLIC EDUCATION SHOULD BE THE SAME EVERYWHERE SO THAT IT COULD ACT AS A BALANCE FOR SOCIETY AND HELP EVERY STUDENT REACH HIS OR HER INDIVIDUAL POTENTIAL.

MANN'S IDEAS WERE VERY INFLUENTIAL, AND IN 1852, MASSACHUSETTS PASSED A COMPULSORY ATTENDANCE LAW. BY 1900, 34 STATES HAD DONE THE SAME, AND IN TEN YEARS, 72 PERCENT OF AMERICAN CHILDREN ATTENDED SCHOOL.

AT THIS MOMENT OF EXPANSION IN BOTH INDUSTRY AND THE EDUCATIONAL SYSTEM, AN INTELLECTUAL MOVEMENT BASED ON THE PRINCIPLES AND LESSONS OF MASS PRODUCTION CAPTURED THE IMAGINATION OF DECISION MAKERS IN AMERICA.

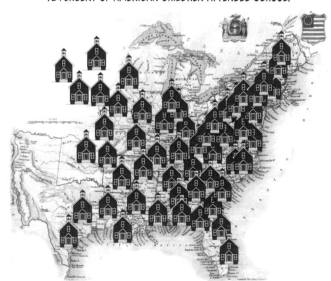

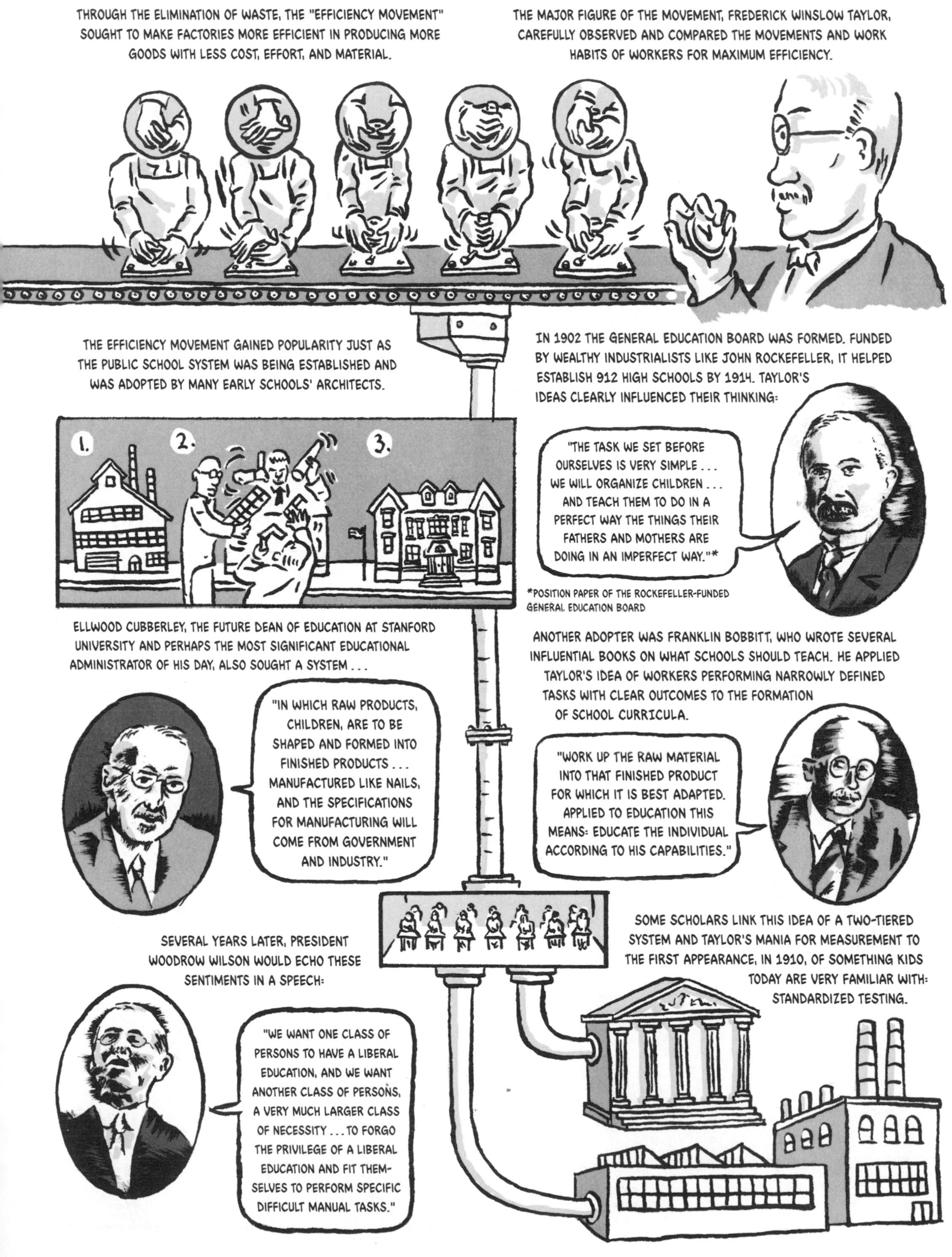
THROUGH THE ELIMINATION OF WASTE, THE "EFFICIENCY MOVEMENT" SOUGHT TO MAKE FACTORIES MORE EFFICIENT IN PRODUCING MORE GOODS WITH LESS COST, EFFORT, AND MATERIAL.
THE MAJOR FIGURE OF THE MOVEMENT, FREDERICK WINSLOW TAYLOR, CAREFULLY OBSERVED AND COMPARED THE MOVEMENTS AND WORK HABITS OF WORKERS FOR MAXIMUM EFFICIENCY.
THE EFFICIENCY MOVEMENT GAINED POPULARITY JUST AS THE PUBLIC SCHOOL SYSTEM WAS BEING ESTABLISHED AND WAS ADOPTED BY MANY EARLY SCHOOLS' ARCHITECTS.
1.
2.
3.
IN 1902 THE GENERAL EDUCATION BOARD WAS FORMED. FUNDED BY WEALTHY INDUSTRIALISTS LIKE JOHN ROCKEFELLER, IT HELPED ESTABLISH 912 HIGH SCHOOLS BY 1914. TAYLOR'S IDEAS CLEARLY INFLUENCED THEIR THINKING:
"THE TASK WE SET BEFORE OURSELVES IS VERY SIMPLE . . . WE WILL ORGANIZE CHILDREN . . . AND TEACH THEM TO DO IN A PERFECT WAY THE THINGS THEIR FATHERS AND MOTHERS ARE DOING IN AN IMPERFECT WAY."*
*POSITION PAPER OF THE ROCKEFELLER-FUNDED GENERAL EDUCATION BOARD
ELLWOOD CUBBERLEY, THE FUTURE DEAN OF EDUCATION AT STANFORD UNIVERSITY AND PERHAPS THE MOST SIGNIFICANT EDUCATIONAL ADMINISTRATOR OF HIS DAY, ALSO SOUGHT A SYSTEM . . .
"IN WHICH RAW PRODUCTS, CHILDREN, ARE TO BE SHAPED AND FORMED INTO FINISHED PRODUCTS . . . MANUFACTURED LIKE NAILS, AND THE SPECIFICATIONS FOR MANUFACTURING WILL COME FROM GOVERNMENT AND INDUSTRY."
ANOTHER ADOPTER WAS FRANKLIN BOBBITT, WHO WROTE SEVERAL INFLUENTIAL BOOKS ON WHAT SCHOOLS SHOULD TEACH. HE APPLIED TAYLOR'S IDEA OF WORKERS PERFORMING NARROWLY DEFINED TASKS WITH CLEAR OUTCOMES TO THE FORMATION OF SCHOOL CURRICULA.
"WORK UP THE RAW MATERIAL INTO THAT FINISHED PRODUCT FOR WHICH IT IS BEST ADAPTED. APPLIED TO EDUCATION THIS MEANS: EDUCATE THE INDIVIDUAL ACCORDING TO HIS CAPABILITIES."
SEVERAL YEARS LATER, PRESIDENT WOODROW WILSON WOULD ECHO THESE SENTIMENTS IN A SPEECH:
"WE WANT ONE CLASS OF PERSONS TO HAVE A LIBERAL EDUCATION, AND WE WANT ANOTHER CLASS OF PERSONS, A VERY MUCH LARGER CLASS OF NECESSITY . . . TO FORGO THE PRIVILEGE OF A LIBERAL EDUCATION AND FIT THEMSELVES TO PERFORM SPECIFIC DIFFICULT MANUAL TASKS."
SOME SCHOLARS LINK THIS IDEA OF A TWO-TIERED SYSTEM AND TAYLOR'S MANIA FOR MEASUREMENT TO THE FIRST APPEARANCE, IN 1910, OF SOMETHING KIDS TODAY ARE VERY FAMILIAR WITH: STANDARDIZED TESTING.

IN 1904, FRENCH PSYCHOLOGIST ALFRED BINET DEVELOPED A TEST TO SEPARATE INTELLECTUALLY NORMAL STUDENTS FROM THOSE WITH DISABILITIES. HE WARNED THAT THE TEST WAS NOT SUITABLE AS A WAY TO RANK THE MENTAL WORTH OF ALL STUDENTS.

HIS WARNING WOULD GO UNHEEDED. IN 1916, AMERICAN PSYCHOLOGIST LEWIS TERMAN, A EUGENICIST* AND COLLEAGUE OF CUBBERLEY'S AT STANFORD, INTRODUCED A TRANSLATED VERSION OF THE TEST TO SCHOOLS IN THE U.S. BUT HE USED IT TO SEPARATE STUDENTS WHO . . .

"OUR PURPOSE IS TO BE ABLE TO MEASURE THE INTELLECTUAL CAPACITY OF A CHILD WHO IS BROUGHT TO US IN ORDER TO KNOW WHETHER HE IS NORMAL OR RETARDED."

"CANNOT MASTER ABSTRACTIONS BUT THEY CAN OFTEN BE MADE INTO EFFICIENT WORKERS."

*EUGENICS WAS AN EARLY-20TH-CENTURY "BIO-SOCIAL" MOVEMENT THAT ADVOCATED THE MANIPULATION OF THE GENETIC STOCK TO IMPROVE HUMANS. AFTER IT WAS EMBRACED BY THE NAZIS AND INFLUENCED THEIR POLICY OF "ETHNIC CLEANSING," THIS PSEUDOSCIENCE FELL OUT OF FASHION.

BY THE 1920s, OVER A MILLION CHILDREN WERE TAKING IQ TESTS EVERY YEAR. DUE TO THEIR AIR OF SCIENTIFIC CERTAINTY, THESE TESTS INSPIRED CONFIDENCE, DESPITE QUESTIONS LIKE:

IQ TESTS WERE EMBRACED AS A TOOL OF "SCIENTIFIC MANAGEMENT" AND, IN 1941, WERE USED AS ONE OF THE MODELS FOR THE SCHOLASTIC APTITUDE TESTS (SATs).

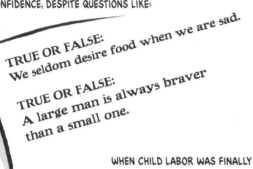

TRUE OR FALSE: We seldom desire food when we are sad.

TRUE OR FALSE: A large man is always braver than a small one.

WHEN CHILD LABOR WAS FINALLY BANNED IN 1938 AND ALL CHILDREN MADE THE TRANSITION FROM THE FACTORY TO THE SCHOOL, SCHOOL LOOKED MORE LIKE A FACTORY THAN EVER.

THE USE OF BELLS TO MARK PERIODS, THE SORTING OF CHILDREN INTO GRADES AND SKILL LEVELS, THE DIVISION OF SUBJECTS, AND THE EMPHASIS ON MEASUREMENT ALL REFLECTED THE INFLUENCE OF THE EFFICIENCY MOVEMENT SPAWNED BY TAYLOR'S STUDIES.

AND IT'S QUITE POSSIBLE THAT TAYLOR'S STUDIES HAD ANOTHER EFFECT: THE CREATION OF RECESS.

BRIIIIING

TAYLOR DISCOVERED, AMONG OTHER THINGS, THAT WORKERS COULD PERFORM MORE EFFICIENTLY OVER LONG PERIODS OF TIME IF THEY TOOK REGULAR BREAKS.

BRIIIIING

AS EARLY AS 1884, EDUCATORS ADVOCATED FOR "THE SURRENDER TO CAPRICE FOR A BRIEF INTERVAL" AS A WAY TO ENCOURAGE THE "SUSPENSION OF THE TENSION OF THE WILL POWER."

RECESS SEEMS TO HAVE ALWAYS BEEN A PART OF THE SCHOOL DAY . . . AT LEAST UNTIL RECENTLY.

THE INTERNATIONAL PLAY ASSOCIATION REPORTED IN 2005 THAT 40% OF AMERICAN SCHOOLS ARE REDUCING OR ABOLISHING RECESS IN ORDER TO PREPARE FOR STANDARDIZED TESTS.

SCHOOL DISTRICTS IN GEORGIA, NEW YORK, ILLINOIS, NEW JERSEY, AND CONNECTICUT ARE CHOOSING TO ELIMINATE RECESS. IN FACT, SOME DISTRICTS ARE BUILDING NEW SCHOOLS WITHOUT PLAYGROUNDS.

THOUGH SAFETY AND LIABILITY FEARS PLAY A PART, THE PRESSURE FOR STUDENTS TO DO BETTER ON STANDARDIZED TESTS IS THE PRIMARY REASON FOR THIS CHANGE. OR AS ONE SUPERINTENDENT PUT IT,

"WE ARE INTENT ON IMPROVING ACADEMIC PERFORMANCE AND YOU DON'T DO THAT BY HAVING KIDS HANG ON MONKEY BARS."

IN 2001, CONGRESS PASSED THE NO CHILD LEFT BEHIND ACT (NCLB). THE LAW REQUIRES ALL PUBLIC SCHOOLS TO USE STANDARDIZED TESTS AND PENALIZES SCHOOLS WHOSE STUDENTS DON'T GET HIGH ENOUGH SCORES.

IF THE SCHOOLS DON'T IMPROVE TEST SCORES, THEY FACE "CORRECTIVE ACTION," WHICH MIGHT INVOLVE FIRING ALL THE TEACHERS AND EXTENDING THE LENGTH OF THE SCHOOL DAY. IF THAT DOESN'T WORK, THE SCHOOL MAY BE CLOSED COMPLETELY.

GIVEN HOW HIGH THESE STAKES ARE, IT'S NOT HARD TO SEE WHY SCHOOLS WOULD CUT RECESS IN FAVOR OF STUDY TIME.

SCHOOL CLOSED BY FEDERAL ORDER

BUT SOME RESEARCH SUGGESTS THAT THIS IS A BAD IDEA. A 2002 STUDY BY THE CALIFORNIA DEPARTMENT OF EDUCATION SHOWED THAT CHILDREN WHO WERE PHYSICALLY ACTIVE SCORED BETTER ON TESTS.

A 2005 STUDY BY THE UNIVERSITY OF ILLINOIS SUGGESTED THE SAME, FINDING THAT KIDS PERFORMED BETTER ON COGNITIVE TASKS, MATH, AND READING COMPREHENSION WHEN TESTED RIGHT AFTER BEING PHYSICALLY ACTIVE FOR 20 MINUTES.

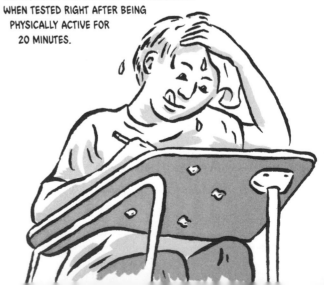

THIS RESEARCH SUPPORTS WHAT MANY TEACHERS BELIEVE: THAT STUDENTS, ESPECIALLY BOYS, GET FIDGETY AND HAVE TROUBLE CONCENTRATING WHEN THEY CAN'T BE PHYSICALLY ACTIVE. AS ONE FIFTH GRADER IN CHICAGO SAID:

"SOMETIMES, IT'S JUST REALLY HARD TO SIT SO LONG. YOU JUST WANT TO BE FREE."

ADDITIONAL RESEARCH SUGGESTS THAT OTHER SUBJECTS, WHICH ARE BEING CUT TO MAKE MORE TIME FOR TEST PREPARATION—MOST NOTABLY DRAMA, MUSIC, AND THE VISUAL ARTS—MAY ACTUALLY CONTRIBUTE TO HIGHER TEST SCORES.

SINCE 2007, ALMOST 71% OF SCHOOLS HAVE REDUCED SOME INSTRUCTION TIME IN SUBJECTS SUCH AS HISTORY, ARTS, LANGUAGE, AND MUSIC, IN ORDER TO GIVE MORE TIME AND RESOURCES TO MATHEMATICS AND ENGLISH.

BUT A REPORT BY THE ARTS EDUCATION PARTNERSHIP LOOKED AT 62 STUDIES BY NEARLY 100 RESEARCHERS AND FOUND THAT INVOLVEMENT IN THE ARTS HAD A POSITIVE EFFECT ON STUDENT TEST SCORES, GRADES, SOCIAL SKILLS, AND MOTIVATION.

SOME ARTS ADVOCATES, HOWEVER, SAY IMPROVING TEST SCORES IS BESIDE THE POINT. ESPECIALLY SINCE STANDARDIZED TESTS DON'T MEASURE WHAT THE ARTS MIGHT BE BEST AT TEACHING.

STANDARDIZED TESTS, BECAUSE THEY USE MULTIPLE CHOICE AND NOT ESSAYS, TEST WHAT SOME EDUCATORS CALL "CONVERGENT THINKING," THE ABILITY TO NARROW OPTIONS TO ONE CORRECT ANSWER. THE ARTS ENCOURAGE THE OPPOSITE, "DIVERGENT THINKING."

"STUDENTS WHO STUDY THE ARTS SERIOUSLY ARE TAUGHT TO SEE BETTER, TO ENVISION, TO PERSIST, TO BE PLAYFUL AND LEARN FROM MISTAKES, TO MAKE CRITICAL JUDGMENTS AND JUSTIFY SUCH JUDGMENTS."

"NOT EVERYTHING HAS A PRACTICAL UTILITY, BUT MAYBE IT'S EXPERIENTIALLY VALUABLE. LEARNING THROUGH THE ARTS PROMOTES THE IDEA THAT THERE IS MORE THAN ONE SOLUTION TO A PROBLEM, OR MORE THAN ONE ANSWER TO A QUESTION."

ELLEN WINNER AND LOIS HETLAND OF PROJECT ZERO, AN ARTS-EDUCATION PROGRAM AT THE HARVARD GRADUATE SCHOOL OF EDUCATION

ELLIOT EISNER, A PROFESSOR EMERITUS OF EDUCATION AT STANFORD UNIVERSITY

CONVERGENT THINKING IS CLEARLY AN IMPORTANT PART OF KNOWLEDGE, ESPECIALLY IN SUBJECTS LIKE MATH AND READING. BUT IS EMPHASIZING IT EXCLUSIVELY THE BEST WAY TO PREPARE KIDS FOR FUTURE EMPLOYMENT IN A RAPIDLY CHANGING WORLD?

MANY OF THE FACTORY JOBS THAT PUBLIC SCHOOLS WERE DESIGNED TO PREPARE STUDENTS FOR HAVE MOVED TO OTHER COUNTRIES WHERE PEOPLE WILL WORK FOR LESS MONEY.

AND MANY OF THE JOBS THAT PEOPLE DO IN THE UNITED STATES DIDN'T EXIST 20—OR EVEN 10—YEARS AGO.

SO, MANY EDUCATORS TODAY THINK THAT WE NEED TO SHIFT SCHOOLS TOWARD ENCOURAGING CREATIVITY, AS WELL AS BOTH CRITICAL AND CONCEPTUAL THINKING ABILITIES.

WHICH MEANS SHIFTING THEM AWAY FROM A FACTORY-BASED MODEL THAT SPLITS UP SUBJECTS, REGIMENTS EVERY MOMENT, AND EMPHASIZES LIMITED AND MEASURABLE OUTCOMES.

BECAUSE MAYBE THE LESS SCHOOLS LOOK LIKE FACTORIES AND THE MORE THEY LOOK LIKE PLACES OF EXPLORATION AND EXPERIMENTATION, WITH ROOM FOR CREATIVITY AND PLAY, THE BETTER PREPARED KIDS WILL BE FOR THE FUTURE, WHATEVER IT MAY BE.

You know what a standardized test is—it's one of those tests that for some reason is more important than all the rest. The one your teacher makes you study extra hard for and that you take only once a year. It's that fill-in-the-bubbles test, where you need a bunch of sharpened 2B pencils for your answers to count. This one, though, is a standardized test that's a little different. That's because you don't have to study for this one. You're already living it.

STANDARDIZED CHEATING

DIRECTIONS:

Read each question and choose the best answer. Then fill in the circled letter for the answer you have chosen.
PLEASE NOTE: WHATEVER YOU DO, DON'T LOOK FOR THE CORRECT ANSWERS IN SMALL PRINT BELOW THE QUESTIONS.

1. WHO HAS BEEN CHEATING MORE ON STANDARDIZED TESTS LATELY?

(A) Good students

(B) Bad students

CORRECT ANSWER:
(A) Educators have seen dishonesty rates rise among "gifted" students, who are under pressure to do well.

2. STANDARDIZED TESTING IS ALSO CALLED "HIGH STAKES" TESTING. WHAT'S SO "HIGH STAKES" ABOUT IT?

(A) If you fail, a puppy dies.

(B) Lower scores from students could mean that teachers lose their jobs and schools lose their funding. Some "failing" schools are even shut down because of low scores.

(C) That's a typo. It should read "HIGH STEAKS."

CORRECT ANSWER: (B)

3. WHO IS CAUGHT CHEATING ON STANDARDIZED TESTS AFTER THE TESTS ARE COMPLETED?

(A) Students

(B) Teachers

(C) Principals

(D) I knew it—it's the school janitor!

CORRECT ANSWERS: (B) & (C) "I've never seen so many cheating scandals as there have been in the last few years," said Diane Ravitch, former assistant secretary of education of the U.S.A. And the cheaters she was talking about were TEACHERS! A recent cheating scandal involving teachers and principals in the Atlanta, Georgia, school system was "of historic proportions." Not so surprising when your job is at steak . . . er, stake.

4. WHAT CLUES DO INVESTIGATORS LOOK FOR WHEN THEY ARE TRYING TO CATCH CHEATING TEACHERS?

(A) A lot of erasing on the tests

(B) The same pattern of answers on different students' tests

(C) A sudden jump in students' scores from last year

(D) The same error repeated in a series of "corrected" answers, indicating that the cheating teacher is "correcting" the tests with the WRONG ANSWERS!

(E) All of the above

CORRECT ANSWER: (E) In the 56 Atlanta schools under investigation, 178 educators were ultimately caught cheating. There were stories of teachers organizing "erasure parties" where they would all get together after school to alter their students' answers (though not always to the right ones).

5. TEACHERS AND PRINCIPALS WHO ALTER THEIR STUDENTS' TESTS ARE HELPING THEIR STUDENTS.

(A) TRUE

(B) FALSE

CORRECT ANSWER: (B) The cheating will catch up with students once they get a teacher who isn't cheating (around 5% of teachers are cheaters). The students end up paying the price when their scores suck the next year.

6. WHAT DID NEARLY 9,000 NEW YORK CITY PUBLIC SCHOOL STUDENTS HAVE TO DO WHEN A COMPANY THAT MAKES STANDARDIZED TESTS MARKED THEIR CORRECT ANSWERS AS WRONG?

(A) Lots of push-ups

(B) Nine months of hard labor

(C) Worst of all, summer school

CORRECT ANSWER: (C) Even though the company had been alerted to the problem eight months earlier, they said nothing at first when student scores dropped dramatically, and the New York City school chancellor was fired. Formerly a big fan of standardized testing, today the ex-chancellor says that what the company did was "lie." Or, you could say, "cheat" ... both him out of a job and the kids out of their summer.

7. IS THERE ANYTHING ELSE OUT THERE THAT'S ALSO CHEATING STUDENTS OF THEIR FREE TIME?

(A) YES

(B) NO

CORRECT ANSWER: (A) Yes, and it's called HOMEWORK. It's cheating students of their valuable not-working time!

8. SPECIFICALLY, WHAT KIND OF TIME IS HOMEWORK CHEATING KIDS OUT OF?

(A) Time to relax and eat dinner with their family

(B) Time to tell their family about their day

(C) Time to play games with their family

(D) Time to go outside and play with friends

(E) Time to do nothing

(F) All of the above

CORRECT ANSWER: (F) Two studies, one from 1999 and the other from 2006, found that homework was "robbing children of time to play, explore, and socialize." In a national survey conducted by the University of Michigan, family meals were cited as "the single strongest predictor of better achievement scores and fewer behavioral problems for children ages three to twelve." In fact, family mealtime was considered a better predictor of success than time spent studying.

9. HOW MUCH HOMEWORK DO ELEMENTARY SCHOOL KIDS GET?

(A) Only 10 minutes a day, and it involves a lot of crayons

(B) Instead of a 15-page reading assignment, students lift the book over their head 15 times

(C) Double the amount they did 30 years ago

CORRECT ANSWER: (C) By 2003, almost the same proportion of younger (64%) as older (68%) children spent some time studying, and there's been no noticeable decline since then. So how come? It probably all stems from a 1983 report by the National Commission on Excellence in Education that determined America was a nation "at risk" because school kids' scores were falling behind the rest of the world.

10. HOW MUCH HAS THE INCREASE IN HOMEWORK OVER THE YEARS INCREASED READING SCORES?

(A) 25%

(B) 15%

(C) 5%

(D) What? LESS than 5%!

CORRECT ANSWER: (D) The National Assessment of Educational Progress (known as the "Nation's Report Card") found the scores among fourth- through eighth-graders have "barely budged" since a commission report that called American kids "at risk." Another report from 2007 found "student achievement has remained stagnant and our K–12 schools have stayed remarkably unchanged."

11. AN HOUR'S WORTH OF HOMEWORK A NIGHT WOULD TRANSLATE INTO AN INCREASE IN YOUR ENGLISH GPA OF

(A) A full grade point

(B) Half a grade point

(C) Two-tenths of a point? A measly 0.20?

(D) Try 0.13

CORRECT ANSWER: (D) That's how little improvement was found in a large-scale study of high school students. Researchers found that a student with a 3.0 grade point average in English would go from a B minus to . . . a B minus (just not quite as minus).

12. WHICH OF THESE STATEMENTS ABOUT HOME-WORK IS TRUE?

(A) Homework is a swell way for young children to practice how to do homework.

(B) Homework helps kids to do in-depth learning of what they are studying in the classroom.

(C) Homework is great because students don't know what to do with themselves after a long day at school.

CORRECT ANSWER: (A) There is no reason for young kids to do ANY homework, according to education expert Harris Cooper, except to get them used to doing MORE homework when they get older. If you chose (B), then check out Cooper's studies, which show that elementary school kids get more benefit studying with their teachers than doing homework and "almost zero" correlation between better achievement and homework. Other research shows countries with less math homework tend to have students with higher math test scores. "I don't think anyone except senior high school students should be doing a couple of hours of homework," says associate professor Richard Walker (Sydney University's education faculty), whose research has found most kids are "overloaded" with after-school assignments.

13. WHAT IS THE HOMEWORK ASSIGNMENT THAT CORRELATES WITH THE HIGHEST TEST SCORES?

(A) Writing out definitions from the dictionary

(B) Building a diorama of the Coliseum

(C) Memorizing poetry

(D) Reading for pleasure

CORRECT ANSWER: (D) "Reading for pleasure is the single most important activity associated with higher children's test scores," according to a 2001 study titled "How American Children Spend Their Time."

14. AN AVERAGE OF 20% OF A STUDENT'S TIME IS SPENT ON HOMEWORK. HOW MUCH TIME IS SPENT ON TRAINING A TEACHER IN THE SUBJECT OF ASSIGNING HOMEWORK?

(A) On average, a year-long class

(B) On average, a semester-long class

(C) On average, a week-long workshop

(D) Er, how about an hour-long special class?

(E) No time

CORRECT ANSWER: (E) Hard to believe it, but Kylene Beers, president of the National Council of Teachers of English, has to admit that "colleges of education simply don't offer specific training in homework." Or, as Harris Cooper puts it, when it comes to homework, "Teachers are winging it." Which is why most kids wind up with an assignment whose whole point "isn't to learn, much less to derive real pleasure from learning," according to Alfie Kohn (author of *The Homework Myth*). "It's something to be finished."

15. WHAT SINGLE GROUP IS PUTTING THE MOST PRESSURE ON SCHOOLS TO CONTINUE TO INCREASE THE AMOUNT OF HOMEWORK?

(A) Evil teachers

(B) Mentally disturbed students

(C) Parents

(D) Companies that make spiral notebooks

CORRECT ANSWER: (C) "At the moment homework [is] an add-on because parents want it," claims Richard Walker (who, if you've been reading the answers—hint, hint—you should know has recently concluded a big survey on homework).

16. LEAH WINGARD, A LINGUIST AT THE UNIVERSITY OF CALIFORNIA, VIDEOTAPED 32 FAMILIES INTER-ACTING OVER A PERIOD OF MONTHS AND DISCOV-ERED ONE QUESTION PARENTS ALMOST ALWAYS ASKED FIRST WHEN THEIR CHILDREN ARRIVED HOME FROM SCHOOL. WHAT WAS THAT QUESTION?

(A) How are you feeling, honey?

(B) Did you have a nice day, sweetie?

(C) What did you learn today, dear?

(D) So . . . how much homework do you have?

CORRECT ANSWER: (D) As Alfie Kohn (remember, *The Homework Myth* author) also notes from the videos, the conversations between parents and kids usually don't focus on what the homework is about, but only "how long it will take to do . . . and the ways in which activities will be scheduled around [it]." And in a survey of more than 1,200 parents of kids ranging from kindergartners to high schoolers, Kohn says, "exactly half reported that they had had a serious argument with their child about homework in the past year that involved yelling or crying."

HOW TO SCORE THE TEST

1 to 4 correct answers: Go back and erase the mistakes, then change them to the correct answers.

5 to 14 correct answers: What are you waiting for? See above.

15 or 16 correct answers: Relax, they probably won't shut down your school.

IN RECENT YEARS, MANY SCHOOL ADMINISTRATIONS HAVE EXPLORED THE USE OF TV AS A TEACHING TOOL. SOMETIMES THE STUDENTS, LIKE THOSE AT GLOBE HIGH SCHOOL IN PHOENIX, ARIZONA, LEARN THEIR LESSONS TOO WELL.

LIKE AN ESTIMATED SIX MILLION HIGH SCHOOLERS NATIONWIDE, THE STUDENTS AT GLOBE START THEIR DAY WITH A TELEVISED NEWS PROGRAM, CHANNEL ONE, FOLLOWED BY COMMERCIALS.*

*ONE STUDY SHOWED THEY REMEMBERED THE COMMERCIALS BETTER THAN THE NEWS FEATURES.

IN 2008, TRUTH, AN ANTI-TOBACCO AD CAMPAIGN, FEATURED SOME EDGY SLANG DESIGNED TO CAPTURE TEENS' ATTENTION.

IT DIDN'T CAUSE MUCH OF A STIR UNTIL A STUDENT WROTE ABOUT THE ADS IN THE SCHOOL NEWSPAPER, USING THE PHRASE IN THE HEADLINE.

THE PRINCIPAL SEIZED AND DESTROYED ALL 700 COPIES OF THE PAPER. HE EXPLAINED HIS ACTION BY CITING THE OFFENSIVE HEADLINE AS WELL AS AN EDITORIAL DESCRIBING A "SULLEN AND GLOOMY ATMOSPHERE" AT THE SCHOOL AND A LACK OF MOTIVATION AMONG STUDENTS AND TEACHERS.

AS IT TURNS OUT, THE PRINCIPAL MAY HAVE BEEN WITHIN HIS RIGHTS, AND THE JUSTIFICATION FOR THIS RIGHT IS A CONCERN FOR THE EDUCATIONAL ATMOSPHERE THAT THE STUDENT WAS WRITING ABOUT.

IN 1983, THREE JUNIORS AT HAZELWOOD EAST HIGH SCHOOL IN ST. LOUIS, MISSOURI, WANTED TO PUBLISH AN ARTICLE THEY WROTE ON DIVORCE AND TEEN PREGNANCY IN THEIR SCHOOL NEWSPAPER.

WHEN THE PRINCIPAL CENSORED THE ARTICLE, THE GIRLS WENT ALL THE WAY TO THE SUPREME COURT TO PROTECT THEIR FIRST-AMENDMENT RIGHTS OF FREEDOM OF EXPRESSION. THE CASE WAS HEARD IN 1987.

BUT THE SUPREME COURT RULED AGAINST THE GIRLS, STATING THAT THE SCHOOL NEWSPAPER IS AN EDUCATIONAL TOOL, NOT A PUBLIC PLACE FOR EXPRESSING AN OPINION, AND CENSORSHIP IS ALLOWED IF IT IS JUSTIFIED BY AN EDUCATIONAL CONCERN.

REPRESSION
SUPPRESSION
TRANSGRESSION
ULTIMATUM

THEY ALSO RULED THAT THE SAME RIGHT TO CONTROL STUDENT SPEECH APPLIES TO PLAYS, YEARBOOKS, SPEECHES, AND EVEN ART SHOWS AND CREATIVE WRITING ASSIGNMENTS.

WHILE THE DECISION REQUIRES THE SCHOOL TO SHOW AN EDUCATIONAL CONCERN IN ORDER TO CENSOR, CRITICS SAY THAT THE JUDGES' RULING IS TOO VAGUE TO PROTECT STUDENTS' FIRST-AMENDMENT RIGHTS.

JUSTICE WILLIAM BRENNAN, IN DISSENT TO THE DECISION, SEEMED TO AGREE:

"SUCH UNTHINKING CONTEMPT FOR INDIVIDUAL RIGHTS IS INTOLERABLE FROM ANY STATE OFFICIAL.

"IT IS PARTICULARLY INSIDIOUS FROM ONE TO WHOM THE PUBLIC ENTRUSTS THE TASK OF INCULCATING* IN ITS YOUTH AN APPRECIATION FOR THE CHERISHED DEMOCRATIC LIBERTIES THAT OUR CONSTITUTION GUARANTEES."

*MEANS "INSTILLING" OR "TEACHING."

THE STUDENT PRESS LAW CENTER, A FREE SPEECH ADVOCACY GROUP, HAS REPORTED A 350% INCREASE IN CALLS FOR HELP SINCE THE HAZELWOOD DECISION.

THERE HAVE BEEN REPORTS OF CENSORSHIP OF STUDENT ARTICLES ABOUT ENVIRONMENTAL ISSUES, SCHOOL BOARD ELECTIONS, FREE SPEECH, AND EVEN A STUDENT EDITORIAL AGAINST THE HAZELWOOD DECISION. ALL, IT MUST BE ASSUMED, WITH THE JUSTIFICATION OF EDUCATIONAL CONCERNS.

THE SAME CONCERNS RENATO TALHADAS, A HIGH SCHOOL SENIOR IN FLORIDA, RAISED IN HIS ARTICLE "WHEN TEACHERS GO BAD." HE NAMED ONLY GOOD TEACHERS, BUT THE ARTICLE WAS STILL CENSORED BY HIS PRINCIPAL.

THE PRINCIPAL, ACCORDING TO TALHADAS, HAD HIS OWN EDUCATIONAL CONCERN. HE WANTED THE SCHOOL TO HAVE A "POSITIVE ATMOSPHERE" DURING STANDARDIZED TESTING.

Back in the 1960s, the American Educational Research Association warned that whenever homework takes away from "time devoted to sleep, it is not meeting the basic needs of children and adolescents." The association understood that without proper snooze time, it's hard for kids to remember all those facts and figures that teachers are always trying to cram into their brains. But here's the really weird part: as kids become older, the way they sleep changes, so that they end up getting less rest just when they need it the most. The result . . .

sleep over

BAD TIMING

Everyone agrees that babies need their naps and little kids should be asleep by nine, but when it comes to teenagers, bedtime can become battle time. Don't blame it on adolescent rebellion, though—blame it on teens' rebelling bodies instead. As kids enter their teens, Mother Nature literally resets their biological clocks. Teens start producing the hormone that makes you sleepy,

called melatonin, a lot later . . . usually around 11 P.M. (or beyond). Even worse, teen melatonin continues a-flowin' into the next morning, making it almost impossible to drag teens out of bed before noon. But because teens are still basically kids, they continue to need that extra hour of sleep they did when they were younger (on average, anyone between ages ten and seventeen should be getting around nine and a half hours of shut-eye a night; grown-ups, on the other hand, can usually get by on seven to eight hours). And no slumber can make you lumber . . . transforming teens into what Cornell University psychologist James B. Maas describes as "walking zombies" (according to the National Sleep Foundation, only about 15 percent of American adolescents are getting an adequate amount of sleep every night). But when these teen zombies shamble down the hallway, moaning "Brains . . . brains," it's likely they're crying out for their own.

MENTAL BLOCK

With many high schools in the U.S. starting around 7:20 A.M., it's easy to do the math to see how sleep-deprived these kids are—although maybe not that easy if you're one of those sleep-deprived teens. In a chapter on sleep called "The Lost Hour," the authors of *NurtureShock* write that when kids are given standardized tests on weekdays, there's a seven-point drop in their IQs compared to their scores if the test is given on a weekend, when they're able to wake up later. In another major study, shaving off one hour of sleep transformed sixth-graders into fourth-graders—literally a difference of "two years of cognitive maturation and development." Research focusing specifically on high schoolers discovered that an A student usually got an extra fifteen minutes of sleep over a B student, who, in turn, slept fifteen minutes more than a C student (and so on . . . down the sleep-deprived grade scale). But IQ isn't the only thing lowered by missing sleep. Teens' happiness drops right along with their intelligence. If they're getting less than eight hours, the rate of clinical-level depression doubles! In fact, as many sleep scholars have discussed, the traits that drive parents crazy about their teens—moodiness, being exhausted all the time, acting distant and impulsive—are all symptoms of acute sleepiness! When a kid is sleepy, it scrambles the part of the brain where positive memories are processed, while another area of the brain where bad emotions, such as fear, are stored is stimulated. Sleep scarcity may even contribute to the dramatic increase in attention hyperactivity disorder (a 22 percent jump from 2003 to 2007), according to a new study that tracked British children for six years. Not just how kids think or feel, but how they look can also be affected, claims snooze investigator Dr. Eve Van Cauter: "Lack of sleep disrupts every physiologic function in the body," which can ultimately lead to obesity. So don't blame watching TV or playing video games for American kids' weight gain (an analysis of 8,000 families since 1968 showed no increase in weight with an increase in TV, anyway). Blame it on lack of sleep! In studies of high school and middle school kids, "the odds of obesity went up 80% for each hour of lost sleep." How about a new diet plan: snooze and lose? And there's still one other way that lack of sleep can have a negative impact on high school kids—emphasis on IMPACT. Drowsy drivers make lousy drivers, and teens are often driving to and from school, sports events, or home from late-night parties. With only six or seven hours of sleep, according to the American Automobile Association, drivers are "twice as likely to be involved in a 'drowsy driving' accident as are those who got eight hours of shut-eye." If you've slept less than five hours, your risk goes up 400 percent! So who's asleep at the wheel when it comes to keeping kids safe? Maybe the answer to that "lost hour" of sleep is really simple.

LATE FOR SCHOOL

In Edina, Minnesota, they shifted the start of the school day from 7:15 to 8:30 A.M., and it's even later in Minneapolis (8:40 A.M. in high schools and 9:10 A.M. in middle schools). What they didn't do was change the overall length of the school day (so don't get your hopes up, kids). Thousands of students were affected by the switch, and according to a comprehensive study by the Center for Applied Research and Educational Improvement, the results were pretty impressive. There were improvements in health (fewer trips to the school nurse), overall well-being, and academic performance. Tardiness was down, attendance was up, and so were graduation rates. Research showed that the suburban students usually went to bed at their regular time, meaning that they gained roughly an extra hour of sleep per night, which they said allowed them to "get more homework done during the day because of increased alertness and efficiency." At the Edina high school, top-scoring kids' SATs "shot up," going from under 1,300 to 1,500 points in that year. "Truly flabbergasting" is how the startled College Board's executive director described it to the news. While that's the biggest study to date, there have been others showing similar results, like the one in a Massachusetts middle school, where younger teens got an extra hour of sleep and "had less difficulty staying awake in school, and had better grades" than students at a similar school that continued to make kids drag their sorry butts into class at 7:15 in the morning. More recently, at a private Rhode Island high school, administrators started school half an hour later, and kids' health, attendance, and mood improved. Even though that may not sound like such a big difference time-wise, researchers say that it's around dawn that teens are in their deepest state of sleep, so adding that extra thirty minutes can keep them from being so groggy in the morning. And in what could be the most dramatic data to date, in Fayette County, Kentucky, a start-time change from 7:30 to 8:30 A.M. found a decrease in car accident rates for 16- to 18-year-olds, compared with an actual increase in the rate for the rest of the teens in the state. Seems like these statistics should be eye-opening for school administrators, but unfortunately, start times aren't designed with students in mind. For instance, school districts looking to save some cash often double up on bus routes and deliver teens to school first, then pick up the younger kids—even though it's the young'uns who function better in the morning. Teachers also prefer the early hours because there's less traffic on the road when they drive to school, and coaches think ending classes later in the day will mess with their after-school games. Given that administrators report how much "calmer" well-rested students are, maybe teachers should rethink their position . . . which they did, in the case of Rhode Island. Despite "considerable resistance" from coaches and teachers before the change, the faculty voted "overwhelmingly" in favor of keeping the later start time after the study was completed. Maybe kids aren't the only ones whose intelligence increases with an extra hour of rest.

UNLESS THEY ARE TAUGHT AT HOME, ALL KIDS HAVE TO GO TO SCHOOL.

81.5 MILLION KIDS IN AMERICA GO TO SCHOOL FIVE DAYS A WEEK.

AND EVERYBODY AGREES THAT EVERY KID'S SCHOOL SHOULD HAVE A SAFE, RESPECTFUL, CARING, AND POSITIVE LEARNING ENVIRONMENT.

THE QUESTION IS: HOW DO YOU ACHIEVE SUCH AN ENVIRONMENT?

ONE STRATEGY IS TO HAVE VERY CLEAR RULES AGAINST THE THINGS THAT DISRUPT LEARNING—THE TWO MOST OBVIOUS BEING VIOLENCE AND DRUGS.

AND IN ORDER TO MAKE SURE THE STUDENTS FOLLOW THESE RULES, THEY MUST BE ENFORCED STRICTLY AND WITHOUT EXCEPTIONS.

THIS MEANS NO EXCEPTIONS FOR NOT KNOWING THE RULES, ACCIDENTAL MISTAKES, AND UNFORESEEN SITUATIONS.

PRINCIPAL

THIS STRATEGY HAS BECOME POPULAR ENOUGH THAT IT HAS A NAME, A NAME THAT PERFECTLY CAPTURES THE IDEA . . .

ZERO

SPOKANE, WA: An eight-year-old, Terry Wilson-Spence, was suspended for having two tiny plastic G.I. Joe guns at school.

MONUMENT, CO: Middle-schoolers Breana Crites and Alyssa McKinney were suspended for ten days after one made the mistake of lending the other her inhaler.

LOS ANGELES, CA: A seven-year-old schoolboy was suspended for carrying a gun-shaped toy key fob because it violated the district's policy on "weapon possession."

SAFFORD, AZ: Thirteen-year-old Savana Redding was subjected to a strip search when she was suspected of bringing prescription-strength ibuprofen to the school.

KEY to THREATS

Toy Guns

Hugging

Flatulence (Farts)

Other "Weapons"*
*Including pointed fingers (human and chicken), gun-shaped paper, model rockets, miniature baseball bats, plastic knives, paring knives, flags, wallet chains, chili peppers, and a drawing of a gun.

Legal Drugs†
†Including asthma inhalers, aspirin, zinc lozenges, antacids, and mouthwash.

TOLERANCE

"There is zero intelligence when you start applying zero tolerance across the board. Stupid and ridiculous things start happening."
—Juvenile court judge Steven Teske, who is working to reshape zero tolerance policies in schools

IRVINGTON, NJ: Hamadi Alston, eight, found an L-shaped piece of paper in a schoolbook. After using it in a game of "cops and robbers," he was questioned and then turned over to police. He spent five hours in police custody and had to make two court appearances before charges were dropped.

CURTISVILLE, PA: Five-year-old Jordan Locke was suspended from kindergarten for a day for violating the school district's weapons policy. The five-inch plastic ax that came with the firefighter costume he wore for Halloween was a "serious problem."

LAKELAND, FL: An eighth-grade student was suspended for three days for repeatedly farting on the school bus. "It wasn't even me," said 15-year-old Jonathan Locke. "It was a kid who sits in front of me." Locke should be thankful he wasn't arrested, like the 13-year-old in STUART, FL, who "continually disrupted his classroom environment" with his frequent farts.

JONESBORO, AK: An eight-year-old was suspended from school for three days for pointing a breaded chicken finger at a teacher and saying, "Pow, pow, pow."

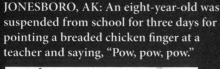

THE TERM "ZERO TOLERANCE" ORIGINALLY CAME FROM A FEDERAL ANTI-DRUG LAW ENFORCEMENT POLICY USED IN THE 1980s.

FROM THE BEGINNING, THE IDEA WAS TO PUNISH BOTH MAJOR AND MINOR DRUG CRIMES HARSHLY IN ORDER TO SEND A MESSAGE TO CRIMINALS.

DAT'S HARSH.

I SENTENCE YOU TO ... HOLD ON A MINUTE ...

ONE ASPECT OF THIS POLICY IS CALLED "MANDATORY MINIMUM SENTENCING," WHICH MEANS JUDGES HAVE TO APPLY PRESET PUNISHMENTS NO MATTER WHAT THE CIRCUMSTANCES ARE.

"ZERO TOLERANCE" SEEMED TO CAPTURE THE PUBLIC'S IMAGINATION, AND BY 1989, SCHOOL DISTRICTS IN NEW YORK, CALIFORNIA, AND KENTUCKY HAD MANDATORY AUTOMATIC EXPULSION FOR DRUGS, FIGHTING, OR VIOLENCE.

THEN CONGRESS PASSED THE FEDERAL GUN-FREE SCHOOLS ACT OF 1994, REQUIRING AUTOMATIC ONE-YEAR SUSPENSION AND NOTIFICATION OF THE POLICE FOR ANY STUDENT CAUGHT POSSESSING A FIREARM.

IN 1997 IT WAS AMENDED TO COVER ANYTHING THAT COULD BE USED AS A WEAPON, AND SOON THE IDEA OF ZERO TOLERANCE WAS EXPANDED BY LOCAL SCHOOL DISTRICTS TO COVER DIFFERENT OFFENSES.

A STUDY DONE FOR THE DEPARTMENT OF EDUCATION FOUND THAT BY 1998, AT LEAST ONE COMPONENT OF THE POLICY WAS IN 80% OF SCHOOLS.

ZERO TOLERANCE BEGAN TO BE APPLIED TO MANY THINGS BESIDES GUNS AND DRUGS, INCLUDING OTHER WEAPONS, CELL PHONES, PHYSICAL CONTACT, AND IN SOME SCHOOLS, ANYTHING INTERPRETED AS "DISRUPTIVE BEHAVIOR."

THE NATIONAL TRAGEDY OF THE COLUMBINE HIGH SCHOOL SHOOTINGS BROUGHT ZERO TOLERANCE TO A NEW LEVEL, WITH SCHOOL OFFICIALS IDENTIFYING AND PUNISHING POTENTIALLY VIOLENT STUDENTS.

SIX MONTHS AFTER COLUMBINE, IN NOVEMBER 1999, A 13-YEAR-OLD BOY IN PONDER, TEXAS, WAS ARRESTED AND HELD IN JUVENILE DETENTION FOR FIVE DAYS AFTER HE WROTE A HALLOWEEN HORROR STORY ABOUT A SCHOOL SHOOTING. THE STORY HAD RECEIVED AN A+.

ACCORDING TO THE FATHER OF A STUDENT PUNISHED FOR DRAWING A GUN IN 2007, ARIZONA SCHOOL OFFICIALS MENTIONED THE COLUMBINE SHOOTINGS TO POINT OUT THE SERIOUSNESS OF THE SITUATION.

THE DISTRICT SPOKESMAN SAID THE CRUDE SKETCH WAS "ABSOLUTELY CONSIDERED A THREAT," AND WAS THUS PUNISHABLE. THE 13-YEAR-OLD BOY WAS SUSPENDED FOR THREE DAYS.

AS RECENTLY AS MARCH 2012, COURTS UPHELD THE SIX-DAY SUSPENSION OF A NEW YORK STATE FIFTH-GRADER FOR A CRAYON DRAWING DEPICTING AN ASTRONAUT BLOWING UP A SCHOOL WITH MISSILES.

IN THE DECISION, ONE JUDGE NOTED THE NEED TO CONFRONT SCHOOL VIOLENCE . . .

". . . GIVEN THE RECENT WAVE OF SCHOOL SHOOTINGS THAT HAVE TRAGICALLY AFFECTED OUR NATION."

ANOTHER ATTEMPT TO CONFRONT THIS VIOLENCE HAS BEEN THE WIDESPREAD PRACTICE OF ASSIGNING POLICE OFFICERS TO SCHOOLS. NEARLY HALF OF ALL PUBLIC SCHOOLS HAVE POLICE OFFICERS ON SITE.

PARTICULARLY IN URBAN SCHOOLS, LAW ENFORCEMENT STRATEGIES SUCH AS CAMERAS, METAL DETECTORS, PROFILING, AND A HEAVY RELIANCE ON SECURITY HAVE BECOME MORE COMMON.

CRITICS SAY THIS TREND CREATES A CLIMATE WHERE STUDENTS ARE TREATED MORE LIKE CRIMINALS THAN KIDS AND CAN LEAD TO ALL SORTS OF PROBLEMS.

WHEN 12-YEAR-OLD ALEXA GONZALEZ WROTE "I LOVE MY FRIENDS ABBY AND FAITH. LEX WAS HERE 2/1/10 :)" ON A SCHOOL DESK IN THE BRONX, SHE WAS ARRESTED.

"I DIDN'T WANT THEM TO SEE ME BEING HANDCUFFED, THINKING I'M A BAD PERSON."

AT FULMORE MIDDLE SCHOOL IN AUSTIN, TEXAS, A 12-YEAR-OLD GIRL WAS FINED $150 FOR "DISRUPTING CLASS." THE POLICEMAN, WHO WORKED IN THE BUILDING, WAS CALLED WHEN THE GIRL SPRAYED HERSELF WITH PERFUME IN CLASS.

A POLICE OFFICER IN SAN MATEO, CALIFORNIA, PEPPER-SPRAYED AN "AGITATED" SEVEN-YEAR-OLD SPECIAL EDUCATION STUDENT WHEN HE WOULDN'T GET DOWN FROM A BOOKSHELF HE HAD CLIMBED.

PERHAPS THE MOST DISRUPTIVE INCIDENTS INVOLVING POLICE AND SCHOOLS ARE NOT THE RESPONSES TO PARTICULAR EVENTS BUT PLANNED SECURITY SWEEPS FOR WEAPONS AND BANNED CELL PHONES.

LIKE WHAT HAPPENED ON NOVEMBER 17, 2006, AT WADLEIGH SECONDARY SCHOOL IN NEW YORK CITY. POLICE INSTALLED METAL DETECTORS BEFORE SCHOOL FOR THE 880 STUDENTS TO PASS THROUGH.

DOZENS OF OFFICERS SEARCHED STUDENTS' BACKPACKS, CONFISCATING CELL PHONES, iPODs, FOOD, SCHOOL SUPPLIES, AND OTHER PERSONAL ITEMS.

OFFICERS SELECTED SOME STUDENTS FOR WAND SCANNING, FORCING THEM TO LEAN AGAINST THE WALL AND SPREAD THEIR LEGS AND ARMS. OVER A THIRD WERE MARKED LATE FOR CLASS, AND ATTENDANCE DROPPED 10 PERCENT.

STUDENTS AT AVIATION HIGH SCHOOL WERE SUBJECTED TO SIMILAR TREATMENT ON OCTOBER 24, 2006, WHEN ALMOST 30 POLICE VANS AND CRUISERS SURROUNDED THE HIGH SCHOOL.

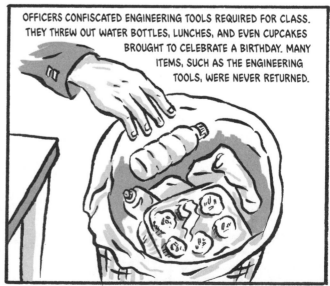

AVIATION HIGH SCHOOL

OFFICERS CONFISCATED ENGINEERING TOOLS REQUIRED FOR CLASS. THEY THREW OUT WATER BOTTLES, LUNCHES, AND EVEN CUPCAKES BROUGHT TO CELEBRATE A BIRTHDAY. MANY ITEMS, SUCH AS THE ENGINEERING TOOLS, WERE NEVER RETURNED.

AT THE COMMUNITY SCHOOL FOR SOCIAL JUSTICE, STUDENTS WERE FORCED TO REMOVE ALL CHIN AND EYEBROW PIERCINGS, AND A TEACHER TAKING PICTURES OF THE SECURITY SWEEP WAS FORCED TO TURN OVER HER FILM.

"MY STUDENTS WERE NOT THE ONLY ONES TREATED LIKE CRIMINALS TODAY . . . CAN WE PLEASE NOT TREAT ALREADY-STRUGGLING, INNER-CITY TEENAGERS WHO HAVE GOTTEN THEMSELVES TO SCHOOL LIKE THEY'VE COMMITTED A CRIME?"*

*LEAH WISEMAN FINK, ENGLISH TEACHER

THERE WAS A SIMILAR SWEEP AT CURTIS HIGH SCHOOL IN STATEN ISLAND, NEW YORK. IN ADDITION TO CELL PHONES AND iPODS, THE OFFICERS CONFISCATED THE TONGUE RING OF ONE TENTH-GRADER, CLAIMING THAT IT COULD BE USED AS A WEAPON.

"THIS IS RIDICULOUS. THIS IS SO UNNECESSARY. THIS ISN'T A SCHOOL ANYMORE; THIS IS RIKERS."†

†A PRISON IN NEW YORK

PRINCIPALS AND OTHER ADVOCATES HAVE COMPLAINED THAT OFFICERS ARE ARRESTING STUDENTS FOR THINGS THAT WOULDN'T EVEN GET THEM SUSPENDED AND MAKING TYPICAL TEEN BEHAVIOR CRIMINAL.

"USING PROFANITY—I'M NOT SUPPOSED TO SUSPEND A CHILD FOR THAT."

IN ONE CASE, PRINCIPAL MICHAEL SOGUERO AND A SCHOOL AIDE WERE ARRESTED WHEN THEY TRIED TO DISSUADE AN OFFICER FROM ARRESTING A STUDENT FOR SWEARING.

"YET AN OFFICER CAN ISSUE A SUMMONS FOR THAT AND EVEN PUT A CHILD IN CUFFS AND CALL IT DISORDERLY CONDUCT."

THE PRINCIPALS' COMPLAINTS SEEM TO BE SUPPORTED BY THE FACTS, AS SEEN IN THIS CHART COMPILED BY THE NEW YORK CIVIL LIBERTIES UNION.

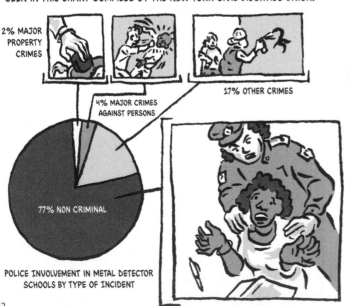

2% MAJOR PROPERTY CRIMES

4% MAJOR CRIMES AGAINST PERSONS

17% OTHER CRIMES

77% NON CRIMINAL

POLICE INVOLVEMENT IN METAL DETECTOR SCHOOLS BY TYPE OF INCIDENT

BECAUSE SO MANY OF THESE INCIDENTS HAVE HAPPENED AT SCHOOLS WITH HIGH MINORITY POPULATIONS, CRITICS SAY THERE IS AN ELEMENT OF RACISM INVOLVED.

"I AM AN IMMIGRANT, AND IN MY SCHOOL, MOST STUDENTS ARE BLACK OR LATINOS. EVERY DAY, WE ARE TREATED LIKE WE ARE CRIMINALS."

18-YEAR-OLD NADIA OUEDRAOGO, PROTESTING AT POLICE HEADQUARTERS IN NYC

INDEED, A 2008 AMERICAN PSYCHOLOGICAL ASSOCIATION TASK FORCE FOUND EVIDENCE THAT MORE STUDENTS OF COLOR GET SUSPENDED OR EXPELLED, EVEN THOUGH THEY DON'T SHOW HIGHER RATES OF DISRUPTIVE BEHAVIOR.

THE TASK FORCE ALSO EXAMINED THE DATA TO INVESTIGATE SEVERAL KEY ASSUMPTIONS OF ZERO-TOLERANCE POLICIES.

FOR INSTANCE, SUPPORTERS OF ZERO TOLERANCE SAY IT CREATES A BETTER SCHOOL CLIMATE BECAUSE IT REMOVES TROUBLEMAKERS.

BUT THE RESEARCH FOUND THAT THE SCHOOLS WITH HIGHER RATES OF EXPULSION AND SUSPENSION ALSO HAVE WORSE RATES OF ACADEMIC ACHIEVEMENT.

IN FACT, ONE STUDY MADE THE POINT THAT STUDENTS HOPING TO AVOID SUSPENSION MIGHT BE BETTER OFF CHANGING SCHOOLS RATHER THAN CHANGING THEIR BEHAVIOR.

ANOTHER ASSUMPTION IS THAT THE HARSH PUNISHMENT ACTS AS A WARNING TO STUDENTS, WHICH WILL RESULT IN BETTER OVERALL BEHAVIOR.

BUT IT DOESN'T SEEM TO HAVE THAT EFFECT, GIVEN THAT SCHOOLS WITH HIGHER SUSPENSION RATES ALSO HAVE HIGHER DROPOUT RATES.

163

SOME SCHOOLS DO OFFER AN ALTERNATIVE TO SUSPENSION AND EVEN LET THE STUDENT HAVE A CHOICE . . .

WHEN 17 ALABAMA HIGH SCHOOL STUDENTS WORE PROM DRESSES THAT VIOLATED THE SCHOOL DRESS CODE, THEY WERE GIVEN THE CHOICE BETWEEN SUSPENSION OR PADDLING. ONLY ONE CHOSE SUSPENSION.

ADVOCATES OF PADDLING, OR CORPORAL PUNISHMENT, SAY THAT IT'S A GOOD ALTERNATIVE TO SUSPENSION. "AFTER ALL OTHER TECHNIQUES OF BEHAVIOR CORRECTION HAVE RUN THEIR COURSES, THE PADDLE MAY BE THE ONLY THING LITTLE JOHNNY TRULY FEARS."

KATHLEEN KRUMNOW, ENGLISH TEACHER, ROYSE CITY HIGH SCHOOL, TEXAS

BUT NOT EVERYONE AGREES. TENIKA JONES WAS UPSET THAT HER FIVE-YEAR-OLD SON WAS PADDLED BY THE PRINCIPAL IN HIS SECOND WEEK AT HIS PRESCHOOL IN FLORIDA.

"IF I WOULD HAVE HIT MY SON HOW SHE HIT HIM, I WOULD HAVE BEEN IN JAIL."

"I CRIED ALL THE WAY HOME. IT WAS REALLY HARD."

JONES WAS ESPECIALLY UPSET BECAUSE SHE HAD CHOSEN NOT TO SIGN A PAPER TO GIVE THE SCHOOL PERMISSION TO HIT HER SON. BUT IT TURNS OUT THE SCHOOL DIDN'T NEED HER PERMISSION ANYWAY.

"IF THE SCHOOL BOARD AND THE PRINCIPAL SPECIFICALLY AUTHORIZE CORPORAL PUNISHMENT, IT CAN BE ADMINISTERED LAWFULLY AGAINST THE PARENT'S WISHES.

"THEY'RE IMMUNE BOTH CIVILLY AND CRIMINALLY BY LAW."*

*ROBERT RUSH, AN ATTORNEY AT THE LAW FIRM REPRESENTING JONES

IN FACT, SCHOOLS ARE THE ONLY INSTITUTIONS IN AMERICA THAT ARE LEGALLY ALLOWED TO BEAT PEOPLE. NOT PRISONS, MENTAL INSTITUTIONS, OR THE MILITARY—ONLY SCHOOLS IN THE 19 STATES THAT STILL PERMIT CORPORAL PUNISHMENT.

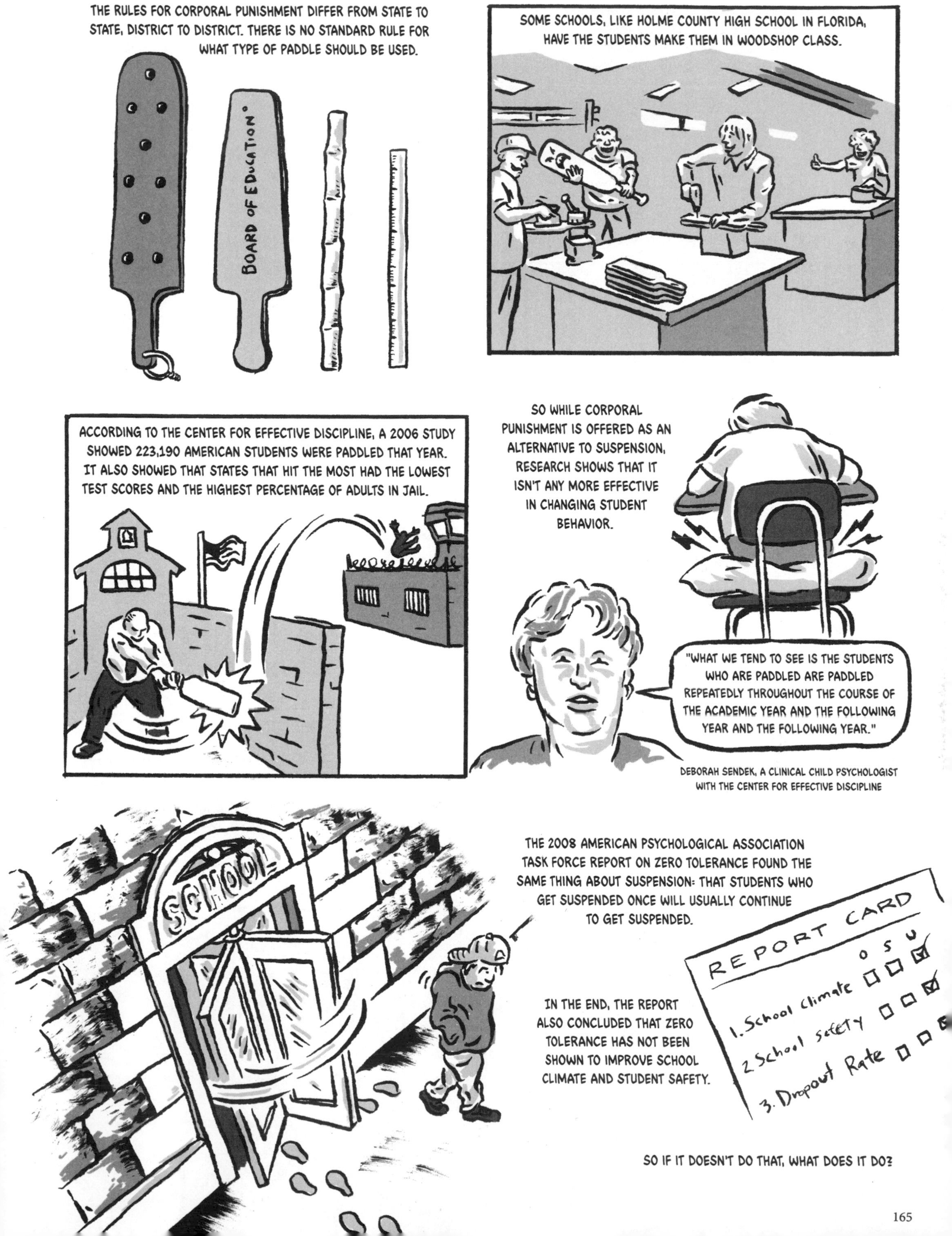

THE RULES FOR CORPORAL PUNISHMENT DIFFER FROM STATE TO STATE, DISTRICT TO DISTRICT. THERE IS NO STANDARD RULE FOR WHAT TYPE OF PADDLE SHOULD BE USED.
BOARD OF EDUCATION
SOME SCHOOLS, LIKE HOLME COUNTY HIGH SCHOOL IN FLORIDA, HAVE THE STUDENTS MAKE THEM IN WOODSHOP CLASS.
ACCORDING TO THE CENTER FOR EFFECTIVE DISCIPLINE, A 2006 STUDY SHOWED 223,190 AMERICAN STUDENTS WERE PADDLED THAT YEAR. IT ALSO SHOWED THAT STATES THAT HIT THE MOST HAD THE LOWEST TEST SCORES AND THE HIGHEST PERCENTAGE OF ADULTS IN JAIL.
SO WHILE CORPORAL PUNISHMENT IS OFFERED AS AN ALTERNATIVE TO SUSPENSION, RESEARCH SHOWS THAT IT ISN'T ANY MORE EFFECTIVE IN CHANGING STUDENT BEHAVIOR.
"WHAT WE TEND TO SEE IS THE STUDENTS WHO ARE PADDLED ARE PADDLED REPEATEDLY THROUGHOUT THE COURSE OF THE ACADEMIC YEAR AND THE FOLLOWING YEAR AND THE FOLLOWING YEAR."
DEBORAH SENDEK, A CLINICAL CHILD PSYCHOLOGIST WITH THE CENTER FOR EFFECTIVE DISCIPLINE
SCHOOL
THE 2008 AMERICAN PSYCHOLOGICAL ASSOCIATION TASK FORCE REPORT ON ZERO TOLERANCE FOUND THE SAME THING ABOUT SUSPENSION: THAT STUDENTS WHO GET SUSPENDED ONCE WILL USUALLY CONTINUE TO GET SUSPENDED.
REPORT CARD
O S U
1. School Climate
2. School Safety
3. Dropout Rate
IN THE END, THE REPORT ALSO CONCLUDED THAT ZERO TOLERANCE HAS NOT BEEN SHOWN TO IMPROVE SCHOOL CLIMATE AND STUDENT SAFETY.
SO IF IT DOESN'T DO THAT, WHAT DOES IT DO?

AT ITS WORST, CRITICS SAY THAT ZERO TOLERANCE PUSHES KIDS INTO THE JUVENILE JUSTICE SYSTEM BY CRIMINALIZING DISRUPTIVE STUDENT BEHAVIOR THAT USED TO BE HANDLED IN THE SCHOOL.

FOR AVERAGE STUDENTS, WHO AREN'T DISRUPTIVE, THE STRICTNESS OF ZERO TOLERANCE MAY MAKE IT MORE DIFFICULT TO MEET THEIR DEVELOPMENTAL NEEDS AS TEENS.

NEEDS LIKE MORE FREEDOM, CLOSE ADULT RELATIONSHIPS, AND INTELLECTUAL INDEPENDENCE.

THIS CAN ULTIMATELY LEAD TO STUDENTS WHO FEEL ANXIOUS, ALIENATED, AND UNFAIRLY LABELED AS A THREAT TO SAFETY.

WHICH ISN'T THE SAFE, RESPECTFUL, CARING, AND POSITIVE LEARNING ENVIRONMENT THAT ZERO TOLERANCE SET OUT TO ACHIEVE.

PRECISELY THE TYPE OF ENVIRONMENT THAT STUDENTS AT FREDERICK DOUGLASS ACADEMY IN DETROIT, MICHIGAN, MAY HAVE BEEN LOOKING FOR.

IN MARCH OF 2012, 50 SENIORS STAGED A PROTEST, WALKING OUT OF CLASS IN THE MIDDLE OF THE DAY.

WHAT DO WE WANT ??

AN EDUCATION!!

TEACH US!

WHEN DO WE WANT IT??

NOW!

WHAT THEY WANTED WAS AN EDUCATION.

WHAT THEY GOT WAS SUSPENDED.

HAIR BANS

Years before the words "zero" and "tolerance" were ever paired, things could still get pretty hairy when it came to school suspensions. In fact, the fur could really fly when it concerned a student's head. Not what was inside it . . . but what was on top.

1800s: Most schools don't hassle with hair in the nineteenth century, unless the kids happen to be Native Americans. Then the missionary-run boarding schools lop off the boys' long braids as a way to "help" them assimilate into the dominant white culture. No need for hair bands if you ban long hair, right?

1950s: Lurid accounts of gang violence and middle-class kids on "crime sprees" lead the U.S. Senate to investigate the rise of juvenile delinquency (remember, the problem turns out to be comic books!). Principals across the nation hope that by controlling "greaser" fashion (as the oily hairstyle popular among kids is known), they'll somehow control their students, too. Many schools adopt the Buffalo Plan (named for the city of Buffalo, New York, where it originates), which includes a list of

"don'ts" for hairdos: hair can't cover eyebrows, ears, or collars, and beards, mustaches, and goatees must be shaved off. Most schools forbid the popular "duck tail" cut, and the length and width of sideburns are carefully regulated.

FEBRUARY 1964: The world's first "boy band," the Beatles, appears on the popular *Ed Sullivan Show*, and American girls go wild. But boys also like the band, and the Beatles' "mop-top" haircut catches on, so much so that thousands of young males grow their hair longer in imitation of their rock idols.

FALL 1964: Edward T. Kores, a Westbrook High School student in Connecticut, refuses to comb his Beatles-inspired bangs off his forehead and is suspended. This is only the beginning of a long wave of long-hair bans—but there's one big difference from the bans in the 1950s: Now students start fighting back. . . .

JANUARY 1966: One teacher in San Diego, California, takes matters into his own hands and cuts a student's long hair in class. He's sued by the student for assault and battery, even though the teacher claims the school administration gave him permission to clip the kid. They settle out of court.

SEPTEMBER 1966: Three members of a Dallas, Texas, rock band, Sounds Unlimited, are not allowed to enroll in school because they refuse to trim their locks. They sue, becoming the first high-school haircut case to be taken to the Federal Circuit Courts of Appeals (and eventually the U.S. Supreme Court). During the trial, the principal states that, if allowed to attend school, "the length and style of the boys' hair would cause commotion, trouble, distraction and a disturbance." Sounds Unlimited records a protest song about being kicked out of school called "Keep Your Hands Off It," which plays on the local radio station several mornings in a row.

FALL 1966: Five boys are barred from regular classes at their Oyster Bay, Long Island, high school due to the length of their hair. They are forced to stay on the previously unoccupied fourth floor of the school building so that they can't be seen or heard by the other students. Their parents are warned that the children could upset the "morale" of other kids. Around the same time, in Forest Hills, New York, two senior honors students are similarly isolated from other students until they get "suitable" haircuts. Their graduation

from school is jeopardized because they can't take gym class and therefore won't receive the necessary credits to pass. They refuse to cut their hair, and the New York Civil Liberties Union files a petition with the State Education Commissioner on their behalf. Their separation from other students, the principal asserts, is because the boys' "grooming was disruptive of the learning system." The superintendent of schools thinks otherwise, and orders the boys returned to class (despite the principal's fear that this could encourage "anarchy").

NOVEMBER 1967: A High Bridge teacher hacks off a student's hair but escapes the fate that befell the instructor sued for assault in January 1966 for the same action. This time around, the case is dismissed thanks to the corporal punishment provisions of school law in New Jersey.

DECEMBER 1968: Eighteen boys are bused to a local barber shop, against their wishes, by a high school in Concord, New Hampshire.

SPRING 1969: This is a big year for protests, and according to a House of Representatives report, nearly 70 percent of

those protests involve dress codes and hair restrictions. By this time, over 100 hair cases reach the U.S. Circuit Courts of Appeals, and nine cases climb all the way to the U.S. Supreme Court. Student councils across the land begin adopting what becomes known as the High School Bill of Rights, which declares that students are protected by the same rights as adults under the United States Constitution. The most famous of all the Supreme Court dress code rulings also happens this year: *Tinker v. Des Moines Independent Community School District*. The court rules seven to two in the landmark case, affirming the status of students as citizens. The case began in 1965, when school officials in Des Moines, Iowa, boot out two high school boys and one junior high school girl for wearing black armbands to school in protest of the Vietnam War. They violate a recently instated school policy against political demonstrations, but the Supreme Court rules that wearing the armbands is protected by the First Amendment as a form of free speech. Justice Abe Fortas, who writes the majority opinion, states, "It can hardly be argued that either students or teachers shed their constitutional rights at the schoolhouse gate." He adds, "In our system, state-operated schools may not be enclaves of totalitarianism." Fortas comes within a hairbreadth of granting full rights to students, as requested by their High School Bill of Rights, but unfortunately, armbands are one thing and hair bands (at least for guys) are another. "The problem posed by the present case does not relate to the regulation of the length of skirts or the type of clothing, to hair style, or deportment," the justice concludes.

SEPTEMBER 1969: Seventy-six percent of adults think high schools should be allowed to rein in the hair length of their students, according to a *Good Housekeeping* magazine poll. Just 21 percent think kids have a right to wear their hair however they care to.

FALL 1970: Following summer vacation, Chesley Karr returns to high school in El Paso, Texas, referring to his new lengthy locks as a "freak flag," which he feels aligns him with the "peace or hippie movement." But Karr's "freak flag" puts him in the crosshairs of his gym coach's sights; he is barred from class. Twenty-one of Karr's fellow students decide to back him up by refusing to submit to a school regulation shearing; all but Karr give in when threatened with suspension. Karr sues the school in federal court with the support of both his parents and some ACLU lawyer friends they know. During the trial, an assistant principal testifies that Karr's behavior is out of line, asserting, "Any good army has discipline" (though he doesn't explain why high school is like the army). Another administrator from Irvin High School testifies the long-haired students have brought "outsiders" to the school with "sinister" motives, mentioning a visit from one subversive group called GIs for Peace (oh, there's the army part). Karr's coach explains his reason for keeping him out of class, observing how some students would switch seats "because the long-haired boys smelled." In November, the presiding judge rules in favor of Karr and his hair, stating his style choice is "constitutionally protected" and that the school's ban could undermine youth's "respect for society's laws or rules." But when the school successfully appeals the case, the rule is reinstated. Hundreds of kids from high schools around the district assemble in front of the district headquarters to protest, carrying signs reading SMASH THE SCHOOLS and HELL NO, LET IT GROW.

1970s to 1980s: To make a long-hair story short, as the 1970s progress, people prominent in the public eye—movie stars, sports figures, and politicians—start flying their own, more stylish versions of "freak flags." This results in long hair becoming more acceptable for society in general and for teens in particular. Then, in the 1980s, when those teens grow up and some start teaching, their students rebel in a totally different way. "Believe it or not, a lot of kids are . . . wearing suits to school," Dr. Joan Raymond, a Yonkers, New York, principal, explains in 1984. "There's a totally different attitude. . . . In many cases, the difficulty is that they're being taught by people who are wearing braids and long hair." By the 1990s (maybe because the kids wearing suits grow up and become teachers) the Bad Hair Days will return. But the reasons for suspensions won't be nearly as . . . clear-cut.

MAY 1991: Hair spray is banned from some Florida schools in Broward County for fear of "allergic reactions, explosions in restrooms and, in some cases, an aerosol attack."

SPRING 1995: After getting a buzz cut just days before his Sacramento school's graduation ceremony, straight-A student Ben Sharpe, thirteen (who is scheduled to speak at the event), is banned from participating. His hairdo is deemed too short, in violation of the California school's policy. "It isn't shaved," Ben protests, "the barber used clippers!"

WINTER 1996: Stephanie Henry and Anne Muhleisen, two Syracuse, New York, middle school students, are sent home because of their distracting hair color (one is maroon, the other pink). School officials say they also fear the "potentially hazardous" effect on school air quality (hair dye you could die for?). Jessica Wasilenko, one of three students protesting the suspensions, wonders why, if the school is so serious about "environmental problems," they aren't rounding up "anyone with hair dyed brown or blond."

FALL 1997: The Texas Supreme Court upholds the Bastrop, Texas, school district's right "to set different grooming standards for boys and girls." Back in 1990, third-grader Zachariah Toungate was forced out of class because of his wispy ponytail. For four months, Zach was isolated in a small room, eating lunch separately and playing alone at recess, until his frustrated parents pulled him out of school and sued. "The bottom line," Zach's lawyer says, "is that unless they show that long hair disrupts the learning process, then their long-hair rule isn't any good." But the court supports the school's "bottom line" (which, by the way, is that hair can't hit the bottom of a kid's collar).

FALL 2002: "I like pink hair," sixteen-year-old Sarah declares. "It's part of how I want to express myself." Her school expresses itself by suspending her. To keep Sarah in the pink, her mom relocates the family to another Houston neighborhood—one with a color-blind hair code.

MAY 2009: Labette, Kansas, school superintendent Dr. Chuck Stockton explains how his district tries to "balance a student's . . . individual right of expression with the expectations . . . of each of the teachers, of parents and other students." To achieve this "balance," a teacher shaves off the Mohawk of a six-year-old boy, thereby balancing the top of the student's head with the close-cropped hair on his sides.

SEPTEMBER 2009: The ACLU is at it again, this time defending a kindergartner's hair-related separation from the rest of the school. But a federal judge rules that the Needville, Texas, Independent School District violated the boy's constitutional rights, because his long locks reflect his Native American religious beliefs.

DECEMBER 2009: Seven-year-old Lamaya Cammon likes to play with her long,

bead-adorned braids. That's why one of them had to be cut off—to teach Lamaya a lesson, according to her teacher. Afterward, the teacher who did the clipping is taught a lesson, too: She's charged with disorderly conduct and fined $175.

AUGUST 2011: "Unnatural" hair colors and "extreme makeup" are banned from Florida's Lake County school district. Repeat offenders will be barred from extracurricular activities. Pink and purple hair is out, according to school spokesperson Chris Patton, as is "eyeshadow that goes way off the side of your face almost like how a rock star would have."

JANUARY 2012: Seventeen-year-old J. T. Gaskins is growing his mane for Locks of Love, a charity that uses donated hair to create wigs for young chemotherapy patients who have lost their own tresses due to cancer treatments. Having survived leukemia as an infant, J.T. is just trying to give a little (hair) back. His charter school in Burton, Michigan, doesn't care and suspends him for breaking their "off the ears and out of the eyes" policy. "The fact that he's ready to talk about everything he went through, his strength . . . I can't deny him that," his mother, Christa Plante, explains. J.T.'s school, on the other hand, can deny him graduation unless he trims his Beatlesque bangs.

FOOD FOR THOUGHT

WITH ALL THE RULES AND SECURITY IN SCHOOLS THESE DAYS, YOU'D THINK KIDS WERE GOING TO JAIL, NOT SCHOOL. ONE THING'S FOR SURE, THEY'RE EATING LIKE THEY ARE (WELL, ALMOST . . . A KID'S LUNCH COSTS A WHOLE SIX CENTS MORE THAN A PRISONER'S).

PRISON

SCHOOL

AVERAGE CALORIES PER INMATE: 1,300–1,450

AVERAGE COST: $2.62

AVERAGE CALORIES PER STUDENT: 1,400

AVERAGE COST: $2.68

¾ CUP OF STARCH

ONE BEVERAGE

½ CUP OF VEGETABLES

ONE SERVING OF BREAD

3 TO 4 OUNCES OF MEAT*

ONE SERVING OF FRUIT OR DESSERT

ONE STARCH ITEM

MILK

8 OUNCES OF MILK

ONE SERVING OF BREAD (PASTA)

½ CUP OF VEGETABLES OR FRUIT

1½ TO 2 OUNCES OF MEAT†

*AND PINK SLIME! THAT'S THE NAME OF A CHEAP MEAT-FILLER PASTE MADE OF BEEF SCRAPS, FAT, AND CONNECTIVE TISSUE, WHICH IS THEN SUPER-HEATED AND BLASTED WITH AMMONIA GAS. THE STATE OF GEORGIA ONCE RETURNED NEARLY 7,000 POUNDS OF THE STUFF TO A MANUFACTURER BECAUSE IT STANK SO BAD THEY WERE AFRAID TO FEED IT TO THEIR INMATES.

†AND PINK SLIME! YOU DON'T THINK SCHOOLS WOULD DARE DEPRIVE KIDS OF THAT DELICIOUS AMMONIA FLAVOR? ACTUALLY, IF YOU'RE IN NEW YORK CITY, BOSTON, HOUSTON, AND NEW JERSEY, THE STINKY STUFF HAS BEEN PHASED OUT; IF YOU'RE NOT, WELL . . . ENJOY!

While it seems clear from the chart on the previous page that prisoners and students share similar diets, that comparison is not suggesting the two groups are the same when it comes to how they live their lives day to day. After all, one group must learn to survive a harsh system of constant surveillance under the watchful eyes of their appointed controllers. They experience a high level of scrutiny so all-encompassing that even their lousy lunches have before-and-after photographs taken of them to be analyzed by experts. Which is nothing like what the other group experiences— you know . . . the prisoners. They sure have it a lot easier, at least when it comes to having their meals monitored. Just compare criminals to the poor students in San Antonio, Texas, who must munch their lunches while eyed by a "calorie camera" installed in their cafeteria. Sure, the idea sounds totally, um, out to lunch,

but the school insists it's the best way to battle childhood obesity. Here's how it works: Each student has a special tray bearing a unique bar code that is photographed by the all-seeing "calorie camera" (along with whatever is piled on the plate). After the kids choke down what they can of the cafeteria gruel and return their tray, the camera takes another photo of the plate, as well as the identifying bar code. Computer software then crunches the nutrients consumed by each kid. Guess a picture's worth a thousand words, or in this case, $2 million, since that's what this federal program costs. Imagine if that money was put toward more nourishing meals (you heard me, Sloppy Joe Fridays!). Sounds like a half-baked idea when you think that the government could have just asked the kids what they ate and saved the dough. Still, surveillance-wise, it isn't too bad, since the camera is angled to shoot only the tray. And the students are well aware of their monitoring because the dietary data is also sent to their parents. What would be creepy, though, is if it were done secretly, and instead of taking pictures of their food, they were snapping photos of their faces. Thank goodness the San Antonio schools aren't trying something like that.

HIDE & PEEK

VILE, YOU'RE ON CANDID CAMERA

But in the Bronx, New York . . . that's exactly what one assistant principal is up to! "They don't even realize that we're watching," laughs

the AP at Intermediate School 339, while spying on his pupils during a 2009 *Frontline* documentary called "Digital Nation." Even more surprising than his snooping is that when the show originally aired, no one even batted an eye over Dan Ackerman's activities. It wasn't until another school spy scandal broke a few weeks later (more on "WebcamGate" below) that people started getting upset. Ackerman bills himself as a "former technology coach," so you'd think he'd know better when we see him peering through his remote camera to watch a girl combing her hair as she uses her Mac's Photo Booth application as a mirror. Giving a whole new—and twisted—meaning to the phrase "keeping an eye on students," Ackerman then demonstrates how he "always [likes] to mess with them and take a picture" by remote-controlling the software (at the last second, the girl ducks out of the way). Luckily, like the girl in the *Frontline* piece, "nine times out of ten" the students usually become aware of Peeping Dan and dodge the camera before the picture can be taken. Ackerman claims his spying techniques are all about monitoring students' laptops for "inappropriate use" and that he likes to interrupt students' instant-message conversations "with his own message, telling them to get back to work." Now, if you're wondering if anyone is monitoring the schools for their own inappropriate use of technology, you'll have to look someplace other than the Bronx. Someplace like Tennessee, specifically Overton County, where upset parents sued the school system for allowing their kids to be filmed while they were changing clothes in the Livingston Middle School's locker rooms! Back in 2003, when a student visiting from another school for an interscholastic basketball game spotted a "suspicious device," he asked Livingston school officials what was up. While they downplayed the kid's questions, they had more difficulty calming the parents' concerns, and after a few months of hammering

away at the school, officials finally admitted what was going on. In the end, the parents went to court to discover that the hidden cameras had reportedly captured students (ages 10 to 14) "in various stages of undress." Wow—what could possibly be worse than being spied on in your school?

TRAPTOPS

How about being spied on in your bedroom . . . by your school! That's what the aforementioned "WebcamGate" scandal was all about, though it began with a seemingly kindly act, when Pennsylvania's Harriton High distributed 2,300 laptops to its students to use for free. Well, almost free, except for the price of their privacy. That's because, occasionally, the school liked to secretly monitor their students at home (off campus . . . yet on camera). In mid-February 2011, fifteen-year-old Blake Robbins was pulled out of class and accused of "improper behavior" by the assistant principal (no, not the same assistant principal as in the Bronx, though both of them may have shared certain "principles" when it came to a student's privacy). Now, what was really shocking to the student was that the "improper behavior" his assistant principal was accusing him of had taken place in his own bedroom, which is how Blake and his parents (and eventually the rest of the world) discovered he was being cyber-stalked by his school. The assistant principal's allegations were based on photos that were taken by the laptop showing Blake partaking in "suspicious substances" (later, these turned out to be Mike and Ike's "suspicious" fruit-flavored candy). Learning this really pushed his parents' buttons, so they pushed back, filing a class-action lawsuit against the school system. When "WebcamGate" went public, more Harriton High students came forward to report their

own strange experiences of laptops' green "active" lights mysteriously flashing on and off at home. While the school admitted to having activated the devices forty-two times over a fourteen-month period, they denied that they were invading students' privacy, claiming the software that allowed them to remotely access the webcams was used only as a way for them to locate missing computers "in case of theft." Oddly, Blake had never reported his laptop stolen . . . which is why the FBI decided to become involved in the case. In the course of their investigation, school employees admitted they sometimes

forgot to turn off the cameras, which might explain why the computers captured and sent more than 65,000 images to school district servers. But was it all just an accident? Did the school simply get their wires crossed when it came to operating the high-tech cameras? According to some very incriminating e-mails the parents' lawyer uncovered, it sounds like school officials knew exactly what they were doing. It was like a window into "a little . . . soap opera," one staffer said in an e-mail to Carol Cafiero, the administrator running the program. "I know, I love it," Cafiero wrote back. In the end, the school admitted recording students, chat logs, and the websites they visited, as well as reviewing and sharing the secret laptop snapshots with others. Blake received $175,000 in a settlement with the school, and two other students were given $10,000 each the following year. "My family and I recognize that in today's society, almost every place we go outside of our home we are photographed and recorded by traffic cameras, ATM cameras, and store surveillance cameras," Blake said following the settlement. "This makes it all the more important that we vigilantly safeguard our homes, the only refuge we have from this 'eyes everywhere' onslaught." Not surprisingly, the district has dropped its tracking program.

SHOW AND TELL

But maybe, in the right situation, surveillance at school can be GOOD FOR YOU. That is, if it's a kid who's using tech to turn the tables on a BAD teacher, which is what fifteen-year-old Julio Artuz did after his own parents refused to believe him when he told them an instructor at his New Jersey school was constantly bullying him. The special-needs student secretly videotaped a typical encounter with his abuser at the Bankbridge Regional School (apologies ahead of time for the *bleeping* language, but then these are pretty nasty grown-ups talking). "Don't call me special," Artuz tells the teacher, while filming their heated exchange. "What?" the teacher screams. "Oh my God, *bleeping*. What does the sign on the front of the school say? Special education!" When Artuz tries to stick up for himself, the teacher threatens, "I will kick your *bleep* from here to kingdom-come, until I'm 80 years old." But once the story hit the news in November 2011, it was the teacher who got a kick . . . out of the classroom (though he was put on paid leave). "The actions depicted on the video," the school later announced, "do not reflect [our] mission or culture." Good to hear, but, unfortunately, they come very close to reflecting the actions of another special-needs teacher and in-class aide at an Ohio middle school, whose verbal abuse was exposed by a bullied student using a tape recorder hidden under her clothes. "No wonder you don't have any friends," the aide is heard telling the student. "No wonder nobody likes you." The teacher—who had the student in her class for THREE YEARS—is recorded questioning the girl's intelligence ("Are you that *bleeping* dumb? You are that dumb?") and later taunts her about not exercising enough. "Don't you want to do something about that belly?" she sneers. While the aide resigned, the teacher was only temporarily removed from class (this time unpaid). At least she had to go back to school herself, to take classes to help her recognize bullying and child abuse (of course, she could just look in a mirror . . . or listen to that tape over and over again). The family was awarded $300,000 in damages in a civil lawsuit against the school district. Perhaps that's just what society needs: more students willing to give schools a taste of their own twisted tech . . . thereby teaching them a lesson.

I'LL SAY WHATEVER I WANT TO. YOU DON'T LIKE IT... OH WELL. WHAT ARE YOU GOING TO DO?

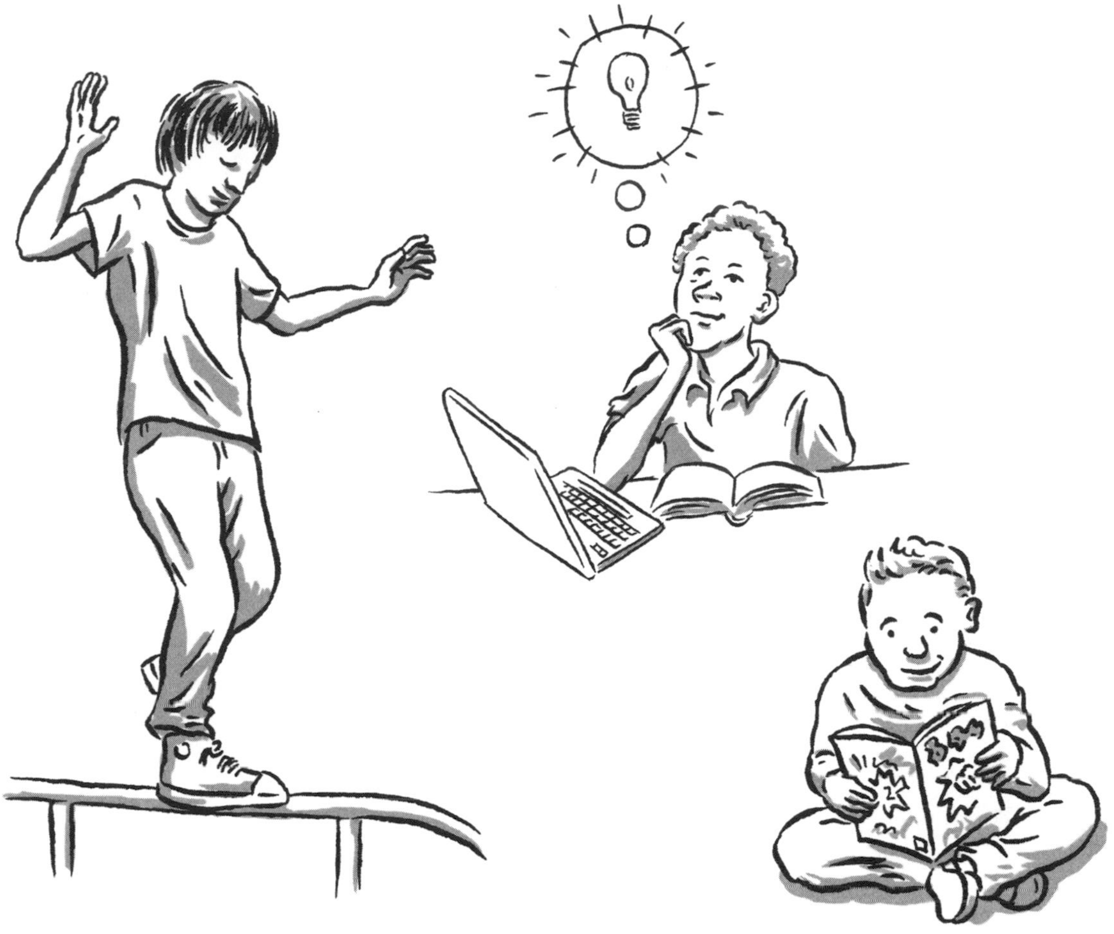

GOOD FOR YOU

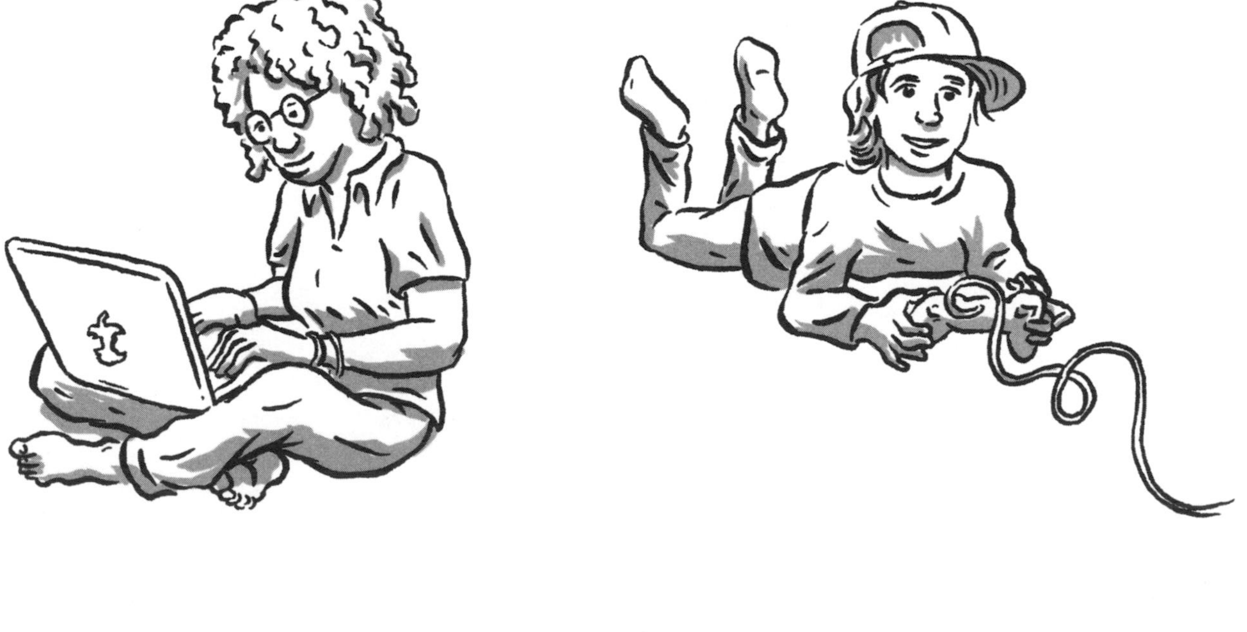

FOR AS LONG AS ADULTS HAVE BEEN STOKING FEAR AND LIMITING THE THINGS KIDS LOVE, THERE HAVE BEEN SOME KIDS WHO PUSH BACK.

PRINTED IN THE SAME MAGAZINE AND QUOTED IN SEVERAL COMIC BOOKS PUBLISHED BY COMICS LEGEND STAN LEE, IT IS STILL ONE OF THE MORE THOUGHTFUL AND WELL-CONSTRUCTED REBUTTALS TO WERTHAM'S ATTACK.

TODAY, YOUTH-STAFFED ACTIVIST GROUPS FIGHT FOR THE REPEAL OF CURFEW LAWS AND AGAINST INTERNET BLOCKING FILTERS.

THE SPLC OFFERS FREE LEGAL ADVICE AND INFORMATION TO STUDENT JOURNALISTS STRUGGLING WITH CENSORSHIP AND FREE SPEECH ISSUES.

WHEN DR. FREDRIC WERTHAM PUBLISHED ONE OF HIS EARLIEST ATTACKS ON COMICS IN A 1948 ISSUE OF THE *SATURDAY REVIEW OF LITERATURE*, 14-YEAR-OLD DAVID WIGRANSKY PUSHED BACK WITH A LETTER.

FIFTY YEARS LATER, FOURTH GRADERS IN MICHIGAN ORGANIZED PETITION SIGNINGS IN RESPONSE TO THE BANNING OF HARRY POTTER NOVELS FROM THEIR CLASSROOM. THE MOVEMENT GREW INTO A NATIONWIDE YOUTH CAMPAIGN, KIDSPEAK, ADVOCATING FOR KIDS' FIRST-AMENDMENT RIGHTS.

OTHER GROUPS LIKE THE AMERICAN CIVIL LIBERTIES UNION AND STUDENT PRESS LAW CENTER (SPLC) HELP KIDS FIGHT FOR THEIR RIGHTS.

WITH CHAPTERS ALL ACROSS THE U.S., THE ACLU HAS SUCCESSFULLY CHALLENGED DOZENS OF YOUTH CURFEW LAWS, ISSUED SCATHING REPORTS ON ZERO TOLERANCE, AND CONTINUALLY HELPS KIDS DEFEND THEIR RIGHTS.

IN 2005, THE ACLU HELPED STUDENTS AT DEER VALLEY HIGH SCHOOL IN CALIFORNIA WIN THE RIGHT TO HOLD A PEACE RALLY THE SCHOOL HAD OUTLAWED.

IN 2010, THEY HELPED GET A COURT SETTLEMENT FOR A HIGH SCHOOLER WHOSE CONFISCATED CELL PHONE WAS SEARCHED BY SCHOOL AUTHORITIES.

THE ACLU BACKED A SIXTH GRADER IN MINNESOTA WHO SUED HER SCHOOL FOR FORCING HER TO GIVE THEM ACCESS TO HER E-MAIL AND FACEBOOK ACCOUNT AND PUNISHING HER FOR THINGS SHE WROTE ONLINE. IN SEPTEMBER 2012, A JUDGE RULED THAT THE SCHOOL HAD INDEED VIOLATED HER RIGHTS.

HOW CONSTITUTIONAL RIGHTS LIKE FREE SPEECH, PRIVACY, AND FREEDOM OF ASSEMBLY (CURFEWS) APPLY TO KIDS WILL CONTINUE TO BE DEBATED FOR MANY YEARS.

OTHER CONCERNS, LIKE VIDEO GAME VIOLENCE, WILL PROBABLY FADE AS A NEW TECHNOLOGY OR MEDIA ARRIVES FOR ADULTS TO WORRY ABOUT, JUST AS CONCERNS ABOUT COMICS FADED.

THE ACLU SEEMED TO HAVE THIS HISTORY IN MIND IN 2012 WHEN IT OPPOSED A POSSIBLE LAW REQUIRING ALL VIDEO GAMES OVER AN E RATING TO CARRY THE WORDS "WARNING: EXPOSURE TO VIOLENT VIDEO GAMES HAS BEEN LINKED TO AGGRESSIVE BEHAVIOR."

IN THEIR STATEMENT, THE ACLU RECOUNTED WERTHAM'S CRUSADE AGAINST COMICS TO ILLUSTRATE "THE DANGER INVOLVED WHEN CONGRESS GETS IT IN ITS HEAD THAT A PARTICULAR ART FORM THREATENS THE WIDE-EYED INNOCENCE OF AMERICA'S YOUTH."

NOWADAYS, THE PARTICULAR ART FORM OF COMICS IS USED TO TEACH LITERACY AND REACH RELUCTANT READERS IN SCHOOLS AND, LIKE JAZZ MUSIC, IT IS RECOGNIZED AS A GREAT AMERICAN CONTRIBUTION TO WORLD CULTURE.

EVEN DR. WERTHAM CAME TO SEE ITS VALUE, WRITING IN HIS LAST BOOK HOW COMICS FAN CULTURE WAS A POSITIVE, FREEING FORCE IN YOUNG PEOPLE'S LIVES.

HE EVEN WENT SO FAR AS TO SPEAK AT THE 1973 NEW YORK COMIC ART CONVENTION, HIS LAST PUBLIC APPEARANCE. HIS SPEECH CELEBRATED COMICS FAN CULTURE AS . . .

"FREE FROM OUTSIDE INTERFERENCE, WITHOUT CONTROL OR MANIPULATION FROM ABOVE, WITHOUT CENSORSHIP, VISIBLE OR INVISIBLE."

THE COMICS FANS FREELY EXPRESSED THEIR OPINION, BOOING HIM FROM THE STAGE.

ON JANUARY 20, 2011, THE COMICS CODE AUTHORITY DIED FOREVER.

RESOURCES

DIRECT-ACTION KID ORGANIZATIONS

CENTER FOR TEEN EMPOWERMENT

teenempowerment.org

"Teen Empowerment hires and trains urban youth, including at-risk youth, to be community organizers," believing that "urban youth represent a valuable, untapped resource" that can help rejuvenate neighborhoods and local institutions.

THE FREE CHILD PROJECT

freechild.org

The Freechild Project promotes kids "leading their communities in activism for social change" and envisions "a society where every young person is engaged in powerful, purposeful, and positive social change."

KIDSPEAK!

kidspeakonline.org

Born out of kids fighting Harry Potter book bans in school, kidSPEAK! now joins youths' free speech battles across the country. "These rights are not as broad as the rights of adults because they have been limited by courts in the United States and elsewhere. However, where these rights exist, kidSPEAK! will help kids fight for them."

NATIONAL YOUTH RIGHTS ASSOCIATION

youthrights.org

A youth-led national nonprofit group "dedicated to defending the civil and human rights of young people," which focuses on curfew laws, corporal punishment, restrictions on video games sales, the spread of the Mosquito, kids' free speech, zero tolerance policies, and lowering the voting age.

PEACEFIRE

peacefire.org

Billing itself as "Open Access for the Net Generation," Peacefire is open to members of any age, as long as they are against "censorship of students and people under 18." One of the first topics the group took on was censorware (because Peacefire was also one of the first groups blocked by it!).

TakingITGlobal

tigweb.org

"An international organization, led by youth, empowered by technology. TIG brings together young people in more than 190 countries within international networks to collaborate on concrete projects addressing global problems and creating positive change."

WHAT KIDS CAN DO

whatkidscando.org

"This popular website features voices and work from the next generation in news stories from across the U.S., highlighting the ability of students to plan, deliver, and learn from serving their community."

YOUTH ACTION NET

youthactionnet.org

This website is a collection of "stories of young people from around the world who are fighting for social justice, opportunity, and equality in their cities and nations, and globally."

YOUTH ACTIVISM PROJECT

youthactivismproject.org

This group "strives to promote youth civic engagement—especially in the areas of school policies, city ordinances, state laws, national legislation, and international issues" and provides a free advice hotline, 1-800-KID-POWER, to help young people's proposals "be taken seriously by the powers-that-be."

YOUTH SERVICE AMERICA

ysa.org

Connects young people ages 5 to 25 to volunteer organizations to serve "in substantive roles." YSA "supports a global culture of engaged youth committed to a lifetime of service, learning, leadership, and achievement."

SUPPORT GROUPS

YOUTH RIGHTS

CONSTITUTIONAL RIGHTS FOUNDATION
crf-usa.org
CRF is "a non-profit, non-partisan, community-based organization dedicated to educating America's young people about the importance of civic participation in a democratic society."

FREE SPEECH/CENSORSHIP

AMERICAN LIBRARY ASSOCIATION
ala.org
The ALA is one of the strongest groups working against kids'-book bans and fighting censorship in libraries. The ALA also sponsors an annual event called Banned Books Week (bannedbooksweek.org). Another part of ALA's site is called the Freedom to Read Foundation. They are the only organization in the U.S. whose primary goal is to protect and promote the First Amendment in libraries.

CENTER FOR DEMOCRACY & TECHNOLOGY
cdt.org
CDT "works to promote democratic values and constitutional liberties in the digital age" by monitoring and advocating on internet-related policy issues, including free speech, privacy, copyright, and government surveillance.

COMIC BOOK LEGAL DEFENSE FUND
cbldf.org
The Comic Book Legal Defense Fund "is a non-profit organization dedicated to the protection of the First Amendment rights of the comics art form and its community of retailers, creators, publishers, librarians, and readers. The CBLDF provides legal referrals, representation, advice, assistance, and education in furtherance of these goals."

ELECTRONIC FRONTIER FOUNDATION
eff.org
"A kind of ACLU for the geek world, EFF is both a legal defense fund fighting for privacy and free speech online, as well as an activist organization that educates the public about the complicated intersection of cutting-edge tech and the legal issues it creates."

ENTERTAINMENT CONSUMERS ASSOCIATION
theeca.com
ECA is a nonprofit "founded to give gamers a collective voice with which to communicate their concerns, address their issues, and focus their advocacy efforts."

THE ESCAPIST
theescapist.com
A website "devoted to the betterment of role-playing games and the education of the public and media of their benefits to society." Features an unofficial homepage for CAR-PGs (the Committee for the Advancement of Role-Playing Games).

FREE EXPRESSION POLICY PROJECT
fepproject.org/issues/harmfulminors.html
This section of the site focuses on issues of youth censorship.

GAME POLITICS
gamepolitics.com
A website (often used by this book's authors for research) covering a number of issues on gaming, including the latest news on game censorship and related legislation.

NATIONAL COALITION AGAINST CENSORSHIP
ncac.org
"NCAC strives to create a climate of opinion hospitable to First Amendment freedoms in the broader community." They also support the Kids' Right to Read Project, which provides "advice and assistance to students, teachers, and others opposing book-banning in schools and communities nationwide," as well as supplying "educational materials to promote community awareness about the right to read" and supporting "local activism by reaching out to students, teachers, booksellers, librarians, journalists, and other community members." Also tracks "book censorship incidents across the country."

PROJECT CENSORED
projectcensored.org
The mission of Project Censored "is to teach students and the public about the role of a free press in a free society—and to tell the News That Didn't Make the News and Why." The group is most famous for its "Top 25 Censored" news stories each year.

STUDENT PRESS LAW CENTER

splc.org

SPLC is "an advocate for student free-press rights and provides information, advice, and legal assistance at no charge to students and the educators who work with them."

PLAY (PLAYGROUND, SKATEBOARD)

AMERICAN ASSOCIATION FOR THE CHILD'S RIGHT TO PLAY

ipausa.org

This group "is a necessary response to an unnecessary evil—the well-meaning, misinformed pundits who are trying to do away with childish things like recess and free play." This group is a part of the International Play Association (IPA), which provides a forum and advocacy "for the promotion of play opportunities."

FREE RANGE KIDS

freerangekids.com

Fighting the belief that children are in constant danger (a site hosted by Lenore Skenazy, "America's Worst Mom" . . . but we mean that in the best possible way).

KaBOOM!

kaboom.org

KaBOOM! is "a national non-profit dedicated to saving play for America's children." Their mission is to work with local communities to help create imaginative play spaces for kids.

SKATE PARK ASSOCIATION OF THE UNITED STATES OF AMERICA

spausa.org

SPAUSA is a group with experienced skaters as members. They have available on the site a good info packet, a link to a skate park directory, and an advisory board to consult if a community or group wants to try to build their own skate park.

TONY HAWK FOUNDATION

tonyhawkfoundation.org

Skateboarder extraordinaire Tony Hawk formed this foundation to support and help fund "recreational programs with a focus on the creation of public skateboard parks in low-income communities."

UNDERGROUND MOMS

undergroundmoms.com

Not moms living in tunnels, but a website whose members call into question "the fear- and safety-obsessed culture of parenting." Many links to similar-minded authors like founding member–mom Lenore Skenazy (*Free-Range Kids*).

US PLAY COALITION

usplaycoalition.clemson.edu

US Play "is a partnership to promote the value of play throughout one's life. It consists of individuals and organizations that recognize play as a valuable and necessary part of a healthy and productive life."

HOMEWORK/TESTING

CHALLENGE SUCCESS

challengesuccess.org

"The Challenge Success program addresses the concern that children and adolescents often compromise their mental and physical health, integrity, and engagement in learning as they contend with performance pressure in and out of school." Challenge Success is an expanded version of the Stanford University School of Education Stressed-Out Students Project.

END THE RACE TO NOWHERE

racetonowhere.com

This is a website for the documentary film *Race to Nowhere*, about the current "pressure-cooker climate that dominates American classrooms." It also has news stories on education and updates on parents and children organizing to oppose high-stakes testing and excessive homework in schools.

NATIONAL CENTER FOR FAIR AND OPEN TESTING

fairtest.org

NCFFOT works to "end the misuses and flaws of standardized testing and to ensure that evaluation of students, teachers, and schools is fair, open, valid, and educationally beneficial."

STOP HOMEWORK

stophomework.com

Stop Homework is a resource-loaded website with anti-homework info, created by Sara Bennett, coauthor of *The Case Against Homework: How Homework Is Hurting Our Children and What We Can Do About It.*

ZERO TOLERANCE (CORPORAL PUNISHMENT)

DIGNITY IN SCHOOLS CAMPAIGN
dignityinschools.org
DSC "unites parents, youth, advocates, and educators to support alternatives to a culture of zero tolerance, punishment, and removal in our schools."

THE HITTING STOPS HERE
thehittingstopshere.com
The goal of this group is to "create national awareness of sanctioned school beatings" and to provide info on the harm they do to children and society.

PARENTS AND TEACHERS AGAINST VIOLENCE IN EDUCATION
nospank.net
NoSpank "takes the position that children should no longer be excluded from the legal protections against assault and battery that apply to adults."

UNLIMITED JUSTICE
unlimitedjustice.com
Campaigns against corporal punishment in schools.

REFERENCES

Here are some of the main sources the *Bad For You* writers have used to create this book. But there's a longer list—a much looooooonger list—available at their website, badforyoubook.com. So, why try to make all the sources available? Because some of this stuff is so over the top, you're probably thinking the writers made it up. On these pages (and at the website) is the proof that "Student Kicked Off Bus Over Passed Gas" really did happen.

COMICS

Hajdu, David. *The Ten-Cent Plague: The Great Comic-Book Scare and How It Changed America.* New York: Picador, 2008.

Heiner, Heidi Anne. *SurLaLuneFairyTales.com*, 2012. http://www.surlalunefairytales.com/talesindex.html.

Jones, Gerard. *Killing Monsters: Why Children Need Fantasy, Super Heroes, and Make-Believe Violence.* New York: Basic Books, 2002.

Pflieger, Pat. "Nineteenth-Century American Children & What They Read: An Anthology of Works for Children, from 1800 to 1872." *MerryCoz.org*, 2012. http://merrycoz.org/kids.htm.

Robinson, B. A. "Conservative Christian Responses to the Harry Potter Books: Introduction & Book Burnings." *Ontario Consultants on Religious Tolerance*, 2005. http://www.religioustolerance.org/pottera.htm.

Wertham, Fredric. *Seduction of the Innocent.* New York, Toronto: Rinehart & Company, Inc., 1953. http://www.dreadfuldays.net/soti.html.

GAMES

Anderson, Craig A. and Karen Dill. "Video Games and Aggressive Thoughts, Feelings, and Behavior in the Laboratory and in Life." *Journal of Personality and Social Psychology*, Vol. 78, No. 4 (April 2000): pp. 772–790. http://web.clark.edu/mjackson/anderson.and.dill.html.

Cohen, Stanley. *Folk Devils and Moral Panics: The Creation of the Mods and Rockers.* London: MacGibbon & Kee, 1972.

Dear, William. *Dungeon Master: The Disappearance of James Dallas Egbert III.* New York: Houghton Mifflin, 1984.

Ferguson, Christopher J. "Blazing Angels or Resident Evil? Can Violent Video Games Be a Force for Good?" *Review of General Psychology, American Psychological Association*, Vol. 14, No. 2 (2010): pp. 1–13. www.tamiu.edu/~cferguson/Blazing%20Angels.pdf.

Kohler, Chris. "How Protests Against Games Cause Them to Sell More Copies." *Wired*, Oct. 30, 2007. http://www.wired.com/gamelife/2007/10/how-protests-ag/.

Kutner, Lawrence, and Cheryl K. Olson. *Grand Theft Childhood: The Surprising Truth About Violent Video Games and What Parents Can Do.* New York: Simon & Schuster, 2008.

Stackpole, Michael A. "The Pulling Report." *RPG Studies .net*, 1990. http://www.rpgstudies.net/stackpole/pulling_report.html.

TECHNOLOGY

Arnett, Jeffrey Jensen. "Suffering, Selfish, Slackers? Myths and Reality about Emerging Adults." *Journal of Youth and Adolescence*, Vol. 36 (Dec. 2006): pp. 23–29. www.faithformationlearningexchange.net/uploads/5/2/4/6/5246709/myths_and_realities_of_emerging_adults_-_arnett_2007.pdf.

Baron, Dennis. *A Better Pencil: Readers, Writers, and the Digital Revolution.* Oxford: Oxford University Press, 2009.

Bell, Vaughan. "Don't Touch That Dial! A History of Media Technology Scares, from the Printing Press to Facebook." *Slate.com*, Feb. 15, 2010. http://www.slate.com/articles/health_and_science/science/2010/02/dont_touch_that_dial.html.

Crystal, David. *Txtng: The Gr8 Db8*. Oxford: Oxford University Press, 2008.

Eibach, Richard P., and Lisa K. Libby (contributors). "Ideology of the Good Old Days: Exaggerated Perceptions of Moral Decline and Conservative Politics," in *Social and Psychological Bases of Ideology and System Justification (Series in Political Psychology)*, eds. John T. Jost, Aaron C. Kay, and Hulda Thorisdottir. Oxford: Oxford University Press, 2009.

Trzesniewski, Kali H., and M. Brent Donnellan. "Rethinking 'Generation Me': A Study of Cohort Effects From 1976–2006." *Perspectives on Psychological Science,* Vol. 5, No. 1 (Jan. 2010): pp. 58–75. http://news.msu.edu/media/documents/2010/03/d86dd7ab-adb0-4887.

PLAY

Adams, Kenneth. "The Effectiveness of Juvenile Curfews at Crime Prevention." *The Annals of the American Academy of Political and Social Science*, Vol. 587, No. 1 (May 2003): pp. 136–159.

Anderson, Linnea M. "The Playground of Today Is the Republic of Tomorrow: Social Reform and Organized Recreation in the USA, 1890–1930s." *The Encyclopaedia of Informal Education (infed.org),* 2007. www.infed.org/playwork/organized_recreation_and_playwork_1890–1930s.htm.

Burke, Mary Kate. "Cops vs. Skaters: Video of Skater Arrest Leads to Investigation." *ABCNews.com*, 2007. http://abcnews.go.com/TheLaw/story?id=3327172&page=1.

Carroll, Aaron, MD, and Rachel Vreeman, MD. *Don't Swallow Your Gum! Myths, Half-Truths, and Outright Lies About Your Body and Health*. New York: St. Martin's Press, 2009.

Dickason, Jerry G. "Playground Movement." *Encyclopedia of Children and Childhood in History and Society*. http://www.faqs.org/childhood/Pa-Re/Playground-Movement.html.

Ellis, Bill. "Legend Trips and Satanism: Adolescents' Ostensive Traditions as 'Cult' Activity," in *The Satanism Scare*, eds. James T. Richardson, Joel Best, and David G. Bromley. New York: Walter de Gruyter, Inc., 1991.

Johnson, Paige L. *Playscapes: A Blog About Playground Design*, 2011. http://playgrounddesigns.blogspot.com.

Ruebush, Mary. *Why Dirt Is Good: 5 Ways to Make Germs Your Friends*. New York: Kaplan Publishing, 2009.

Skenazy, Lenore. *Free-Range Kids: How to Raise Safe, Self-Reliant Children*. San Franciso, CA: Jossey-Bass, 2009.

Widman, Amy. "Kids 'N Safe Play: Regulation, Litigation and Playground Safety." *Center for Justice & Democracy*, Aug. 2008. http://centerjd.org/content/white-paper-kids-n-safe-play-regulation-litigation-and-playground-safety.

THOUGHT

Bronson, Po, and Ashley Merryman. *NurtureShock: New Thinking About Children*. New York: Hachette Book Group, 2009.

Chambliss, John. "Student Kicked Off Bus Over Passed Gas." *The Lakeland Ledger,* March 18, 2009. http://www.theledger.com/article/20090318/NEWS/903185043.

Franklin, Barry M. "Franklin Bobbitt (1876–1956): Social Efficiency Movement, Bobbitt's Contribution." *StateUniversity.com*. http://education.stateuniversity.com/pages/1794/Bobbitt-Franklin-1876-1956.html.

Gatto, John Taylor. *The Underground History of American Education*. New York: The Oxford Village Press, 2001.

Gonzalez, Sarah. "Spanking Lives On in Rural Florida Schools," *NPR.org*, March 13, 2012. http://www.npr.org/2012/03/13/148521155/spanking-lives-on-in-rural-florida-schools.

GOOD graphics and Column Five Media designers. "Do Students Eat Like Prisoners?" Graphic by GOOD; designed by Column Five Media, 2011. http://dev.visual.ly/do-students-eat-prisoners.

Herrick, Andrew Robert. "A Hairy Predicament: The Problem with Long Hair in the 1960s and 1970s." Thesis Submitted to the Eberly College of Arts and Sciences, West Virginia University, 2006.

Johnson, Steven. *Everything Bad Is Good For You: How Today's Popular Culture Is Actually Making Us Smarter*. New York: Riverhead Books, 2005.

Kohn, Alfie. *The Homework Myth: Why Our Kids Get Too Much of a Bad Thing*. Philadelphia: Da Capo, 2006.

Louis, E. "It's Time to Police the NYPD's School Cops." *New York Daily News,* Feb. 18, 2009. http://www.nydailynews.com/opinion/time-police-nypd-school-cops-article-1.390382.

Mukherjee, Elora. *Criminalizing the Classroom: The Over-Policing of New York City Schools*. New York: The New York Civil Liberties Union, 2007. http://www.nyclu.org/pdfs/criminalizing_the_classroom_report.pdf.

Public Broadcasting System. "School: The Story of American Public Education," *PBS.org*, 2001. www.pbs.org/kcet/publicschool/index.html.

GOOD FOR YOU

Raymond, Nate. "Dr. Fredric Wertham." *The Amazing Website of Kavalier & Clay*, 2010. http://www.sugarbombs.com/kavalier/?page_id=14.

KEVIN C. PYLE is the author and illustrator of numerous graphic novels and docu-comics, including *Take What You Can Carry.* He also teaches comics and enjoys hanging around with his wife, son, two cats, and dog in their creaky old house in New Jersey.

SCOTT CUNNINGHAM has written kids' comics for DC, *Archie*, and *Nickelodeon* magazine and parodies for *Mad* magazine. He lives in Brooklyn with his wife, daughter, ten cats, and one dog. He thinks he has enough pets for now.